ENGLISH RECUSANT LITERATURE
1558–1640

Selected and Edited by
D. M. ROGERS

Volume 218

RICHARD BROUGHTON
English Protestants Plea
1621

WILLIAM BELL
The Testament of
William Bel
1632

RICHARD BROUGHTON
English Protestants Plea
1621

The Scolar Press
1974

ISBN 0 85967 202 6

Published and printed in Great Britain by
The Scolar Press Limited, 59-61 East Parade,
Ilkley, Yorkshire and
39 Great Russell Street,
London WC1

NOTE

The following works are reproduced (original size), with permission:

1) Richard Broughton, *English Protestants plea*, 1621, from a copy in the Bodleian Library, by permission of the Curators. A portion of the title-page has suffered slight damage resulting in some loss of text; this passage should **Read**: ' . . . practize of the same supreame spirituall Iurisdiction of the Apostolick See of Rome, and other Catholick doctrines, in the same sence wee now defend them . . . .'

References: Allison and Rogers 159; STC 10415.

2) William Bell, *The testament of William Bel*, 1632, from a copy in the library of Downside Abbey, by permission of the Abbot and Community.

References: Allison and Rogers 86; STC 1802.

ENGLISH

PROTESTANTS PLEA,
AND PETITION, FOR ENGLISH
PREISTS AND PAPISTS, TO THE
preſent Court of Parlament, and all perſecutors of them: diuided into two parts.

IN THE FIRST IS PROVED
by the learned proteſtants of England, that
theſe Preiſts and Catholicks, haue hitherto
been vniuſtly perſecuted, though they haue
often and publickly offered ſoe much, as any
Chriſtians in conſcience might doe.

IN THE SECOND PART, IS PROVED
by the ſame proteſtants, that the ſame preiſtly ſacri-
ſizinge function, acknowledgeing and practize of the
ſame ſupreame ſpirituall Iuriſdiction of the Apoſtolick
See of Rome, and other Catholick doctrines, in the
ſame ſence wee now defend them, and for which
theſe ar at this preſent perſecuted, continued and were,
practized in this Iland without interruption in al ages,
from S. Peter the Apoſtle to theſe our tymes.

Odio habuerunt me gratis
They haue hated me without cauſe,
With permiſsion, Anno 1621.

THE PREFACE
TO AL INDIFFERENT
AND EQVAL READERS.

Ight honorable and the rest, my dearest and moste beloued contrymen, kinred, and frends : I haue by the greate prouidence, protection and mercy of God, liued now amongst you a preist in persecution, little lesse then halfe the life of an aged man : That which remayneth is cheife my debt by nature to die, and make accompt to my highest Kinge, and Iudge, as of late our moste reuerend Arch-preist within these few weekes hath done: whoe (as I interprete his letters) bequeathed as a legacie to mee vnworthie, this chardge: To write, and publish to the world this ensueing treatise, which I name. The protestants Plea, and petition to the Parlament for preists, and papists : (*soe many protestants please to stile Catholicks.*) If this chardge had not beene committed vnto mee by my soe honored and reuerend frend, yett hauinge beene soe longe a partaker of the miseries which english catholicks haue in these tymes endured, and beeing well acquainted with the proceedings of bothe sides, and knowing by certaine experience, that besides their sufferings to their immortall honor, their published bookes by diuers our learned preists haue soe conuinced the vnder standings of our

A 2

grea-

greateſt aduerſaries in all cheife queſtioned things.
That noe proteſtant Bishop or other writer, hath now
after diuers yeares, made any answeare at all vnto
them: and of many former moſte humble petitions of
our learned preiſts and catholicks, both to our proteſtant princes, and parlaments, to haue audience in
diſputation with their beſt learned proteſtant Bishops and doctors, whether they could conuince vs as
guiltie and worthie to bee perſecuted, as we haue
beene, which hither they would neuer graunt, but
haue ſoe longe and greuouſly without any triall or
condemnation, executed and perſecuted vs in ſoe
ſtraunge a maner: and the preſent proteſtant rather
puritane parlament, ſtormeth now more againſt vs,
then the wiſeſt of vs can ſee reaſons to warrant them:
I therefore for the honor of God, and reputation of
his holy church and Religion, the loue of my country,
and to performe my frends requeſt, doe publish this
remembred worke to bee diuided into two parts, and
eyther of them to bee inuincibly proued by the learned proteſtants of this kingdome. In the firſt, becauſe the holye ſcripture ſoe deſcribeth the dutie of
well lyuing men : Declina à malo, & fac bonum,
declyne from euill and to good: I am to proue by
theſe remembred proteſtants, that the catholicks of
England doe moſte religiouſly decline from your Religion, and all participating therein, and their offers conſidered, the proteſtant ſtate doth moſte vniuſtly perſecute them. In the ſecond, to iuſtifie, that
fac bonum, wee doe well, and therein performe the
holy commande of God, in profeſsing the catholicke
                                                      Reli-

Religion, the same with the church of Rome, shall bee demonstratiuely proued by these protestants, and the best Antiquities and monuments they haue of our first true Apostolick Religion, in these kingdomes of our present most honored soueraigne kinge Iames, that not onely those cheifest questions, for which wee ar soe persecuted, as namely holy preisthood, now treason, the sacrifice of the masse so punished, and the spirituall power, and iurisdiction of the see Apostolicke, here now we soe penall and contemptible, but if need require, all other controuersies betweene vs of substance, haue euer from the tyme of S. Peter the Apostle, in euery age, and hundred yeares, vntill these dayes beene practised and continued here, without interruption, in such sence, maner, & meaneinge, as wee catholicks of this kingdome with the church of Rome now doe professe. And here I entreate noe Religious order to take my Title, plea and petition for preists and papists, as any excluding of their holy labours, and deserts, which I embrace and reuerence: for although I will maintaine for them, that monasticall life in England is soe auntient, as the dayes of S. Ioseph of Arimathia, whoe brought it hither, and dyed here with his holy companie in that profession: yett I finde wee had both preists, and Bishops here, in, and of this nation, longe before that tyme, and many Catholick Christians of the same Religion wee now professe, and soe continued vntill this tyme without the least discountinuance or totall interruption; which I dare not to affirme of our Religious men, ceasing for an hundred yeares

A 3

after

after S. Iosephs death : and in the beginninge of Queene Elizabeths tyme, for twenty yeares allmost together, fayled here, when many holy preists were laboureing here in this holy worke : and after some Religious men of the societie had come hither, they went and left vs alone for diuers yeares. Therfore to speake consequently (which I must performe) I must giue this happie prerogatiue to our reuerend preists, whoe neuer fayled or fainted in this cause and contry. They were the first conuerted this kingdome, and did neuer cease. They first tooke this quarrell in hand in the tyme of Q. Elizabeih , and onely were they that neuer gaue it ouer. They principally are they, whoe in the catalogues of our holy writers of this tyme, ar stiled with that honor. They ar the spirituall fathers, and in Christ Iesus haue begoten , both the present Religious, and other catholicks of this kingdome. They, whoe with their holy doctrine, and effusion of their sacred blood , for this moste glorious cause, haue aboue all others (eight or more to one) beene the continuall preachers and propugners of this true faith with vs. They (whoe both in the presence and absence of all religious) haue often offered and humbly sought, publick defence thereof by disputation, against the best learned and selected protestan Bishops and Doctors of this nation. Therfor, leauinge these peculiar honors vnto the Reuerem preists of England, I will with such inequalitie as haue before proposed, maintaine for all preists, Re ligious , and all catholicks , that our holy preist hood , sacrifice of Masse, spirituall Romane ii

risdi

rifdiction , and the like were vfed and continued here
without chaunge , or intermiffion , in the fame
tenure wherein Catholicks now profeffe them,
from S. Peter to thefe dayes, by our proteftant war-
rants and antiquities , and foe I reft

              Your moft loueinge and well
                  wifhing contry man.

TO THE RIGHT HONORABLE
Court of parlament: efpecially fuch as therein bee
perfecutors of Catholicks : and to all other fuch
perfecutors.

A breuiate of the vndoubted truthe of catholick Religion perfecuted in England.

         Right honorable , and the reft.

He penalties , and perfecutions , which
in thefe daies of Proteftants , haue been
heaped vpon , and profecuted againft
the facred preifts , and renowned Catholicks
of England, haue beene foe heauy, and greate
by his Maiefties regall fentence , in publice parlament , that they moued him, to thefe words
of commiferation. *My minde was euer free from*
perfecution , or thrallinge my fubiects in matters of
confcience: I was foe far from encreafing their burdes
with Roboham, as I haue foe much , either as tyme,

        A 4   *occa-*

occaſion , or lawe could permitt , lightned them .
Your Courte well knoweth , what the cauſe of
Roboham was (wee neede ſay noe more , and
what other heauie burdens haue been ſince then
heaped vpon vs; And by your preſent aſſemblie
now againe to bee inuented and added. *in his*
publick ſpeach in his 1. parlam.

You cannot poſſibly bee ignorant what an
eminent man in your houſe , and companie,
hath written of the opinion of the Chriſtian
world, of theſe proceedings: *The ſuffrings* (Syr
Edwine Sandes ſpeaketh vnto you, *in his booke*
of the relation of the ſtate of Religion) and martyr-
domes of Engliſh Catholicks in theſe times , ar ac-
compted to the height of Neroes , and Dioclesians
perſecutions , and the ſuffrings on their ſide , both in
meritts of cauſe , in extremitie of tormerts , and in
conſtancie and patience , to the renowned martyrs
of that heroicall church age. What *Nero* and *Dio-*
cleſian were, amonge the greateſt tyrants , and
perſecutors, your place, and lawe-makers may
not pleade ignorance; neyther what the honor
and glorie of that moſte ſacred preiſthood , ſacrifice and Religions, which ſoe vehemently,
and beyonde example, you perſecute. If all catholicks would bee ſilent, your owne proteſtant Biſhops and Antiquaries haue publiſhed
in Theaters, and hiſtories to the preſent world,
and future poſterities, that the very ſame were
planted and embraced here , in the Apoſtles
tyme, and were neuer chaunged in any mate-
riall

riall thinge , vntill your pretended reformation.
Protest.Bishops in the Theater of Brit. l. 6. Holinsh.
hist. of Engl. in Claud. Cambden in Britan. Godwyn
Conuerf. Parker.antiq. Brit. Grymston booke of Esta-
tes in Engl. Scotland, Ireland.

Yf wee appeale to kings and parlaments,
(whereon you builde,) all the auncient parlaments, lawes and liues of the kings of Scotland,
cry out vnto vs , that after 80. Christian kings
there, king Iames is the first , and onely protestant kinge. The parlaments, lawes, liues of
kings, and histories of England, and Ireland doe
publish vnto vs , that of all his primogenitors
kings of these nations , hee alone is protestant
kinge of them. Hee claymeth nothing from king
Henry 8 Edward 6. or Q. Elizabeth hee enioyeth (and longe and happily God graunt him to
enioy it) this Empire by a better and truer
right, then they could giue him . *Hettor Boeth.*
Vereca. & alij hist. Scot. all English and Irish hist.
With their parlam. &c.

Your histories and the laste wills and testa-
ments of those kings, ar witnesses against them
and your Religion , that they laboured moste
vniustly against the lawe of God, and nature
to suppresse the vnquestionable right of our
soueraigne, and his holy mother . (*Edw. Howes*
preface historial in king. Henr. 8. last will of king
Henr. 8.) All those lawes, parlaments and antiquities ar warrant , that from our first conuersion to Christ , wee had noe other Bishops,
                                                    preists,

preiſt, miniſters, or church ſeruice, which you
call communion , but Romane catholicke Biſ-
ſhops, preiſts (whom you make Traytors) and
ſacrifice of maſſe , for the liuinge and the dead,
now ſoe perſecuted by you , vntill the ſecond
parlament of kinge Edward 6. a childe , moſte
childiſhly began this innouation. (*Parlament
2. Edw. 6. cap. & an. 5. c. 1. Confer. at hampt. court*)
And in Scotland your miniſtry and communion
deuiſed there by that Traytor to God , and
prince , is of a younger ſtandinge , in the yeares
1560. and 1571. (*Commun. booke &c. of the kirke of
Scotland by Iohn knoxe 9. of march. an.* 1560. *and*
1671.) Your Proteſtant Antiquaries muſtar vnto
vs about 1000. approued claſsicall writers , in
this kingdome that be renowned in the chriſtian world; whoe were ſuch preiſts, ſaid maſſe,
preached and proued that Religion they tell vs
of many thouſand Biſhops , by continuall ſucceſſion from our firſt chriſtianitie , of aboue
1000. canonized Saints, of diuers thouſands of
Religious men and woemen , liuing in continuall pouertie , chaſtitie , and obedience : ſince
the tyme of Saint Ioſeph of Arimathia that bu-
ryed Chriſt , and brought monaſticall life into
this kingdome , wee had 700. Religious howſes founded for them , which you haue defa-
ced. *Baleus l. de Scriptor. centur. 1. 2. 3. 4. Ioh. Le-
land. de ſcript. Pitſeus de vir. illuſtrib. ætate 2. 3. 4.
5. &c. Capgrau. & al. de Sainct. hiſto. Angl. paſsim.
Theater of Brit. per tot. Stowe hiſt. Holinsh. hiſtor.
Eng.*

Our Religion builded thofe churches which
you haue referued , & many thowfands which
you haue defaced; Wee enioyed aboue the
third part of England to our Religion 600.
yeares pafte, and after wee had more kings,
Queenes and Princes Saints in this Ifland , and
Ireland, by your owne hiftoryes and kalenders,
then there euer were fince in all the world of
your Religion. (*Tom. 1. 2. 3. Concil.*) Our Religion had for external warrat aboue 20. general
councells. From the firft of Nyce in the time of
Conftantine , our Kinge , Emperour , and con-
tryman , and Sardice , where the popes fuprea-
preamacy , maffe, and preifthood are confirmed,
(*Concil. Nic. 1.can.6.7.Sardic.concil.Theater of Britan. in Brit. Stowe hist. Holinsh. ibid. Camb. Brit*)
which our Brittifh bifhops receued, vntill the
lafte of Trent in the tyme of Q. Elizabeth; to
which our catholicke Bifhop Pates of worcefter , fubfcribed for England for vs , and againft
you , as you proteftant Bifhop telleth vs.
(*Godwyn. Catalog. of Bish. in worcefter in Rich.
Pates*) wee had confequently all holy fathers
and Bifhops prefent in them to warrant vs.
Wee had , and haue, as your Proteftants acknowledge, (*Cafaubon. refponf. ad Cardinal:Peron.
pag. 69. 70.*) all Apoftolicke feas for vs , againft
you, wee had and haue confequently , all thofe
true, and vndeniable motiues of true Religion,
which moued the Chriftian world , to embrace
the

the lawe of Chriſt, to aſſure and confirme vs in this truthe, wee ſee and knowe that this our holy faith accordinge to the foretellinge of Chriſt, his prophets and Apoſtles, is preached and planted in all the worlde, Europe, Africke, Aſia, and America, neuer any Religion in the lawe of nature, of Moyſes, Iewes, Turcks, Tartares, proteſtants, pagans, or other, is, or was at any tyme in anye degree dilated, as it is. *Grymſton Booke of eſtates in k. of Spaine, Europe, Aſia, Africk, America.*

And for externall ſplendor at home, it was ſoe greate, when king Henry 8. began to enuie the glory of it, that he promiſed the parlament (as your proteſtant hiſtories aſſure vs, if it would graunt him power to viſitt the Religious howſes: *Hee would create,* (your proteſtants words) *and mayntayne 40. Earles 60. Barons 3000. knights, and 40. thowſand ſouldiers with skilfull captaines and competent mayntenance for them all for euer, out of the auntient church reueneues, and the people ſhould bee noe more charged with loanes, ſubſides and fifteens.* Of all theſe bleſſings, and benefites wee are ſpoyled, and by your Religion depriued; And not onely wee, that now bee catholicks in England, but all faithfull ſoules allready departed out of this world, and thoſe that are not yet borne, if they ſhall bee of the poſteritie of thoſe holy founders, to bee prayed for, to the end of the world, by thoſe Religious fowndations, and all pore hungry bodyes

there

there releiued with those donations , which protestant tymes haue conuerted to vanities, & that which is vnchristian, to persecute the Religion, which fownded these holy howses. And with such vehemency and cruelty wee ar persecuted, as you haue before acknowledged, your lawes, records, registers, and our miseries, calamities, and martyrdomes haue published to all the world. *Edw. howes in his historiall preface in kinge Henry 8.*

All this you doe vnto vs , vnder pretence that wee will not forsake our holy Religion, soe firmely, and vndoubtedly proued by soe many vndeniable testimonies , in your owne iudgements , that wee cannot bee deceaued, except God (which is vnpossible) can deceaue vs. And in remayninge and persisting wherein, and following and frequentinge that order, which it prescribeth , the sacrifice and Sacraments which it vseth , wee shall by your best learned protestants writing, with your publicke priuiledge , bee sure to bee saued, when contrarywise if wee should bee soe gracelesse, as for feare of torments, and afflictions , to harken vnto you in matters of Religion, the same your best learned protestant Bishops , and others assure vs agayne, wee shall come into a fallible, deceaueable , and actually erroneus Religion, and consequently shall bee damned for euer.
Doue prot. Bish. persswaf. Feild l. of the church pag. 27. 182. Couel.def. of Hooker pag. 68. 73. 76. Feild

pag.

pag. 69. Willet Antilog. 144. Theater of greate Brit. Saxons . Sam. Daniel. hist. &c. Feild pag. 202 Isaac Casaub. praf. responf. ad Card. Peron. Doue persuas. Morton Apolog. part. 2. pag. 315. Willet Antilog. praf. to the Read. vniuersities answeare to the mill. pet. Confer. at Hampt.pag. 47. Protest.Relat. of that conference printed by Ioh. Windet in three seuerall copies 1. 2. 3.

And if God and the truth of his holy cause mayntayned in our bookes, against you , had not inforced and necessitated these your publicke writers , thus publickly to condemne you , and forwarne vs from communicatinge with you, in these affaires : yett the lamentable and desolate experience it selfe in your parlaments of king Henry 8. k. Edward 6. Q. Elizabeth &c. crieth out vnto the world , that all the parlaments and princes supreame heads of Religion by you, haue beene deceaued , and deceaued all , that followed them in these things. Kinge Henry 8. was the first (*parlament of k. Henr. 8. after an. Reg. 22.*) and was herein contrary to all antiquitie , contrary to K. Edward his sonne (*Parlam. Edw.6. 1.2.3.*) daughter Elizabeth (*parlam.* 1: *Elizab. iniunctions of Q. Elizab. an. 1.*) and kinge Iames. (*Articles of Relig. ann. 1561.*) and to himselfe by diuers parlaments, and his Religion dead with him , and condemned by you. Kinge Edward was contrary to his father , his sister , to you , and to himselfe in diuers publicke parlaments , and his publick
iniun-

iniunctions. Queen Elizabeth was in the same
cafe of contradiction, to her father, brother, to
you, and herfelfe by publicke practice , parlament, proclamations, and iniunctions , in leffe
tyme then three quarters of one yeare. And
touchinge that peece of her firft parlament,
wherein fhee condemned the maffe, there was
not one diuine, Bifhop or other, that gaue confent, or could giue it vnto her, but all againft her.
And their extrauagant proceedings therein,
were fuch , as they bee related by your owne
Antiquaries, Cambden , Howes , and others,
that Paganifme , Turcifme, Epicurifme, Iudaif-
me, Atheifme , or any other herefie , might as
eafely haue beene fettled here, as proteftantifme
was : which is not here to bee entreated. King
Iames our prefent foueraigne is generally taken to bee too too wife, and learned, to learne
Religion of fuch Tutors. *Cambden in Apparat
ad Annal. & in annal. in Elizabeth. Howes hiffo-
riall preface in Q. Elizabeth and others.*

Kinge Henry the 8. defired at his death , as
proteftant hiftories fufficiently infinuate , and
diuers then liueing in his Court haue teftified,
to bee reconciled to the church of Rome , and
in one of his lafte Acts the infcription of his
Tombe, doth playnely omitt, and relinquifh
for euer his pretended fupreamacie. And his
laft will and teftament (*Howes fup. in k. Henr. 8.
Stowe an. vlt. Henr. 8. in his lafte will & teftament*)
ordeyned preifts , & maffes , (foe odious now,
and

and cheifeſt cauſe pretended of our perfection, *to continue in England to the end of the world, willinge and chardgeinge* (the words of his will) *prince Edward his ſonne, all his executors, all his heires and ſucceſſors that ſhould bee kings of this Realme, as they will anſweare before almightie God, at the dreadfull day of iudgment, that they, & euerie of them doe ſee it performed. (Exempl. an. 1. Edw. 6. die 14. Februar.)* Kinge Edward 6. was but a child, but both hee and his protectors by which hee was ruled, ſhould haue beene ruled by this will, yet as proteſtants vſe to doe, preſentlie breakinge it, for their worldly ends, and breingeing in the proteſtant Religion. (*Foxe to. 2. Acts and monum. in k. Henr. 8. and an. 1. Edw. 6.*)

The cheife Actor, and Author of thoſe proceedings, the Duke of Northumberland Lord protector, when hee came to dy, renownced proteſtant Religion for hereſie, and as your proteſtant hiſtories tell vs, (*Stowe hiſtor. an. 1. of Queene Mary. and others.*) was reconciled vnto, and dyed in the vnitie and faith of the Romane church. For Queene Elizabeth, ſhee, as ſome noble men, and diuers ladyes of honor can informe you, and ſome haue ſoe teſtified, died noe good proteſtant, neither could endure the ſight of her proteſtant Biſhops, at that time: and proteſted in her life to the lady Saint-Iohn widowe to the Lord Oliuer Saint-Iohn of Bletſoe, *Deus teſtis*, ſoe ſhee confidently related, and ſaid ſee could ſhew that Queenes letters

ters to that purpofe, that fhe would haue liued a
Catholike , but for her ouer-ruling Proteftant
Counfaile : naminge fome of them, no happie
members of this kingdome ; which your Proteftant hiftorians giue way vnto , that fhe did very
often, before fuch men by politick deuifes with-
drew her from it ; frequent *the Sacraments* of
Confeffion , of the *bleffed bodie of Chrift , Maffe,
and the rites of Catholike Religion* (*Edw. Howes
hiftoricall preface in Queene Elizabeth* (and Protefted in publicke Parlament , *neuer to vexe or
trouble the Romaue Catholikes, concerning any difference in Religion* Like was the cafe of William
Cecile, Lord Burleigh hir greatCounfailor,both
for his Religion, in that time ; and at his death,
charged his fonne *Robert* Earle of Salisbury,ne-
uer to perfecute any of that Religion. Thus hee
aknowledged to a worthy and noble witneffe;
who , as God is witneffe, fo hath teftified.

We doe not , we will not conteft, with our
prefent,moft honoured,wife, and learned Soueraigne; neither enter into his priuat iudgement:
But if any the beft learned proteftant - Archbi-
fhops,or Bifhops you haue, will iuftifie all thofe
publicke fpeaches, wittings , and bookes which
goe vnder the name of our King , to proceede
from him;if it will pleafe him to giue way vnto
it, they fhall haue maintained againft them , that
by thofe publifhed writings, 'it is damnable for
them to perfecute vs, and we in confcience cannot , if to gaine a thoufand worlds , be of your

pro-

proteſtant Religion. And we humbly hope this
nothing derogateth to his prudentMaieſtie: for
we openly and willingly write,that concerning
all your beſt learned Bishops, and others that
haue written;as namely W*hitguiſt*,and *Bancroſt*,
of Canterburie , *Bilſon*, and *Andrewes* of Win-
cheſter , *Doue, Barlowe,Godwine , Field, Bridges,
Hooker, Couell,* and all the beſt ſtudents amongſt
you, were in iudgement far from perſecution of
Catholikes, and as far from aſſurance,that they
themſelues were in trueReligion. It is no vaine
boaſting now to write it ; becauſe in all contro-
uerſiall poynts , we haue many yeares ſince inuincibly prooued it by your beſt learned Proteſtant Bishops and Doctors, (*Proteſtants Recan-
tation in matters of Religion. l. 1.& l. 2. Proteſtants
Demonſtrat. for Catholikes Recuſancy ,&c.*) both
in generall; that neither Scriptures ,Traditions,
Counſels,Apoſtolike Churches, Fathers, or any
authoritie in diuine matters is for you,but all a-
gainſt you , that you haue not,neither hereafter
by your Religion can poſſibly find, any Rule or
direction to bring you into trueth : That there
is not,nor can be any true and competent Iudge
or Conſiſtorie with you to decide theſe contentions , and bring you into the right way. That
there is neither true Bishop, Prieſt, or Cleargie
man in your Congregation : That in all particular queſtions betweene vs, you are in error.
  All theſe things ſo inuincibly prooued by
your ſelues , that now after diuers yeares, our
                                    bookes

bookes receaue no anſwere at all: And your beſt
learned are ſo far from taking this charge in
hand, that but for diſgraces of theſe times with
you , they would in their liues and health,
not liue in your wauering religion, but be reconciled to the Romane Church , as many of them
laetly at their deaths haue bene. And now in
this your Parlament time , to moue you and
London , to know the trueth, the late Proteſtant Biſhop thereof, Doctor *King*, in his life
for externall cariage, a great perſecutor of Prieſts
and Catholikes, a little before his death did
playnely denounce your Religion to be damnable, renounced (as wee haue prooued before of
all ſuch) that he was any Biſhop or Cleargie
man : was penitent for hs proteſting hereſie, &
humblie at the feete of a Prieſt, whom he had
formely perſecuted, confeſſed his ſinnes , receued Sacramentall abſolution at his handes, and
was reconciled to the Catholike Romaine
Church, of which he had in his life bene ſo vehement a perſecutor. Zealouſly and openly proteſting, there was nc ſaluation to be had out of
that holy Catholike Romane Church. Therefore wee neede not to diſpute theſe matters a-
new.

But becauſe by the preſent tempeſts you raiſe
againſt vs in this your Parlament , we are aſſured that your ſtorming perſecutions are not
ceaſed, if your wils and anger can maintaine
their bluſtringe , therefore we cannot but ſtill

defend our innocencie, and humbly admonish
you that by these courses you offer, and doe, &
we receaue and suffer wrong. And because you
see and know, you are neither able to instruct
vs, or your selues, persisting in persecution, you
fall into that lamentable estate, preached vnto
you out of Pulpit by your now Archbishop of
Yorke (D. *Matthewes Serm. before the Parlament*)
and in publike Parlament denounced by his
Maiestie: *Persecution without instruction, is but tyrannie* (K• *Iames speach in Parlament.*) That you
cannot, or vncharitably will not (both leade to
that damnable estate) we are now euidently to
demonstrate to you, and make knowne to the
world for our owne excuse ; which we can doe
by no better or more certaine meanes in this
case, then publish and make knowne to our dearest contrey, that from the first beginning of
these your persecutions, broached and borne in
the first Parlament of Queene Elizabeth, wee
haue in all humble and best meanes we could,
requested, and sought for instruction, from your
best learned Bishops, Doctors, and instructors,
among you, if we be in error by many and sundry petitions to our Protestant Princes, Parlaments, and others, that were in chiefe place and
command, to procure it, if there had bene any in
your Religion that could performe it. If you
had that could, and would not, your estate is
more then dangerous : if you haue none, can instruct vs, which you make apparant, if you still
                                                    persist

perfift imperfecution. You heare our King and
your Archbishop call vnto you: *Correction Without inftruction , is but tyrannie.*

Therfore in this firft part of this Proteftant
plea , and petition of your beft learned Proteftants in both parts to be vndeniably proued, &
iuftified by them ; wee propofe fome of thofe
moft humble fuites and petitions, we haue by
the beft warrant fpirituall we had in England,
our moft Reuerend Archprieft , his learned
Priefts , chiefeft renowned Catholikes , prefented,to procure , and obtaine this inftruction,
in conference and difputation , with your beft
learned Proteftant Bifhops and Doctors , and
with fuch vnequall conditions on our behalfe,
that except the Catholikes of England hab bin
affured,they were in trueth, and their difputant
Priefts could not be inftructed by any the beft
learned in your Religion , they could not in
confcience haue made fo large and difaduanta-
geous offers vnto you, as their feuerall petitions
and fuits will witneffe: Except you will thinke
(to flatter your felues) that thefe renowmed
Priefts and Catholikes, did doubt of their Religion (which their martirdomes and fufferings
for it, do inuincibly reproue) and appeale to you
for inftruction, which you denying, and yet fo
perfecuting them , can neuer free your felues
from that dolefull condition remembred by
our gratious King and your Archbifhop ; you
will further receaue in this firft part fuch iufte
B   and

and moſt reaſonable and vnanſwereable reaſons
by the Religions , and proceeding of all your
ſupreame heades in ſpirituall buſines vntill his
maieſties time (wherein ſilence will be vſed)
King *Henry* 8. King *Edward* the 6. and Queene
Elizabeth ; that as they are ſet downe by your
beſt proteſtant writers , we cannnot yeelde to
you in matters of Religion; neither you in conſcience, either perſecute vs in theſe things, or
your ſelues ſecured in that profeſſion.

How Catholicke Religion was vniuſtlye ſup-
preſſed by Queene Elizabeth , not one Spi-
rituall perſon hauing voyce in Parlamente
conſenting : no diſputation or ordinarie defence
thereof permitted to the Catholike Biſhoppes
and Cleargie : and their duitifull loyaltie not-
withſtanding, and their pietie honoured by their
proteſtant enemies .

IN THE firſt yeare and Parlamente of
Queene Elizabeth , when our aunciente
holy Catholike Religion was ſo vnholily , and
irreligiouſly ſuppreſſed , and the new Proteſtant maner and faſhion , by her authoritie receaued , as partly before remembred, from our
ProteſtantHiſtories , and will by them more
amplie be declared hereafter : All the Catholike Biſhops of England then liuing ſo farre
oppoſed againſt it , that as a Proteſtant Antiquarie relateth , obſeruing the willfull and
inci-

indirect proceedings of her, and some few of her secret Councellours, and aduisers in that so importunat businesse, far aboue the compasse, calling, and correction of a yong woman, and laye men, diuers of them vrged to proceede to excommunicate that Queene at that time. (*Cambd. Annal. in Eliz.ab.p.37.* But others which preuailed, aduised to reserue it to the Pope of Rome : And they all ioyntly contradicted that innouation, and then and there offered, as all protestant historians agree (*Stowe and Howes hist. an. 1. Eliz. Holinsh. hist. of Engl. Ib. Theater of Brit.an. 1.Eliz. Cambd.in Annal.supra.*)publickly to defend and maintaine by disputation, against all aduersaries whatsoeuer, their holy professiõ and religion, and to that purpose assigned and appointed these disputants : *The then Bishop of Winchster, the Bishop of Lichfielde, the Bishop of Chester, the Bishop of Charlile, who had crowned her, the Bishop of Lincolne, Doctor Cole, Doctor Harpessfield, Doctor Langdal, and Doctor Chadsey.*

But that protestãt Q. & her fauorites knowing the weaknes of their cause to be such, and how their chiefest chãpions had bene not long before in publike schooles at Oxford, in the time of Queene *Marie* so shamefully conuinced, by some of these Catholikes, that they were hissed by the learned Auditors, durst not ioyne with thē in tryal(*Foxe in Q. Mary, Crã.&c*) But the Parlamẽt begining on or about the 23.of Ianuary, they had so prepared theyr way before, that almost in the beginning of that Parlament, they obtained their purpose , for the receauing their new Religion, and effected it in the very first Acte or law of that Parlament (*Statut. an. 1. Eliz. cap.2.*) and would neuer harken to any motion, or petition for disputation , vntill the laste day of March (*Stowe, Howes. Holinsh. vt sup.*) almost two moneths after they had thus vtterly excluded the Popes authoritie, and the catholike religion , vsed and practised here in this kingdome, euer since the time of Pope *Elutherius*, and King *Lucius* , as the catholikes offered in Parlament to maintaine , foruteene hundred yeares togeather , without interruption *Feckh. orat. 1. Elizab.*) and publicke Masse and seruice of the church to haue bene here so long, celebrated in the latine tongue. And would not then condiscend to any disputation at all, except the catholikes would accept , (to write in Protestants words ; That, *Baconus in Theologicis parum versatus, pontificij infestissimus, & ordinis vindex, tanquam iudex præsideret* : Bacon(*a layman*) *vnskilful in diuinity a most infestuous enemy to Papists, and persecutor of their order, should be iudge* (*Camden Annall.* pag. 27.

And if we may beleeue the present protestant Archbishop , the director of M. *Francis Mason* in their booke of confecration, among so many essentiall matters controuersed betweene the Protestants and vs, they would not dispute any one at all, but onelie three, concerning some ceremoremonies. (*Fran. Maſon in præf. of their booke of cō-ſecrat. and pag.* 103.) 1. *About common prayer ın the Latine or vulgar tongue* 2. *Of the power of Churches to change ceremonies. The third and laſt ; whether communion was to be miniſtred in both kindes* and the triall of theſe three ceremonies, to be made by a fourth moſt ſtrange ceremonie, in diſputation, *onely to be put in writting, within two daies warning at the moſt, vnum & alterum dicm de quæſtionibus præmoniti* ; as your antiquarie writeth, *and deliuered to their ſaid offenſiue enemy, Sir* Francis Bacon (*Cambden annal. pag. 27.*) A thing ſo ridiculous and vnequal, in the iudgement of all learned and wiſe men, that if it had bene offered before Catholike religion was there condemned, it could not in conſcience, either by thoſe learned Biſhops and Doctors, or the moſt learned that euer were in the Church of Chriſt, nor by the holy Apoſtles themſelues if they had then and there bene, be accepted.

Yet Queene Elizabeth and her aduiſers in this, notwihſtanding that ſhe had in open Parlament before, as before is teſtified by our Proteſtant writers (*Howes hiſtoricall preface in Q. Elizabeth.*) *openly pronounced, that ſhee would neuer vexe or trouble the Romane Catholikes, concerning any difference in Religion* : in that very parlament, where ſhe ſpake theſe wordes and made that promiſe, proceeded to cruell penalties, againſt thoſe Romane Catholikes ; all our holie Biſhops were depriued, impriſoned, or exiled:

(*Stow hiſto. an. 1.Eliz.Holinsh.ibid. Cambden An-nal. an. 1. Elizab. Theatre of Brit. an. 1. Eliz. &c.*
So were all other Eccleſiaſticall perſons that
would not doe, as pleaſed her. Great forfaitures
and puniſhments were impoſed vpon all that
ſhould heare Maſſe, or not be preſent at the
new deuiſed ſeruice, (*Parl. an. 1. Eliz. cap..12.*)
premunire, loſſe of landes, goods, and perpetual
impriſonment, and loſſe of iife alſo, with note
of Treaſon to them, that ſhould denie that ſupreame ſpirituall power to be in her, which
many Proteſtants and learned, both then and at
this time ſaid, and ſay, ſhe was incapable of. All
which notwithſtāding that moſt worthy cleargie in exile, and priſons at home, ſo caried themſelues in all ciuill dutie to that Queene, that
they are in that reſpect recommended and honored by their greateſt Proteſtant aduerſaries
and Perſecutors, and for learning and pietie
dignified and exalted more by theirs and our
enemies, then euer any Proteſtant Biſhop or
Miniſters, which inuaded their holy places
ſinces that time. (*Proteſt. def. of English Iuſtice.
Godwine Catal. in thoſe Bish. Camden in Annal.*)
But of this ſtrange innouation of Religion by
Q. Elizabeth, I ſhal write more largely from
theſe Proteſtants hereafter.

The

The vertu, learning, and dutiful loyaltie of the Se-
minarie or secular (as some name them) Priestes
which came after into England, the vniust perse-
cution of them, and catholikes here, and their
most christian and religious offers and behauiour.

AFter Q. Elizabeth had by profane deuifes
& inuentions of some few irreligeous coũ-
cellors, suppressed the auntient catholike religiõ
of this nation, by such sinister proceedings, as ar
before infinuated, & to the wonder of the christian world, *orbe christiano mirante*, as this Protestant chiefest antiquarie truely noteth *(Cambden*
Ann. p. 39.) for the vncõscionable maner, & effecting herõf: though she shad in opẽ Parlamẽt, as
befor protested, *neuer to vexe or trouble the Roman*
Catholikes, cõcerning any differẽce in Religiõ (Hows
historical preface in Q. Elizabeth) yet being assured, as the truth was, by her *pauculi intimi, her*
very few secret friendes (Cambd. sup.) that except
she became a persecutor, againit her faith & pro-
mife so publikely, and lately giuen, & so ioyne
craft and violence together, the weaknes of her
cause was such, and the learning and conuersa-
tion of life, of those her Protestant ministers,
whom she must imploy in this busines, so vnequall, and inferiour to the Catholike Bishops,
and Cleargie of England, that no hope of such
successe as they sought could bee, except these
holie and worthie men were depriued, imprisoned, banished, or vtterly one way or other,
put

put to silence, in such maner, that after their
deathes , our most sacred order of Priesthood,
which had continued in this nation here , in
honor and glorie , from S. Peter the Prince of
the Apostles , as we haue made demonstrance
in other places , might vtterly and for euer be a-
bolished and extinguished, as these fewe secrete
friends of those designements open Antipriests,
or Antichristians (for the Religion of Christ,
cannot be without the Priests of Christ) plot-
ted and hoped to effect. Your principall protestant Antiquarie , thus relateth that cruell Tragedie. (*Cambden in Annal. lib. pag. 36.*)

*Parlamento dimisso , ex eiusdem authoritate, Epi-
scopis pontificijs & alijs ecclesiasticæ professionis iu-
ramentum suprematus proponitur. Quotquot iurare
abnuerunt , beneficijs, dignitatibus exuuntur, 80. re-
ctores ecclesiarum. 50. prebendarij, 15. præsides Colle-
giorum, Archidiaconi. 12. totidem decani. 6. Abbates
& Abbatissæ , & Episcopi 14. Omnes qui tunc sede-
runt, præter vnum Antonium Landauensem, sedis
suæ calamitatem.*

The Parlament being ended , by the authoritie therof, the oath of the Queenes supreamacie was proposed to the popish Bishops , and all
Ecclesiasticall persons , as many as refused to
sweare, were depriued of their benefices, dignities , and Bishoprickes. 80. Rulers of Churches,
50 Prebendaries. 15. Masters of Colledges , 12.
Archdeacons. 12. Deanes. 6. Abbots, and Abbes-
ses, and 14. Bishops ; all that then remained
                                        except

except one *Anthonie* Bishop of *Landaffe*, the calamitie of his Sea. These Bishops inferiour in
vertue and learning to none in Europe, as your
Protestants acknowledge(*Mason lib. 3. consecrat.
c.1.pag.100. Cambd. in Annal. sup. Stowe histor. an.
1.Eliz. Holinsh hist. of Engl. 16.*) thus deposed and
imprisoned, and there to languish to death, they
thought none could suruyue to consecrat anie
more priestes for England: and all rulers of our
Colledges in our(then renowned) Vniuersities
thus expelled, that would not forsweare themselues in such a sacriledgeous manner, they
thought themselues assured, we could haue no
succession of Catholike students here to enter
into that holy priestly order.

But, *non est counsilium contra Dominum*, there is
no counsayle against our Lord. The prophane
craft and wylinesse of a few wicked men, ioyned with a womans spirititual supreamacie, was
too weake to oppose and battaile against the
heauenly wisdome and will of God. For a very
small number, and those of the meanest then, of
our glorious Cleargie, transporting themselues
to Catholike nations, and by such poore meanes
as they could procure, liueing in collegiall discipline and order at *Doway* in Flaunders, where
our common happie and spirituall Nurse and
Mother is, haue so wounderfull and far beyond
the reach of your protestant polycies and strate-
gems, to the honour of God, and his holy cause,
against you, multiplied and encreased, that the
num-

number and glory of our renowned publikely ſtiled writers , which in this time haue
come from thence, giueth not place to anye
age, ſince our firſt conuerſion to Chriſte (*Pitſ.
de vir:b. illuſtrib. Brit. ætate 16.17.*) our holie
Martirs violently put to death by your Edictes,
and proceedings (*Stowe hiſtor. in Henric.* 8.
Elizabeth. & Iacob. Catalog. martyr. ſub Henric.
8. *Eliz̄. & Iacob.* 1.5.) exceede the number , &
are not exceeded in glorie by any , that hiſtories amonge vs doe remember, or whoſe memories by iniquitie of times are not remaining, except the *nouenius perſecution*, duringe
but nine yeares (*Gildas de excid.*) ours nine-
times as longe, vnder Dioclefian the tyrant.
The Religious men of our Nation , all the ſpirituall Children of that Mother , are nowe
poſſeſſours of manie Religious Colledges,
and Monaſteries, vnder Chatholike princes,and
ſome of them in England , with ſo many of
ours are enrolled in the Catologue of glorious martirs, and a great number here ſtil working in this holy labour with vs. And if to enter into ſcholes with your beſt learned , wee
needed their aſſiſtance, wee doubt not, but diuers of them are both wel able, and alſo readie
to aſſiſt vs.

But wee haue euer bene ſo far from either
needing or requiring it , of them , that when
you gaue vs the greateſt hopes of diſputation , wee neuer ſent for any of our owne

re-

renowned profeſſors lyuing in forraine nations: But as true Prieſts of England are the ſucceſſors of Saint Peter the glorions Apoſtle, and
his holie Diſciples in this Nation , by a continued and neuer yet interrupted Hierar-
chicall ſucceſſion to this daye, as we will iuſtifie againſt your beſt antiquaries, and diuines;
and firſt after our Biſhops by you depriued,
impriſoned, and perſecuted, vndertooke this
quarrell of God in hande againſt you , and
gained many ſoules to Chriſt ; and for no
crueltie or perſecutions you rayſed, or ax-
agerated againſt them , coulde at any time be
forced to forſake that holie combate , they
had vndertaken : But as true Paſtors they ad-
uentured , and gaue their liues for the ſheepe
of our higheſt ſhepheard and redeemer : ſo
to the hazard of the honour of Catholike Religion, if Proteſtants could haue put them to
foyle, in all theſe miſeries and affliЖions , de-
ſtitute of bookes, conference and harbour, oftentimes to hide their heades, yet they were
euer readie to offer , and entreate for tryall,
with vnequall conditions ; and ſo vnequall
and preiudiciall to the diſputante Prieſtes,
and Catholickes of England , that except
they had beene ſo confidente in their cauſe,
that they could not be ouercome, and the Proteſtant Biſhops and DoЖors compleately fur-
niſhed and prouided of all thinges requiſite
to ſuch a conflicte , if their quarrell were
iuſt,

iuſt, had not bene deſperatly diffident in theſe matters; neither might the Catholikes in conſcience haue made thoſe ſuits and offers, or theſe proteſtants without damnable ſhame haue refuſed them : as the petitions themſelues will be euerlaſting witneſſe to the world.

And when the proteſtant ſtate of England had in aboue twenty of the firſt yeares of Q. Elizabeth, afflicted vs with many miſeries, and had put many of our renowned and beſt learned prieſts, M. *Sherwine*, *Foord*, and others, to whom they durſt not graunt priuate diſputation (in the Tower it ſelfe though neuer ſo ſecret) vniuſtly to cruell death : and had vſed M. *Campion*, the glorie of that Societie in England, in ſuch meaſure, neuer allowing him to defende his owne written booke, though neuer ſo priuatly, vntill by tortures and rackes they had almoſt depriued him of his life, and after with many of our learned and holy prieſts, did depriue him thereof; had baniſhed M. *Heywood*, and M. *Parſons* had forſaken England, the three prime Engliſh Ieſuits of that time; And no other religious man either of that, or any other order, but onely prieſts being here; and of them aboue thirtie in priſõ in the Tower, Marſhalſea, Kings-bench and other places : About which time, the 27. yeare of her raigne, Queene Elizabeth was ſo vnmindfull of her promiſe made in her firſt parliament before remembred, that by degrees ſhee clambred vp, to the heigheſt pitch of perſecution

tion, against her Catholike subiects, that she imposed twenty poundes for euery moneth absence, frō that her new seruice (Parl. of Q. Eliz.
tit. Recusancy) at which to haue bene pretent, had
bene damnable sinne and heresie, frō our first
conuersiō to Christ, vntil the yeare of K. Edward
the sixt a child, both by the lawes of the whole
Catholike Church, and of this kingdome.

And not content with this, proceeded to that
contempt of the Priestly dignity of our most
blessed Sauiour and Redeemer, his holy Apostles, and all holy Bishops, and Priests since their
time; that she intended to make it treason; and al
that willingly receaued such men (as Christ our
Sauiour commandeth all men to do) vnder a
great woe and penaltie of losse of libertie, lands,
goods, and life also, which she after enacted for
a law in that Parlament. Whereupon, and for
preuention of so vnchristian proceedings, the
chiefest catholikes of this nation, with the consent and directiō of their learned secular Priests,
then onely here remaining (and no religious
men being at that time, or diuers yeares after
in England) humbly, prefered to that Queene, in
her Parlament time, when shee decreed that
bloody edict, this most christian, and more then
equall petition, following word by word.

TO THE QVEENES MOST Excellent Maieſtie, the humble petition of her Catholike ſubiectes of Englãd in the 27.yeare of her raigne, wherein their innocencie is iuſtified, and their Religion offered to be maintained for holy, againſt all Proteſtants.

MOST mighty, and moſt excellent, our dread Soueraigne Ladie, and Queene : the neceſsitie of our lamentable Caſe hath emboldned, yea neceſſarily enforced vs, your Maieſties Catholike and approoued Loyal ſubiects, to preſent our manifold griefes and miſeries, to the merciful viewe, of your Maieſtie, We could ſtill haue bene contented (as hitherto we haue bene) with ſilence to haue made vertue of exceeding great neceſsities : But now moſt gratious Soueraigne, the Law of God and nature doth Councell vs, to appeale vnto your moſt excellent Heighnes, our head-ſpring and fountaine of mercy, for the lightning of ſome heauy yoakes, which by common reporte we haue iuſt cauſe to feare, are intended shortly to be layed vpon our weakned and wearied neckes.

To ſpeake to ſo potent and prudent a prince, as it may be reported boldneſſe : ſo not to ſpeake in a poore and diſtreſſed ſubiect, may be deemed guiltines. Wee doe therefore, moſt deare Soueraigne, with all humilitie and no leſſ ſorrow, cry out and complaine

that

that our afflicted harts haue conceaued an vnspeake
griefe: For what wound can be more mortall to the
bodie, as treasonable accusations to innocent mindes?
We your Catholike subiects, which hitherto haue
bene, and euer will be, as well carefull to please your
Maiestie, as not to displease almightie God, what lamentable state was euer like to ours, that we poore
wretches in discharging our conscience towarde
God, are reported of, and that before your sacred
Maiestie, to be euill affected towardes your Royall
person, and princely dignities, and that vpon the
vyle action and intend of euery lewed person, wee
must be condemned all for traytors? as it appeareth
in bookes daily printed against vs, wherein we are
most odiously tearmed blood-suckers, and by vncha-
ritable exclamations, it is published, that your Maiestie is to feare so many deaths, as there be Papists
in the land. Would God our harts might be layde o-
pen to the perfect view of your Maiestie, and all the
world, no doubt our thoughts should appeare cor-
respondent to the expectation of so mercifull a
Queene, in all louing, true, and faithfull subiection,
and would giue vs dewe deserte of mercie for our
reward.

For most deare Soueraigne, where our greatest
accusation ryseth vpon our recusancy, or absence
from the Church, which hath deuoyded vs of all your
wonted graces, and speciall fauours, wee take al-
mighty God to wittnesse, that this our refusing and
absenting our selues, is not grounded in vs vpon any
contempt of your Maiesties Lawes, or any other will-

C 2　　　　　　　*full*

full or trayterous intent , but altogether vpon meere
conscience, and feare to offende God. This God knoweth the searcher of all hearts, and to the ende, that
our sincerity and dutifull meaning may appeare the
better; we doe protest before the face of the eternall
God, and Lord of vs all , and doe craue his dreadfull indignation in this worlde, and sentence of
endlesse dampnation to bee our portion in another
worlde, if wee doe practise, speake, or write any
thinge in this poynte, more or lesse in respecte of
anie worldlie pollicie , but onelie as the duety of
euerie good Christian Catholike bindeth him. In
which opinion , if happelie wee bee deceaued,
yet if wee should doe contrarie to that we thinke
in conscience to be right, we may iustly be accompted men voyde of all grace and honesty , pretending
in shew, and thinking otherwise in heart, false dissemblers, hatefull to God and man, and in truth the
most dangerous and worst subiects that may be in a
common wealth, as aptest to any wicked or desperat attempt.

No lesse is verified in the late mosse execcrable
example of that monster Parry , whose detestable endeauours , doe giue euidente testimonye, that
the cruell vypar , euer temporising and makinge
ship-wracke , of all faith and Religion , hathe
thereby at length , loste both taste and habite of
the grace and feare of God. Let such diabolicall
dissimulation , and trayterous thirste after hallowed blood, sinke according to Gods iudgement
to their deserued doome of deepe damnation; we for
our

our parts vtterly deny, that either Pope, or Cardinall hath power or authoritie to commande, or licence anie man to consent to mortall sinne, or to commit, or intende any other acte , contra ius diuinum; much lesse can this dislayall wicked and vnnaturall purpose, by any meanes be made lawefull ; to write , that a naturall subiecte maye seeke the effusion , of the sacred bloode of his annoynted Soueraigne: whosoeuer hee bee therefore spirituall , or Temporall, that maintaineth so apparant sacriledge, wee therein renounce him , and his conclusion as false, deuilish , and abhominable.

But nowe to returne , to our purposed matter , wee doe promise , that wee will hereafter be reddie and willing to resorte vnto Churches, and other places, where publicke exercise of prayer is vsed, if the learned nowe assembled in conuocations, ball bee able by sufficiente groundes of Diuinitie, to prooue to the learned of the catholike Church , that wee (being in Religion Catholike) may without committing mortall sinne , frequent those Churches, where the contrary religion is professed, and exercised. If conscience onely had not pressed vs in this point, those of our Religion would neuer haue suffered therefore so many disgraces, & impouerishments.

And if that the mercifull eyes , of your clement Princely nature, could but see the continual terrours, the streight imprisonment , the reproachfull arraynement, making no difference, in place nor time, betweene murderers, felons, & rogues , and be-

tweene

tweene gentlemen of all degreees, descended of honorable and worshipfull parentage. Their arraignements being onely and directly for matters of conscience, as also the famine, and miserable ende of diuers imprisoned, the pittifull whippings , penaltie of twentie pounde a moneth, by reason wherof many good and worshipful housholders, with their wiues and children are brought to extreame pouertie : Many stand out-lawed , and a number of poore soules remaine prisoners for that cause: beside many other strange distressed Catholikes, whose miseries heretofore not throughly knowen to your Maiestie , haue bene and are digested with mildnesse and tempered with dutifulnesse : hoping that now at length our approoued patience , will mooue your most tender heart to haue some pitie and compassion of vs.

Moreouer (most gratious dreade soueraigne Ladie and Queene) it may please your most excellent Maiestie , to graunt vs the grace and fauour to heare the vnfolding of our greater and more dangerous calamitie hang ng ouer our heades. For as much as nothing is more often and deepely to be called to our mindes then the frailtie of men , and how we apt and prone we are to all sinne and wickednesse : for the staye and remedie whereof our Lord and Sauiour Iesus Christ , hath instituted and left behinde him , moste holy and blessed sacraments , for the comfort of mankinde , and hath commanded the vse of them to be continued and preached in the Catholike Church , as the

con-

conduits of his graces , without the which the be-
nefits of his deare passion cannot ordinarily descende
or be applyed vnto vs , as by which we are receaued,
confirmed, remitted, fedde, gouerned, multiplyed and
absolutely prepared to life euerlasting.

These benefites are to be valued at no lesse
price to vs , then they were to our forefathers , who
religiously esteemed the want of them more dan-
gerous and discomfortable, then death it selfe.
The ordinary ministers whereof are , and alwaies
haue bene, Catholike Bishops, and Priests, lawfully
called and anoynted , to that charge and spirituall
authoritie, whom by diuine ordinance we are bound
to heare, receaue and obeye, with dew honour, and
reuerence, and to seeke vnto them as to the dispen-
fers of the mysteries of God , for counsel and helpe
howe to liue and die in the loue and fauour of him,
who hath power to cast both the body and soule
of his enemies , into the perpetuall torments of hell
fier.

In consideration of all which necessary poynts,
and for the humble and true purgation of our selues,
we doe protest before the liuing God , that, all and e-
uery Priest, or Priests, who haue at any time conuer-
sed with vs, haue recognissed your Maiestie their vn-
doubted and lawful Queene : Tam de iure, quam
de facto. *They speake reuerently of you : They duely*
pray for you ; they zealously exhort your subiects to
obey you; they religiously instruct vs, to suffer patienly
what authoritie shall impose on vs; yet they precisely
admonish vs , that it is an heresy condemned by

gene-

generall Councels, for any *subiect to liste vp his hand against his annoynted. This is their doctrine, this they speake, this they exhorte* ; *and if wee knowe, or shall knowe, in anie of them one poynt of treason, or treacherous deuise, or any vndecent speach, or any thought iniurious to your Royall person* : *wee doe binde our selues by oathe irreuocable, to bee the first apprehenders and accusers of such.*

If nowe (*most Gratious Ladie*) *these Priestes, who haue not at any time bene detected, accused or charged, with anie acte, or deuise of treason, shall offerre to continue within this your Realme, and for so doing, shall be adiudged traitours, be it for their comming hither, or continuance here, or for practising, or administring of the blessed Sacramentes onelye* : *then consequently, wee your faithfull and louing subiectes are like to bee capitallie touched with the same, treason* : *and wee knowe by no possible meanes, how to cleare and keepe our selues from it. For when the Prophets, and annoynted Priests of God, mooued by zeale to gayne soules, doe repayre hether, to distribute Spirituall comfortes, according to euerie mans neede* ; *and comming to our gates to craue naturall sustenance for their hungrie and persecuted bodies, promising vs also ghostlye foode, and medecine for our vncleane soules* : *What shall wee nowe doe* ? *we doe verily beleeue them to be Priestes of Gods Church, wee*

doe

doe certainelie knowe, that they doe daylie praye
for your Maiestie . Their predecessoures in that
calling haue ministred Baptisme , and Confirmation vnto your Maiestie , annoynted you Queene,
and ordinarily and rightlye placed you in your
Royall seate, as all your Maiesties ancestours haue
bene.

O poore wormes ! what shall become of vs!
what desolatione are wee brought vnto ! O God
of Heauens, Earth and Men witnesse with vs ,
and pleade our cause. O moste lamentable con-
ditiòn, if wee receaue them, by whome we know
no euill at all ; it shall bee deemed Treason in
vs: if wee doe shutte our doores and denie temporall reliefe to our Catholique Pastours , in respecte of their function , then are wee all, alrea-
die iudged most damnable Traytours to Almightie God , and his holie members, and are moste
guiltie of that curse, threatned to light vpon such
as refuse to comfort and harbour the Apostles and
disciples of Christ saying whosoeuer shal not receaue
you, nor heare your wordes , truely it shall be easier
for them of the lande of Sodome and Gomorra
in the daye of iudgemente, &c. againste which
irreprooueable sentence , wee maye in noe wyse
wrastle.

Beholde (most gratious and Liege Soueraigne) into
what streight we are plunged; be fauourable we beseech your heighnesse, to the liues and soules of
men, it is the force of your Royall word, and the

C 5   prote-

protection of your large prerogatiues , that can onely
diſperſe theſe torments , and direct vs, to the calme
and ſafe hauen of indempnity of conſcience. The
mindes of men , (moſt heigh and royall ſoueraigne)
are vttered in their willes , and their willes with af-
fections are commonly expreſſed in their wordes and
deedes. Let our deedes throughly be examined, and
there ſhall be found harboured, neither in our willes
euill affects : neither in our mindes diſloyal thoughts.
Wherefore with moſt deepe ſighes, proſtrate before
the throne , and at the feete of your Heignes royal
Maieſtie, we with all humilitie, doe ſubmit theſe our
lamentable griefes : and albeit that many wayes we
haue bene afflicted, yet this affliction folloowing (if it
be not by the accuſtomed naturall benignitie of your
Maieſtie ſuſpended, or taken away) will light vpon
vs to our extreame ruine , and certaine calamitie,
that either we (being Catholikes) muſt liue, as bodies
without ſoules, or elſe looſe the temporal vſe both of
body and ſoule.

O moſt mighty Queene , let your excellent and
heauenly vertues now take their chiefe effects, let
your rare and incomparable wiſdome enter into the
conſideration of theſe poynts , and let that Orient
pearle and gratious worke of nature, which in your
royall perſon hath ſo many wealthfull yeares ſhined
amongſt vs , and adminiſtred moſt bright and comfortable beames of graces to al men: Let this vnſpeak-
able and ſingular good nature of yours , deare Ladie
and Queene , delight to worke another thing like it
ſeſſe , or at leaſt diſlike to ſuffer a thing contrary to
                                                                            it

it selfe. Knit the bodie and the soule togeather; Let not vs your Catholike, natiue, english, and obedient subiects stande in more perill, for the frequenting the blessed Sacraments and exercising the catholike religion, and that most secretly then do the Catholikes subiect to the Turke publickly: then do the peruerse and basphemous Iewes, haunting their synagognes, vnder sundry Christian Kings openly: and then doe the Protestants enioying their publike assemblies vnder diuers catholike Kings and Princes quietly. Let it not be treason, for the sicke man in the body, euen at the last gaspe, to seeke ghostly councell for the saluation of his soule of a catholike Priest: so shall both soule and body, spirituall and temporal, according to our most bounden dutie serue you truely: and pray for your long and most prosperous raigne effectually. Then shall this your gratious tolleration found out your most famous memory so triumphantly to all nations, that the same shal be preserued of record from age to age, and consecrated to endles glorie and renowne.

Accept most mercifull Prince our faithfulnes, regard our dutiful hearte, despise not our sincere affection. Let our rehearsed miseries be relieued with your renowned mercies; accompt those subiects to be vndoubtedly faithful in whose accusations and liues, hath appeared a chiefe and special care not to offend God. It nowe behoueth vs most humbly to craue your maiesties gratious pardon: for that we haue not obserued the vsuall breuitie of supplications, being destitute of friendes to speake in our behalfe; wee

are

are driuen to ſet downe ſomewhat largly by writing
that which might by ſpeach with les tediouſnes bene
vttered Finally we make our huble petitiōs, that your
excellency wil giue vs ſuch credite and affiance to our
words & othes, that we may frō henceforth be deemed cleere & voy e of al ſuſpition, both in thought,
word & deed:to refraine publick places of prayers, only for feare to ſal into dānable ſin,& not in any hope
or regard of any worldly preſermēt or policy. Secōdly
to haue that pittiful conſideration, & remorſe of our
calamities, as may be thought moſt expedient to the
comfort of vs afflicted, and moſt agreeing with your
M.moſt gratious pleaſure & good likeing.Thirdly &
chiefly, not to ſuffer any law to be made, whereby
Catholike Prieſts of this realme ſhall be baniſhed,&
their receiuers highly puniſhed.   Grant, O merciful
Q.that we may do the works of mercy & charity to
Gods Prieſts,ſo long as they pray for your M. & vſe
thēſelues dutifully:we are the more encouraged thus
boldly to entreat with your M.becauſe in former yeare
it hath bin deliuered in pulpets, & publiſhed by bookes
late printed,& other wiſe diuulged,that your clemēcy
neither hath, nor will puniſh any of your catholike
ſubiects for their cōſcience,in matters of religiō only.
For our parts what ſucceſſe ſoeuer ſhal grow vnto vs
by reaſon of this our huble ſupplication,we do adui-
ſedly & firmely vow to God, that your M. ſhal finde
ſuch ſubects, as God requireth, and your M.deſireth.
That is moſt louing, moſt loyal, and moſt dutiful.Our
Lord God preſerue your M. to our ineſtimable ioye,
and your endleſſe felicitie.Amen.

                                    The

*The Parlaments vniuſt proceeding againſt Prieſtes
and Catholiks, and perſecution without all cauſe
by their owne iudgements.*

Itherto the petition of the Catholikes
of England penned by the reuerend Prieſts
in that time, and by their aſſent preſented to
Queene Elizabeth, and to her handes deliuered
by M. *Shelly,* in the 27. yeare of her raigne, as
ſhe walked in her Parke at Greenewich, and at
the time of the Parlament then holdé, by which
Parlament, all Engliſh men made Prieſts ſince
the feaſt of the natiuitie of S. Iohn Baptiſt, in
the firſt yeare of her raigne, were made Traytors, and the receiuers of them fellons. The
ſame M. *Shelly* for his preſuming to deliuer it
vnto that Queene, not acquainting her priuie
Councell there-with before, and for no o-
ther cauſe, as hee often proteſted, was by
Sir Francis Walſingham then chiefe Secretarie, committed cloſe priſoner to the Mar-
ſhallſey, where he dyed; which was the ſumme
of the anſwere made vnto this moſt humble
and religious petition, which notwithſtanding,
that Queene and her Parlament then proceeded in making that cruell Lawe, as commonly
the Proteſtants ſince haue preſumed: Although
M. *Robert Apreece* of Waſhingly in Hunting-
ton ſhire lately deceaſed, and in his life, a worthy Confeſſor, did often affirme before diuers &
credi-

credible witneſſes , approuing it againe not
three weekes before his death in the preſence of
many, being thereof of purpoſe demanded, that
the Earle of Kent which then was , and preſent
in that Parlament, did conſtantly affirme that
Queene Elizabeth did not confirme that ſta-
tue , but ſaid *I' a viſera* , which diſabled it to
be a lawe.

He teſtified further (God is called to witnes
of this true relation)that a gentleman named M.
*Hambdon,*at that time gentleman vſher of *Brome-
ley* , then L. Chancellour, and preſent when the
Queene came to allowe or diſallow the lawes,
then entreated , and aſſuredly iuſtified to the
ſame M. *Apreece,*and diuers other gentlemen aſ-
ſembled togeather at a ſupper that very daye,
that this Bill was not paſſed by the Queenes
cõſent, but ſhe ſaid as the Earle before affirmed;
and that which giueth more ſtrength for this to
be ſo. The ſame M. *Apreece* confirmed vpon his
owne knowledge, that this ſtatute was not put
in the written copie or Catalogue of the lawes
that paſſed in that Parlament, & was diuulged,
& ſo continued a fourthnight together in common acceptance, without contradiction.

But howſoeuer the trueth of this is , moſt
true, and too true it was and is, that by onely
pretence of ſuch a lawe, many holy and worthy
Prieſtes haue bene moſt cruelly put to death,
and moſt grieuous afflictions rayſed and proſecuted againſt the Catholikes of England by that
onely

onely warrant. Yet this Queene sometime before her death , or at least some of her priuie Councell, gaue some hope of a mittigation, thinking perhaps that after her death, his maiestie that nowe is , being vndoubtedly by his true and most lawfull right to succeede , could no be so well pleased to finde the Catholikes of England, which had endured so much for their constant defence of the most vnquestionable title of him, and his holy mother, to be so grieuously afflicted by the Protestants estate of this kingdome, which had not bene so friendly and fauourably vnto it. Therefore some hopes were giuen to the Archpriest of England then, that his Priestes should at the laste haue disputation with their Bishops and Doctors ; and this was so credibly related and denounced vnto him, that two seuerall times he sommoned & appoynted foure of his learned Priests to vndergoe that combate. His assigned disputants were these: D. *Weston.* D. *Smyth.* D. *Tho.* W*right* and M. *Richard Broughton* . Three of these also hee appoynted to dispute, D. *Smith,* M. W*right* and M. *Broughton* at the Parlament in K. *Iames* his time, when the new oath was enacted , and for the fourth assigned Doctor *Bishop.*

And to confirme further this relenting disposition in that Queene , and the wisest of her counsell, besides that which is written before, those Priestes whom hee that writeth for the new oath vnder the name of M. *Roger* Widdring-

ton

ton doeth vntruely challenge for his opinion, as both their late Apologie to the contrary, the martirdome of ſome of them for onely refuſing it (as namely M. *Robert Drury*) and the confeſſion and acknowledgment of that author himſelfe vpon certaine knowledge doe teſtifie, they ſtill iuſtifie that the councell of Q. Elizabeth promiſed quietnes and tolleration, vpon Prieſts acknowledgement of temporal obedience vnto her, which none denyed: and this was the motiue as theſe Prieſtes haue often proteſted (for I am none of them) that they were willing to yeeld ſo much as their ſpiritual bond and dutie to the See Apoſtolik which they except, would permit to Queene Elizabeth then their Soueraigne.

Neither can wee without great aſperſion of diſhonour, and all hope of all kinde of penitencie in that princeſſe be of other minde. For hauing publickly ſo proteſted in parlament, neuer to vexe or trouble anye Romane Catholike for matter of Religion , her caſe (euen by proteſtants iudgement, not to perſecute for Religion) ſhould be too deſperate by their owne proceedings, eſpecially if we a little reflect vpõ that, which all the chriſtian world can witneſſe both for prieſts and Catholikes, and our proteſtant hiſtories, themſelus thus deliuer vnto vs in theſe wordes: Elizabeth ſucceeded her ſiſter, & began her raigne with ſo generall applauſe, as her ſiſter did, by reaſon the Cleargie, the Nobilitie

bilitie, and most of the commons were Romane Catholikes, who neuerthelesse, although they knew her full determination, was to alter their setled course in Religion, yet they all with one consent being set in the Parlament house, when the certaine newes was brought thē of Queene Maries death, they acknowledged her immediate right, and presently declared the same by diuers Proclamations, and forth-with prepared themselues to performe their homage and fealtie, which shee gratiously accepted. (*Howes Historical preface in Queene Elizabeth. Stowes Historie. anno 1. Elizabeth. Cambden in apparal. Annal.*)

Thus these Protestant historians, and these renowned Bishops, Priests and Catholiks were so far from raysing the least resistance against her, when as we see they might easily haue kept her from being Queene, if they would haue proceeded as Protestants vse to do, that those holy Bishops, as your greatest Protestant antiquarie writeth (*Cambden annal. pag. 27.*) though they both thought Queene Elizabeth at that time to deserue the censure of Excommunication, and that they had power and authoritie to infliĉt it on her, yet they refrayned to doe it, leaste by that meanes the people and subieĉts of England would take armes against her, and so depose her, being by them excommunicated. And thus tender of this Queenes safety and quiet (though after excommunicate, and for her birth

D by

by our Proteſtant hiſtorians and ſtatutes themſelues not in the beſt eſtate, were all Prieſts of
England, after that not onely at that time of the
ſtatute againſt them, they were all moſt free and
innocent, as is iuſtified in the petition before, &
confirmed by our Proteſtant hiſtorians, which
cannot charge any one Prieſt of thoſe dayes
with temporall diſobedience; but euer after
continued in the ſame dutie and loyaltie, not a-
ny one accuſed of the contrarie, except they wil
inſtance in M. *Ballard*, for the buſineſſe of the
Queene of Scotland, and her ſonne his Maieſtie
that now raigneth, and long and happely may
he raigne amongſt vs, which we thinke for their
dutie they owe to our Soueraigne and King
Iames, Proteſtants ſhould not be haſtie to vrge:
and if they ſhould, and that matter were as the
Proteſtants then pretended, yet but one Prieſt
in 44. yeares, ſeruing for their purpoſe, they
may now acknowledge how vnequal and vniuſt a thing it was, to condemne ſo venerable &
heigh a function, generally for ſo an heynous
offence, when they finde none guiltie by their
owne proceedings.

And this innocencie of Prieſtes was that,
which in thoſe latter dayes of Q. Elizabeth ſo
inforced that Queene and her councel, ſo cun-
ningly as they could with their politike reputation, not to be altogether contrary to themſelues, and not ingeniouſly acknowledge the
wrongs and iniuries they had offered and done

to

to that sacred vocation, to stay the fury, and mit-
tigate the rage of their former persecution,
by occasion whereof, and Priestes prooued thus
innocét, diuers religious men, which spareingly
before (as those of the Societie) or not at all (as
the Monkes of the order of S. Benedi&, had vi-
sited England) resorted hither in some numbers
in those latter dayes of that Queene. And thus
much of the honor and loyaltie of P*r*iests, and
vndeniable trueth of the Religion t*h*ey taught
in her time.

'Howe the Priestes and Catholikes of England, ne-
uer deserued the least persecution or affliction,
vnder our Soueraigne King Iames *, but rather*
fauour, honour, and reuerence.

NOW let vs come to the time of our
dread leige and Soueraigne King *Iames*: as
the world well knoweth, the affection and
dutifull loue of the Priests and Catholikes of
England toward his Maiesties right and most
vndoubted true title to this kingdome, in the
dayes of Queene Elizabeth , yet euer performing due obedience vnto her, was not inferiour to the best Protestants of this nation : so it
pleased his Maiestie without any exception of
Priest or Papist, generally to speake in publike
Parlament of this whole Iland. *I am the husband,*
and all the whole Ile is my lawful wife : I am the
head, and it is my bodie: I am the Sheepheard, and it

D 2 *is my*

is *my flocke*(*King Iames parl.1.ſeſſ.1.*)He therefore
accounteth vs poore members of this his wife,
his bodie,& flocke, for being but one husband,
head and ſhepheard,he hath but one wife,body
and flocke by that relation.And at his entrance
hither, by his regall teſtimonie, wee that be
prieſtes and Catholikes applauded and embraced it with as great ioy and alacritie, as thoſe
that were Proteſtants , and of his Religion, as
they pretende : his Maieſtie tearmeth it (*ſeſſ. 1.*
ſupr.parl 1.) *a ioyfull and general applauſe;and vn-
expected readines of our deſerts , memorable reſolution, moſt wonderfull coniunction, and harmonie of
our hearts , in declaring and embraceing our vndoubted King and gouernour at his firſt entrie into
this kingdome, the people of all ſortes rid and ran,
other flew to meete him; their eyes flaming nothing
but ſparkles of affection, their mouthes and tongues
vttering nothing but ſounds of ioye , their hearts,
feete, and all the reſt of their members in their ge-
ſtures, diſcouering a paſsionate longing, and earne-
ſtnes to meete and embrace,their new Soueraigne.*

Thus it pleaſed him to embrace vs in generall, as his moſt louing and dutifull ſubiects:
and in particular thus he pittied our former afflictions, and intended to mitigate and relieue
them: *my minde*(ſaith he) *was euer free from perſecution or thralling my ſubiectes in matters of
conſcience.* (*King Iames in Parlament*) therefore
of himſelfe he did not thinke vs worthie to
be perſecuted or inthralled, but rather lightned

ned of thofe miferies, as his next wordes a warrant: *I was fo far from encreafing their burdens with Roboam, as I haue fo much, as either time, occafion, or lawe could permit, lightned them.* And in his cenfure againft *Conradus Vorftius* the Dutch heretike, recounting the differences betweene proteftants and vs, hee findeth not one for which we may be perfecuted, but the contrary.

At his comming in, he fet the Catholikes and Prieftes at libertie, gaue free pardons vnto all of them, both priefts and others, that would fue them foorth, and paye foure or fiue Nobles at the mofte for them to the Lorde Chancellour: In thofe pardons, hee remitted both the guilt and danger from priefthood, and much more then any of vs had tranfgreffed in, he ftiled vs as our dignities, difcentes, or callings were, gentlemen, prieftes, or of what degree, dignitie, or preeminence foeuer he were, his belooued fubieƈts: which wordes and ftate are incompatible with the name of Treafon: in thofe pardons hee pardoned whatfoeuer could be in any rigour interpreted to be within the daunger of that Lawe, both our comming into England, and abyding and remayninge neere: fo that by pardon being dead, they cannot poffiblie be reuiued, becaufe the graunt is irreuocable. Our comming in, was but one indiuiall aƈte and offence in Lawe, and fo remitted, cannot be offence: our continuance,

D 3 and

and remayning so long as we doe not reiterate
it againe, by going foorth, and comming in the
second time, is also but one particular, singular,
and indiuidual action, without discontinuance,
one *ens fluens*, as all such not interrupted be: an
hower, a daye, a weeke, a moneth, a yeare, a
life, an age, and the like. This all philosophie, &
common reason (whereon our common law is,
and must be founded) teacheth vs. Thus diuers
protestât, & good lawyers haue answered: thus
his Maiestie esteemed, when hearing of a priest
named M. *Freeman*, put to death for his priesthood, by the Iudges of Warwicke, soone after
his Maiesties comming hither, with signe of
sorrow answered: *Alas poore man, had he not foure
nobles to buye his pardon*: by which he concluded, that a priest being pardoned for his priesthood, could not after for being a priest be put
to death, or tearmed a traytour, or indanger his
friends and receauers, but was a free and lawfull
true subiect, from that imputation. His Maiestie
also allowed the times of Constantine for times
of true Religion, and the Roman Church then,
and after, to be the true, & our mother Church,
and not to be departed from.

Then wee may not so vnder-value the learning and iudgement of our learned and Soueraigne in diuinitie, and histories, but he well
knoweth (which no learned man is ignorant
of) that in the time of Constantine, the Church
of Rome had the same holy sacrifice of Masse,
and

and the fame holy facrifycing priefthood, which
now it hath, which I will hereafter demon-
ftrate by the beft learned proteftant antiquaries
of this nation, as alfo that the Church of Rome
at the reuolt of King Henry the 8. was the fame
in all effential things, which it was in that prefixed time of Conftantine; And to be liberal to
my needy proteftant contrymen in this cafe, I
fay, that the Church of Rome, & the Religion of
the Priefts of England, their priefthood, and facrifice of the Maffe, is the fame which were in
Rome, and in this Iland alfo in S. Peters time, &
in euery age without interruption fince then,
vnto thefe dayes of Proteftants. And if we may
beleeue *Ifaac Cafaubon,* the ftipendarie cham-
pion for the Proteftants of England, who faith,
ab ore regis accepi, and *hæc eft Religio Regis Angliæ* , *&c.*(*Ifaac Cafaubon contra Cardinal Pe-
ron.Pag.5* .*51.52.*) *I haue it from the Kings mouth,
this is the Religion of the King* , *this is the Religion
of the Church of England:The fathers of the Primatiue church did acknowledge one facrifice in chriftian Religion, that fucceeded in the place of the facrifice of Mofes. The facrifice offered by Priefts, is
Chrifts bodie and the fame obiect, and thing.Which
the Romane Church beleeueth.*

These and fuch things troubled the heads of
fome great Proteftant perfecutors in England,
(their confciences being guiltie of fome-what
not good) that they coulde not enduer the
leaft clemency of his Maieftie towards his loy-

all

all and trueſt catholike ſubiects , but olde ſtra-
tagems and tragedies of Queene Elizabeths
time, muſt needes be renewed and playde a-
gaine, to bring not only the Catholikes of England, but their holy religion(if poſſiblie it could
be done)into obloquie, eſpeciallie with his gratious Maieſtie : and thereupon an execrable and
moſt damnable treacherie by gunpowder was
to be inuented, for a few wicked & deſperatly
minded men to doe, whom many proteſtants
tearmed papiſts; although the true Prieſts and
Catholikes of England knew them not to bee
ſuch, nor can any proteſtant truely ſay, that any
one of them was ſuch a one, as their lawes and
proceedings againſt vs, name Papiſts, Popiſh
recuſants, or the like. What he was, papiſt or
proteſtant, rich or poore, noble or vnnoble, of
Courte or countrey, that was inuentor of this
horrible deuiſe, I will not diſcuſſe, but referre all
indifferently minded men, and of iudgement
able to diſcerne the probable trueth in ſuch a
cauſe, to the hiſtorie and circumſtances thereof,
as they are ſet downe by the Proteſtant hiſtorian, M.Ed.Hows(*hiſtor. of Engl. in King Iames.*)

But to graunt to our Proteſtant perſecutors,
for argumenrs ſake (that which I may not) and
they will as hardly proue, that this wicked in-
terpriſe was firſt inuented by *Catesby*, and ſome
of his conſorts, and that diuers of them were
papiſts, and had acquaintance with the chiefe
Ieſuite then in England, who at leaſt in confeſſion

fionknew of this conspiracie, & did not reueale it: that there were foure of this côpanie arraigned for the conspiracie, three gentlemé (though two of these, *Fauxe* and *Keyes* were but feruing men) as the fourth, *Thomas Bates* ftyled yeomâ. that one Knight and three Efquires concealed it, of which the Knight was fo ignorant, that as the Proteftant relator of this matter faith, at his death he fpake thefe wordes (*Howes fupr. in Sir Edward Digby*) *If he had knowne it firft to haue bene fo fowle a treafon, he would not haue concealed it, to haue gayned a world:* Which he could not haue truely faid, if he had knowne it in particular, & in it felfe a moft horrible damnable thing; and the reft as this author writeth, dyed penitent; *and befought all Catholikes, neuer to attempt fuch a bloodie acte, being a courfe which God did neuer fauour nor profper.* Thofe that were vp in tumult with Catesby, were (as the Proteftants relateth (*Howes fupr.*) *neuer full fourfcore ftrong, befides many of their houfhold feruants (no doubt papifts if their maifters were fo) forfooke them howerlie: yet they diuulged many deteftable vntruths againft the king & ftate, omitting no fcandal which they thought might ferue their traiterous purpofe, & that they were affembled and prepared to fome fpecial feruice, for the aduancement of the catholike caufe, hoping thereby to haue drawne into their rebellion, thofe of that religion, & other wilful malecontents:*

And to make euident, it was rather a madde defperat attempt of one priuate kindred, or acquaintance, then of any religion. Thus it is creedibly recounted by them that knew their diſcents(for I was a ſtranger to them all) *Catesby* and *Tresham* were ſiſters children ; the two *Graunts* brethren, and the elder intermarryed with *Winters* ſiſter, calling his eldeſt ſonne *Winter Graunt*: the *Winters* Grandmother, was ſiſter to the Grádmother of *Catesby* & *Treshame*, and ſo they were kinſmen. *Yorke*, and the *Winters* ſiſters children, by the *Englebies* : the two *Wrytes* long time dependers of *Catesby*, and their ſiſter married to *Percy*: *Catesby*, *Tresham*, *T. Winter*, two *Wrights* and *Graunt* were in Eſſex rebellion. All theſe were yong except *Percy*, who gaue the Piſtoll to his Maiſter the olde Earle of Northumberland in the Tower: And if any of theſe were Catholikes, or ſo dyed, they were knowne Proteſtants not long before, and neuer frequenters of Catholike Sacramentes with any Prieſt as I could euer learne:& as all the Proteſtant courts will witneſſe, not one of them a conuicted or knowne Catholike or rǝ cuſant. And of all theſe remembred of that conſpiracie or acquainted with it, the L. *Mounteagle*, now *L. Morley*, who diſcloſed it, was moſt noted to be a Catholike, as his Ladie and Childrē were.

Therefore ſeeing (as the Proteſtants haue teſtified) no Catholikes could by any deuiſe, be drawne into this matter, not one among ſo many hundreth, or thouſands of knowne Catholikes

likes priuie vnto it,but detesting it when it was
knowne, the *Archpriest* by writing condemning
it presently when he vnderstood it,all his *Priests*
abhorring it,& euery one of thē with the *Arch-
priests* warrant, and the consent of the chiefest
Catholikes in England,and all they in their petitions hereafter condemning it for a most horrible offence (*Archpriest letter of prohibit. Author
of moderat answ. epist. dedicat.to the king. Catholiks petitions to the parlament and chiefe Secretary*)
And not one either Prieste or knowne Catholike,with all those strickt and diligent searches
and examinations then made by the protestant state about it,was either prooued,or pro-
bablie suspected to be guiltie of it : but so farre
freede,that the Lords of the Councel,requested
that a Priest should be appoynted to perswade
and assure *Fauxe* (a chiefe agent in it)that he was
bound in conscience to vtter what he could of
that conspiracie, and M. Tho.Write a learned
Priest did hereupon come to the councell, and
offer his best seruice herein , and had a warrant
to that purpose subsigned with 12.priuie Coun-
cellors hands, which he shewed vnto me, and I
am witnesse of his hauing such a warrant. But as
he said, *Fauxe* had confessed all they could wish
before he could come vnto him , so that no
man of conscience can, or will thinke,but generally al the Priestes and Catholikes of England
did rather deserue fauour, honour, and enfran-
chisement, from all afflictions, for their moste
                                              religious

religious, and holy ſeruing of God, and as loyal obedient and dutiful trueth, alleageance and fidelitie to our proteſtant King and countrey, then the leaſt disfauour for this practiſe.

For if the Prieſtes and Catholikes ſo manie thouſands in England would haue entertayned it, no man can be ſo malicious, and ſimple to thinke, but there would haue bene a greater aſſemblie then foureſcore, to take ſuch an action in hand; and the councell could not be ſo winking eyed, but they would haue found foorth ſome one or other culpable, which they could neuer doe, though ſome of them moſt powreable in it, tentered and racked forth their enuie and hatred againſt vs, to the vttermoſt limites they could extend. To confirme this our innocencie, the kings Maieſtie in his ſecond proclamation againſt that wickedneſſe, calleth all the *confederates, men of lewde inſolent diſpoſition, and for the moſt part of deſperate eſtate* (Proclamat.2. againſt Percy, &c. an. 1605.) and in his third Proclamation, when they were all diſcouered and knowne, thus he proclaimeth and publiſheth: (Procl.3.an.eod.1605.) It appeareth now in part who were the complices in this deteſtable Treaſon, publiſhed by our former proclamations, in their aſſembling together, to mooue our people to rebellion, although perhaps many of them did neuer vnderſtande the ſecrete of his (Percies)abhominable purpoſe. Where wee plainely ſee, that the King and his counſell then knew the complices, and partakers of
that

that villanie, yet they neuer taxed any Priest, or knowne catholike therewith.

And it further proueth, that they which ioyned therein knew not the practise in particular, neither durst the workers of it disclose it to the, least for the vilenes of it, they would haue reiected or reuealed it, as al true Catholiks would haue done. And his Maiestie in publicke parlament, doth free Catholikes as much as Protestants in this inuention, when hee plainelie saith(as trueth is) if it had taken effect, *Protestants and Papists should haue all gone awaye, and perished together* (*Kings speath parl.an.* 1605.) And to demonstrate from his maiesties publike acte, that Priestes and catholikes were as innocent as Protestants, and as the Kings Maiestie himselfe, of this, and all such vilenesse, hee declareth by Proclamation (*Proclamat.die 7. Nouembr.an.* 1605) *We are by good experience so well perswaded, of the loyaltie of diuers subiectes (of the Romane religion) that they doe as much abhorre this detestable conspiracie, as our selfe, and will be readie to doe their best endeauours, though with expence of their blood, to suppresse al attempters against our safetie, and the quiet of our estate, & to discouer whomsoeuer they shall suspect to be of rebellious or trayterous disposition.* Thus his maiestie by good experience hath publickly pronounced.

And though I am no Iesuit, yet religiõ, iustice & charitie draw my pen to write thus much, for the supposed guiltines of M. *Garnet,* superior of
the Ie-

Ieſuits here at that time, we haue but the proteſtants affirmation, and him denying it, and we
haue from the ſame proteſtants, that which rather iuſtifyeth his denial, then their affirmatiō:
for they publiſhed his examination before the
Councell, wherein they ſet downe his opinion
(*H. Garnets examination before the Councel. anno
1605.) That the Pope could not depoſe the king*, and
they adde his reaſon thus; *becauſe the King was
neuer ſubieſt to the Pope* ; which reaſon I doe not
examine, but thus iuſtifie, that if in his jopini-
on, the pope could not depoſe the king; and
the king was neuer ſubieſt to the pope, then the
pope could not licence any man, ſuppoſed a
Catholike, ſo to proceed; for himſelfe could not
by this his opinion ſo doe, much leſſe any papiſt
by his allowance: and if the king was neuer ſubieſt to the pope, he could neuer be ſubieſt to a-
ny papiſt, the popes and his owne ſubieſt. And
whereas the proteſtants condemne ſome other
Ieſuits for this matter, and among them Father
Baldwyne, yet hauing him priſoner diuers years,
vnder their ſtricteſt examination, they at laſt diſ-
miſſed him as innocent and guiltleſſe therein, &
that with honour. And how-ſo-euer the caſe
ſtood with the accuſed Ieſuites, we are euidētly
taught by theſe greateſt authorities, that both
prieſts and catholikes were vpon this pretence
moſt vniuſtly perſecuted ; although beſides all
theſe reaſons, wee by publicke conſent both of
Archprieſt, beſt learned cleargie and Catholikes,
presen-

prefented and offered to maintaine our caufe &
innocencie in thefe humble petitions: and firft
to his maieftie in this maner.

TO THE MOST EXCEL-

cellent and mightie Prince , *our gratious*
and dread Soueraigne , I A M E S by the
grace of God, King of great Britaine, France
and Ireland, in the yeare 1605. iuftifying the
Innocencie of Catholikes, and trueth of their
holie Religion, againft all beft learned proteftant aduerfaries.

Moft gratious Soueraigne.

THe *late intended confpiracie againft the life
of your royall maieftie (the life , vnion, rule, and
direction to thefe vnited kingdomes) was fo heynous
an impietie, that nothing which is holy, can make it
legitimate, no pretence of Religion can be alleaged
to excufe it,* God *and heauen condemne it, men and
earth deteft it, innocents bewaile it, the nocent and
vnhappie delinquents themfelues in repentance haue
lamented it, and your dutiful, religious and learned
Catholikes, Priefts and others, which haue endured moft for their profefsion , holde it in greateft
horror, and will fweare , proteft, premife and performe to your Maieftie, whatfoeuer loyaltie, obedience and dutie , is due from a fubiect to his temporall prince, by the word of God, lawe of nature, or
hath bene vfed by the fubiects of this kingdome,*

to any your christian progenitors from the first to the last : acknowledge and render to your honorable counsel, and all magistrates in ciuili causes, so much honor, reuerence and submission, and to all other protestant subiects, like amitie and neighbourly affection, as if they were of the same Religion, which we professe.

Yet, this is the miserable and distressed state, of many thousands your most loyall and louing subiectes (dread liege) for their faithfull dutie to God, and a Religion taught in this kingdome, and embraced by all your progenitors, and our ancestors, so many hundred yeares; that euery aduersary may preach, & print against vs, and make their challenge, as though either for ignorance we could not, or for distrust of our cause, wee were vnwilling to make them answere, or come to triall: when quite contrarie, we haue often, earnestly, and by all meanes we could, desired to haue it granted, with equal conditions, against the most selected, and best learned doctors of that Religion.

And at this present, when your chiefest Protestant Clergie, Bishops and others is assembled, wee most humblie intreate, this so reasonable a placet, that although they will not (as we feare) euer consent to an indifferent choyce, opposition, and defence in questions: yet at the least, to auoyde the wonder of the world, they will be content, that we may haue publike audience of those articles, opinions and practise, for which we are so much condemned and persecuted. If we shall not be able to defend or proue any position generally maintained in our doctrine, to

be

*be conformeable to those rules in diuinitie, which
your Maiestie and the protestant lawes of England
(we can proser no more) haue confirmed for holie,
the canonicall scriptures, the first generall councels,
the dayes of Constantine, and the primatiue Church,
let the penalties be imposed and executed against vs.
If we performe it, or this petition may not be admitted, we trust, that both our office to God, and dutie
to our Prince, is discharged in this poynt.*

*Your royall person, and that honorable Consistory
now assembled, are holden in your doctrine, to be supreame sentencer, euen in spiritual busines in this
kingdome; we therefore hope, you wil not in a Courte
from whence no appeale is allowed, and in matters
of such consequence, proceede to iudgement, or determine of execution, before the arraigned is summo-
ned to answere, hath receaued or refused trial, is, or
can be prooued guiltie. If we be condemned, and our
cause be iust, and religion true; it is God, & not man,
against whom you proceede in sentence. If our profession be erroneous, and yet for consent with so manie
nations, and so long continuance, it is lesse vnpuni-
shed: you onely pardon the frailtie and ignorance of
earthly men, and fight not with the heauenly. Denie
not that to vs (your euer true and obedient subiects)
in a religion so auntient, which your collegued princes, the King of Spaine, and the Archduke, do offer to
the so many yeares disobedient Netherlandes, vpon
their temporall submittance, in so late an embraced
doctrine : that which the Arrian Emperours of the
Easte, permitted to the Catholikes (Bishops, priestes,*

E   *Chur-*

Churches) tolleration: What the barbarian Vandals often offered, and ſometimes truely performed in A-fricke: What the Turkiſh Emperour in Greece, and Proteſtant Princes in Germanie, and other places, conformable to the examples of Proteſtant rulers, not vnanſwerable to your owne princely pietie, pit-tie, and promiſe, no deguſt to any equally minded Pro-teſtant or Puritane at home, a iubil) to vs diſtreſſed: a warrant of ſecuritie to your Maieſtie in all opinions, from all terrours and dangers. From which of what kinde ſoeuer, we moſt humblie beſeech the inſinite mercie of Almightie God to preſerue your Heighnes, and ſend you, your Queene and poſteritie, all happie-neſſe and felicitie, both in heauen and earth, Amen.

Another petition of the Catholiks of England to his Maieſtie, at the ſame time.

REmember moſt worthie Prince, not onely howe grieuous, but how general the penalties againſt your catholikes be exacted; and yet new threatnings be made, that new & more ſtrange (as nec inter ge-tes) ſhall be ordeyned: The bodies, honors, reputati-ons and ritches of the husbands, to be puniſhed for their wiues religion and ſoules, to which they are neither husbāds nor ſuperiours; children to be taken frō their parents, & parents to be depriued of their e-ducation, which Cathol ke princes doe not, and in conſcience cannot offer to Iewes themſelues, though (in ſome opinions) the ſlaues of Chriſtians. Children, ſeruants, kinſmen and neighbours to be made hired

                                                                        eſpials

espials, to betray their parents, maisters, kindred, in things as vnlawful, which the whole catholik world honoreth for holie. Commendable arts, functions of physicke, and which haue no connexion with religion, to be put to silence in catholikes. The seuere penaltie (twentie pounde a moneth) for not monethly professing the protestant faith in churches (when in all diuinitie the precept of profession of true and vndoubted faith, in se & ex se, bindeth but seldome) is to be encreased. And others of such condition, too many here to be mentioned, and too grieuous and vnnatural: We hope, in your princely opinion, to be concluded by a kings consent vnder fauour, for all. Wee instance in one most heauie, and generall in those of our deceased Queene. All Priestes, though neuer so dutiful or obedient, be censured for traytours, equally with the greatest offendor, in the sinne of treason, when many guiltlesse soules of that sacred order, would not for thousands of worldes once consent to any such, or far inferiour offence. A thing most strange, and beyond all example, that men in respect onely of their calling and function, and that function so reuerenced by all our forefathers, should without further cause be condemned, as guiltie of so detestable a crime.

We defende holy Priesthood to be a Sacrament, which being ordained by God, cannot be changed by man, Pope, Prelate, or humane power, but remaining in all things, substance and doctrine, the same, which in those daies when it was so honorably esteemed of all your Christian progenitors, and when our mo-

ther

ther church kept her firſt integritie by your heigh-
neſſe iudgement, as we are reddie to make defence. It
is the honour of our King in heauen (moſt mightie Soueraigne) for which we continue in combate:
that religion which the whole catholike world in all
generall councels , popes, doctors, and learnedmen,
haue euer profeſſed; wherein this nation (as our
Proteſtants acknowledge) was conuerted, all our
Chriſtian anceſtry embraced, and which all princes
in the ſchoole of Chriſt (of whom your Maieſtie is de-
ſcended) mayntained in theſelues & in their ſubiects.
That which is ſo general, cãnot beſurredred by a ſmal
number, of one kingdome: It is not in the power of
man,to reſigne the honour of God: if it will pleaſe
your Maieſtie to vouchſafe vs licence to requeſt,and
grace to obtaine, that your owne princely ſentence &
cenſure may ſtande, that wee ought not to departe
further from the Romane Church, our mother
Church (by your iudgement)than ſhee is departed
from her ſelfe, when ſhe was in her beſt, and
floriſhing ſtate: And that the time of Conſtantine
was incorrupted in religion , wee humbly againe
offer tryal before your heigneſſe,with equall conditions of ſchooles , againſt the moſt ſelected and choſen
proteſtant Biſhops and doctors of your dominions, to
prooue or defend any, or euery ſubſtantial article,
which wee now profeſſe, to be agreeable vnto (and
not, diſſenting) the knowne publike Catholike
doctrine of that mother Church , in thoſe your
mentioned incorrupted dayes of Chriſtianitie.

    And ſeeing the disfauour and penalties againſt
                                                    laye

laye *Catholikes, are grounded vpon their recusan-*
ce, to be prefent at your proteftant feruice :
wee humblie befeech, it may be called to memorie,
howe they haue protefted in feuerall fupplicati-
ons, one to your Maieftie, before the ende of the
lafte parlament: and the other to Queene *Eliza-*
beth, in the twentie feuenth yeare of her raigne,
to be builded onely vpon feare of offending God.
To which their fo long and manifolde difgraces,
loffes, imprifonments, and fufferings, are fufficient
witneffe: And for further triall thereof, haue of-
fered to repayre to your Proteftant Churches, and
feruice, without further exception, if the learned
of your Religion can, and doe prooue to the lear-
ned of their profeffion, that it may be performed
without offence to God, *which is fo much in the*
opinion of all diuines, as any Chriftian fubiects
can offer in this cafe.

This if your Proteftant Cleargie doe refufe,
or doe not fatisfie fo Chriftian a requeft, we hope
your Maieftie beeing wife, learned, iuditious,
and gratious, will perceaue, that the feueritie
of the lawes againft them, for that caufe, is not
to be put in practife. Thefe things in moft hum-
ble manner, wee commende to your heigheft and
mercifull confideration: And fo defiring of the
Almightie, to grannt all happineffe and profperitie
to your Maieftie, and pofteritie: wee conclude in
all dutifull fubiection, with that auntient Father
(Tertullian in Apollget.) Wee will faithfully
ferue you in your Pallace, we will accompanie

other

other your subiects in the market, wee will
ioyne with them in the fielde, againſt your ne-
mies, onely to you we leaue the Churches.

These two petitions were printed and
preſented to his Maieſtie in the Parlament,
when the new oath was enacted, and the
foure remembred Prieſts appointed by the
Arch-prieſt then to performe that challenge or petition; likewiſe at the ſame time
was preſented to the Parlament, by the
handes of Sir *Francis Haſtings*, and Sir
Richard Knightly, two Puritanes of that
Parlameut, from the chiefe Catholikes of
England, with the allowance of the Arch-
prieſt, and his cleargie ; this petition following to the ſame purpoſe.

The

The humble petition of the chiefe Catholike Recusants of England, presented to
the heigh Court of Parlament, in the
yeare 1605. by the handes of Sir *Francis
Hastings*, and Sir *Richard Knightly*,
then of that house of Parlament: to both
which it was deliuered, by the said Catholikes.

T He proceedings of that heigh Court of
   Parlament, in the daies of our late
Queene Elizabeth, against the Catholike subiects of this kingdome, were for seueritie far
beyond example; which they hoped for manie
most iust, reasonable true causes, & were to receaue their ende, when shee should cease to
liue, and by death, determine her personall
quarrells and contentions against the Religion, and Apostolike power of the Sea of Rome.
Especially by the ioyful and happie entrance &
Coronation of our most honoured King Iames,
most free from those tearmes wherewith she
was intangled, at temporall peace, amitie, and
vnitie with that holy Sea, with the sacred Em-
pyre, all Christian Kings and Princes, by vndoubted royal discent, the most lawful, legiti-
  E 4   mate

mate, and rightful King of all thefe his vnited kingdomes. Wee that be Catholiques in
England, and had euer bene fo true and faithfull to the onely vnited true title of him and
his bleßed Mother, and neuer entred into any
diffotiation againft it, affuredly hoped, hee
would not fingularlie drawe his fword of perfecution againft vs, his moft dutiful, faithful,
and obedient fubiects, in whom he could finde
nothing to reuenge or punish: for he publick'y
protefted in that Court of Parlament: his mind
was euer free from perfecution or enthral-
ling his fubiects in matters of confcience,
and the burthens of Catholikes were rather
to be lightned, then with Roboam to be en-
creafed(king Iames fpeach in parlament.1.
feff.1.)

But feeing all this notwithftanding, your
Parlament now affembled (contrary to our
hopes, and otherwife our deferuings, as wee
hope haue bene)doth rather prefage an intended increafe, then either ceafing, or mittigation of thefe our miferies, and extreame afflictions: we feare leaft filence in vs might be taken as an interpretatiue yeelding or confente,
that we are not altogether vnworthely afflicted, with fo ftrange calamities: for the
vvorld

world cannot otherwise in wisdome censure, that such punishment by so heigh a iudgemēt should be imposed vpon men (subiects, friends, and kinsmen, so generally) except guiltie of some most heinous, or execrable fact or offence against God, our King and countrey. Wherefore you must giue vs leaue in this perplexed case, to contest against you in the humblest & best maner we may, and leaue it a memoriall to potesteritie, that if you persist or proccede in persecution, vve protest before God, and in our consciences, vve shalbe vniustly persecuted. If you vvill continue or encrease persecution, you must pretend some motiue to doe it, and if you desire to cloath or shaddow it, vvith any cloake or colour of iustice, it must be founded vpon some probable conuiction, if our generall deseruing such punishments to be so generally prosecuted against vs, vvhich must needs be some vniuersal disobedience, or disloyaltie in vs all, either temporall to our terrestrial king and contrey on earth, or spirituall to God and the heauenly kingdome; vve know no thirde to vvhom your Religion vvould vvish vs to performe obedience.

For our discharge to the first, vve haue serued now vnder your vigilant, and suruey-

E 5   ing

ing eyes , diuers apprentiſhips in continuall
perſecution;yet from the firſt beginning thereof, vnto this day, you haue not found by all
thoſe narrow ſearches, and ſcrutinies you haue
made, that vve (whom you thus perſecute
vnder the name of Religion) haue bene thus
founde diſloyal to our temporal prince, neither
is that pretended in any of your lawes againſt
vs. And in this late vngratious and helliſh
conſpiracie, if they had bene ſuch as your lawes
and proceedings ſtile Papiſts and Recuſants,
yet his Maieſtie by his publike proclamation
(King Iames Proclamation in Septemb.
an. 1605) giueth that teſtimony of the loyaltie, and loue of his Catholike ſubiects vnto
him, that you vvhich perſecute vs doe not, &
by his regal vvordes cannot accuſe vs therein. And the number of theſe certainely knowẽ
conuicted Catholques, vvhich you perſecute
for religion, and both by his maieſties declaration, and all proteſtant moſt diligent ſearches
and examinations, thus innocent, and vvhich
deteſt all diſloialtie , are 500.to one of thoſe
vvhich you prooue guiltie , by your publike
Courts and recordes. Neither can you finde by
anie ſuch proceedings againſt Catholiques,
that theſe malefactours vvere of the number
of

*of those vvhich you haue so punished and
persecuted for our religion. The Archpriest of
England, and the reuerend priests of his companie (vvho best knew vvho be Catholiques
by their frequenting holie Sacraments) haue
by publike vvritings vtterlie renounced thē,
and condemned their lewed enterprise, for
most vvicked impietie.*

Therefore in conscience and iustice you cannot vpon this pretence, rayse a generall persecution against vs: for in so doing, you should
vniustlie persecute thousāds of these that be as
innocent, as your selues can be, or his Maiestie
himselfe by his owne testimony of vs (King
Iam procl. supr. an. 1605.) Wee are by good
experience so well perswaded of their loy-
alties, that they doe as much abhorre this
detestable conspiracie as our selfe, and will
be reddie to doe their beste endeuours,
though with expence of their blood to suppresse all attempts against our safetie, and
the quiet of our state, & to discouer whom
soeuer they shall suspect to be of rebellious
or trayterous disposition. *This is his Maiesties sentence by good experience of vs his
catholique subiects, your petitioners. Therefore vve are confident, vve rather deserue fa-*
uour

fauour then affliction at your Court. And yet if
contrary to the lavves of this Kingdome, you
vvould say, that the lands, goods, and liues of
delinquents (vvhich vve doe not thinke you
intende, or vve vvill vvish you to spare in
these offendours) doe not satisfie in such cases,
you must notvvithstanding (to conteine your
proceedings vvithin the shaddowe of iustice)
not impose the offence and punishment of the
guiltie, vpon those that be so innocent: The
highest law and rule enacteth : anima quæ
peccauerit, ipsa morietur : and as a great
Counsellour and secretarie of estate hath now
published in print for your direction (solum necis artifices arte perire sua (Rob. Earle of
Salisb. in his booke an. 1605.) Therefore wee
stand so cleare in your owne knowledges and
cosciences frō all temporal disobedience, that in
rigour of iustice, it taketh from you all cause,
and pretence, vvhy these or any afflictions at
all, should be imposed vpon vs , in those respects.

Then you must directlie make your quarrel
to persecute for religion, or recusancie, a depen-
dancie thereof : If Religion bee obiected,
vvee ansvvere as vvee haue euer done , and
desire no further fauour for our Religion (in
                                              your

your owne knowledge here so antient) then
yow obteyned of vs for your owne so new, that
the examples of Queene Marie her time,
(which many of your professiō accompt notwith
standing tyrannicall)may be followed. Let a
cōpetent number of our learned prieſts, be called to any of your vniuerſities,or other publick
place, vvhere the beſt learned of your religion
ſhal giue them meeting:let such queſtions and
prepoſitions as concerne the eſpeciall points in
controuerſie be propoſed, ſufficient time of conſideration allowed, and either ſuch equal conditions granted, as were to your chiefeſt Biſhops
and doctors,in the mentioned time. And if our
catholique diſputation ſhal not be able to iuſtifie
and maintaine our religion and cauſe to be holy, you may at your pleaſure proccede againſt
vs,if we perſiſt therein. You haue long time,
and with grieuous puniſhments perſecuted vs,
yet you would neuer vouchſafe vs ſo meane a
trial and iuſtice in this kinde : Execution (as
you know)before conuiction is prepoſterous and
cruel iniuſtice,& both by your Biſhops and maieſties cenſure in publick, Correction without
inſtructiō is but tyranny.(D. Matthew now
proteſt. Archb.of Yorke,Serm. before the
K.and parl.K. Iames ſpeach in parlament.
	If

If our *Recusancie*, or *refusall* to be present
at your new *church-seruice*, is alledged a pretence against vs, being a practicall acte and
profession of religion, it dependeth vpon the
former question, concerning religion: for neither catholiques nor protestants do teach, that
men so far differing therein as we and you, can
in conscience communicate together in such
things. And no enemie or persecutor of vs can
imagine, or inuent any allegation for this our
refusall, but either obstinacie in our willes, or
ignorance in our vnderstandings :non datur
medium: we cannot conceaue what you can o-
therwise deuise. Our imprisonmēts, losses, disgraces, and seuerest punishments in so manie
yeares, being the whole life of a man, from
time of discretion) the knowne bridles of obsti-
nate people) will condemne all men of too much
will, and little iudgement, that could charge
vs with this former. That which wee haue
offered in religion, freeth vs in the second, and
condemneth our accusers.

And to manifest nowe, (as often wee haue
done before) that we are neither carryed away
by wilfulnesse or ignorance in this debate, wee
haue at sundry times by most earnest suites &
petitions desired and offered and still doe, that
if

if your best learned Protestant Bishops and diuines can, and shall proue vnto the learned of our side, that We may repayre vnto your churches, and there be present at your seruice, without most grieuous offence to God,we vvil vvillingly perfourme it. Wherefore vee hope that you vvho in your owne prof· ssion vvould bee esteemed zealous and religious,vvil iudge this our offer to be such , that no Christians can offer more : And consequently further reflect and consider hovv dishonorable,sham ful, and sinfull it vvould be to your Consistorie,& vvhole ·Religion, to impose and multiplie penalties vpon vs (these offers considered)for not doing those things, vvhich by your ovvne knovvledge, your best learned in diuinitie, on vvhose vvordes and vvarrant you hazard your soules,cannot , nor vvill not, take vpon them , to maintaine , as lavvfull for vs to doe.

But if so many suites,supplications,reasons, and examples vvill not call you to a contrary minde, but you haue set vp your resolution, vvithout any answere or defence by vs, to be our accusers, iudges, and executioners,and singularly vvithout any example at all , in the vvorld, either of Christians , or others,

to perſiſt in vehemencie of perſecution againſt
our religion : *let vs finde you ſo far to harken*
vnto vs, that to retaine the name of lavve-
makers , you vvill retaine ſome proportiō & a-
nologie (as all ſo named muſt doe) vvith the
moſt auntient lavve of God, of nature, nations,
and this kingdome , not to puniſh tvvice one
and the ſame offence. If by ſtrong hand you will
haue that to be offence, which *vve aſſure our*
ſelues is ſo far frō that name and nature , that
the contrary is great and heigh offence to
God; Non conſurgat, duplex tribulatio, *and*
afflixi te, non iterum affligam: *and againe.*
Deus non punit bis in idipſū. *And as a dou-*
ble puniſhments is not to be inflicted for one of-
fence, ſo by theſe lavves, pro menſura delicti
erit & plagarum modus; *vvhich our aunti-*
ent lavves in our great charter of England
follovve: Nullus liber homo amercietur, ſed
ſecundum modum delicti ipſius, ſaluo tene-
mento ſuo (Magna Charta cap. 14.) *Peruſe*
if it pleaſe you, but the heades of the puniſh-
ments prouided againſt vs, for ſundry reſpects,
(queſtionable vvhether any offence or no)and
ſhal perceaue that your lavvs do not impoſe you
or proſecute ſuch ſeuere penalties by many de-
grees vpon ſins, that certainly and by al iudge-
ments

*ments are confeſſed and acknovledged to be
ſinnes, yea, and great ſinnes againſt the lawe
of God, nature, all nations, & this Kingdome.*

*By this we hope you vnderſtand, that if you
wil haue example, either in heauen, or earth
to follow, your perſecutions muſt die, or muſt
diminiſh, for we haue yeelded ful ſatisfactiō to
all your pretended reaſons to perſecute vs. That
which remaineth, wee deſire you to conſider
what a reſemblance there is, or ſhould be betweene yours & the heauēly court, frō whence
the irreuocable law is proceeded, & with great
terror published:* Woe to thē that make vniuſt lawes, and writing, haue written iniuſtice, that in iudgemēt they might oppreſſe
the poore, and do violence to the cauſe of
the humble of my people, that widdowes
might be their prey, and the ſpoyle of fa-
therles. *So beſeeching the almightie, that in
theſe and other cauſes, in that heigh Court
now in hand, you may in ſuch ſort procced, as
may be to his honor and glory, the ſecuritie &
good of his maieſtie, his of-ſpring & poſterity,
and this common wealth, we leaue you to Gods
holy protection.*

　　Your wel-wiſhing Countrymen, kinſmen, alliance, &
　　friēds, the Catholike Recuſāts of this realme of Englād.

F　　　　　　　　　An

An other alſo of the like tenure, which
here enſueth, was then with the ſame aſſent
ſubſcribed with 23. handes of the chiefeſt Catholike gentlemen of England, and preſented
to the chiefe Secretarie of eſtate, potent in thoſe
times in court and councell, and as the Catholikes then feared, not equally effected towards
them, though neuer ſo innocent and wel-de-
ſeruing, who was one of them who with other
of the councell declared to diuers of theſe gentlemen (as they confidently reported vpon their
reputation) that the Kings pleaſure was they
ſhould paye no more the penaltie of twentie
pounds a month for their recuſancie; and after
when hee had perſwaded his maieſtie to the
contrarie, denyed his former aſſertion, of the
releace thereof, although the gentlemen moſt
ſincere and iuſte, ſtill inſiſted and maintayned
that this meſſadge was ſo deliuered vnto them:
which alſo the then Earle of Northampton, L.
Henry Howard, did freely confeſſe & acknowledge to be moſt true. And the ſame Catholiks
were more then iealous, that this practiſe of
cōſpiracie was no great ſecret to that Secretary,
long before diuers of them that were actors in
it, and by him named Catholikes, were acquainted with it. We may not enter into iudgement,
where men are not defamed of ſuch inuentions, to entrappe thoſe they doe not affect: for
the reſt, let M. Howes his hiſtorie of that matter make relation who it was, a great proteſtant
that

that had more , or not much inferiour knowe
ledge of it by his relation, then some that wer
put to death for concealing it. But howsoeuer,
the petition followeth in these tearmes.

TO THE RIGHT HO-
norable , *ROBERT*, Earle of Salis-
burie, chiefe Secretarie of estate to his
Maiestie: the petition of the Catholicks
of England.

IF the corrupted and obscured vnderstan-
ding of men not knowing God,could among
other cloudes and mystes of ignorance , be so
far blinde in that wherein the lawe & light
of nature it selfe doth giue sufficient instru-
ctio to all people and nations,that Princes and
rulers in authoritie are to be honoured and
obeyed: yet the heauenly and supernatural il-
lumination doth clearly deliuer all Christians
(especially Catholikes) from such darkenesse
and want of dutie, giuing knowledge that e-
uerie soule must be subiect to superiour po-
wers; that God is he, per quem reges reg-
nant: and, he that resisteth power, resisteth
the ordinance of God.

Wherefore vvee your Lordshippes humble
suppliants, the Lay Catholiques of this Kingdome, so long probationers for religious causes,
haue euer in our hearts, Wordes and Workes
abandoned all contrarie proceedings, as a Babi-
lonian building and insurrection against the
might and commande of heauen: damnable and
rebellious vnto all regall and princely power,
peace, and vnitie on earth. Therefore being admonished by the vvisest King, that there is as
Well, tempus loquendi, as tacendi: and occa-
sions of these times being such as inforce vs to
speake, least by silence vvee might be censured
by some no equall minded men vnto vs, to be
suspected criminal in that, vvherein as al matters of that nature vve doe, and euer did, by
long-knovvne experience, stande most innocent: vvee therefore protest, concerning the
late conspiracie, that vvee doe condemne it
for a most impious, vnnatural, barbarous, and
execrable offence, against the lavve of nature,
the sacred vvord of God, and the canons and
practise of the holy Catholike Church, Wherein
vvee doe liue: to vvhich, no pretence of ho-
linesse, no petence of Religion, no pretence of
priuate or publicke authoritie, can giue vvarrant to make it lavvful. And vvee take God

10

to vvitnesse that vvee vvere neither con-
senting, cospiring or priuie to that, or any such
wicked designement, but the very remembrance
that any such enterprise should be intended or
deuised by any mã (especially bearing the name
of a Catholike) is the continuall sorrow of our
hearts, and among al tribulations, the obiect of
our greatest griefe.

And for this present, and all future times
we offer, professe, and promise, as great, ample,
true, and faithful obedience, loyaltie, & dutie
to his Maiestie, as though he were a Prince
of our owne religion: as much as any our aun-
cestours in this Kingdome did yeelde to any
his heighnes progenitors, Kings and Princes
thereof, or as is required of Catholike subiects
in other countries to their Protestant rulers,
or as any Protestant subiects obserue or per-
forme to their Protestant or Catholike Soue-
raignes, in ciuill obedience: That neither vvee
can offer, nor his Maiestie or estate require
more of vs, all worlds and generations of mē,
Catholikes, Protestants, Christians, Pagans, &
whatsoeuer in this and all other Kingdomes,
past, present, and to come, wil witnesse for vs.
And for our sinceritie, dutifull and obedient
meaning herein, wee appeale to all our perse-
cutors

cutors, their most strict, politicke, and cunning inquiries and examinations of our behauiour, and carriage from time to time, by which vvee stand as clearely vnspotted, as irreprehensible, as irreprooueable, as dutiful in all ciuil respects and duties, as any Protestant in this Nation.

Therefore, Right honorable, if some fewe vnhappie men of our religion haue made trãsgression of their alleageance, we hope it shalbe no motiue to change your graue and vnresolued minde from thinking it vndue to impose a burthen vpon innocents, for the fact of the guiltie, according to your owne excellẽt speeche heeretofore vsed, and now at this present: Solum necis artifices arte perire sua. And your Lordships most christian desire, of one vniformitie in true religion in this kingdome, bringeth no smale hope vnto vs, that now at last, our so-long and many times in humble maner requested petitions concerning our not comming to your churches, may by your honourable mediation to his Maiestie, be brought to tryall, by the learned of both parties, whether without committing sinne, it may be done by vs, which wee take to be the onely meanes to bring this kingdome to your so-much desired vniformitie in religion.

For

*For if your Protestant novv assembled , or
best learned doctors,can and doe prooue it lawfull to our learned diuines,vve absolutely offer
to performe it, vvithout delay or further exception. And may it please your Lordship to call
to minde , the ordinarie knowne practise of
Catholikes and Protestants in France,Helue-
tie,Germanie and other countries, where they
communicate in ciuill societies,and not in churches, and spirituall communications : vvhich
pleadeth that our refusull is not singular, but
hauing ground and patronage, both from Catholiques and Protestants in this point. Our
confidence now is , that his Maiestie,your honour, and the state , will not take this our
humble and necessarie petition in euill parte,
considering that catholique Emperours, Kings
of France and other Princes, haue granted the
like to their Protestant subiects , and this in
those countries vvhere no other Religion,thē
the Catholique Romane Religion hath bene
publicklie exercised at any time,since their first
conuersion from Paganisme.*

G 4   All

All theſe petitions being preſented according to their titles at that time, though the two
firſt to his Maieſtie were printed, and the booke
after his maner anſwered by D. Norton a Proteſtant Biſhoppe, yet he neuer tooke notiſe of
either of thoſe petitions, or any one ſentence of
them: and the Parlament was as ſilent, for that
preſented vnto it. Onely this Secretary was ſo
much diſtaſted with the gentlemen that ſub-
ſigned it, that hee tolde M. Anthony Skinner,
who preſented it vnto him, that if they were
preſent, he would ſet them all by the heeles,
a puniſhment for rogues, & not for men of their
worth and reputation. There was no other anſwere made to theſe petitions, but onely this,
the oath was enacted , and after proſecuted
with ſuch violence as the world can witneſſe,
ſuch accompt and regarde hath bene made of
our miſerie by theſe Proteſtants.

Whether any reformatiō may be found in the preten-
ded reformers of religion for Catholikes to fol-
low. And firſt of King Henry the 8. with whome
neither Catholikes nor Proteſtants now ioyne in
Religion.

NOW, ſeeing if we be in errour , we cannot poſſible by all meanes we can work,
procure that the learned proteſtant biſhops, and
doctors, who haue controlled all the chriſtian
world in their ſecret aſſemblies, will vndertake

to inſtruct a few Prieſts of England, but ſuffer
in their proceedings many thouſandes of Catholikes by this meanes to be tyrannized ouer
both in boaies and ſoules : let vs returne to the
firſt founders of this religion in England. The
father King Henry the 8. his yong ſonne and
daughter, and ſee if wee can finde any motiue
in their proceedings to mooue vs from our error, if we be in error. And firſt to begin with the
firſt, the father in this new Religion, and ſpirituall power, all Proteſtant antiquaries, *Foxe,*
Parker, Stowe, Holinshed, Cambden, Howes, and
the reſt entreating of this matter aſſure vs, both
that King Henrie the 8. and his fit inſtrument
Cranmer, for a cleargie man, were the principall
and firſt actors in this Tragedie (*Foxe tom. 2. in*
Henr. 8, and Cranmar. Parker antiq. Brit. in Cranm.
Stow hiſt. in Henr. 8. Holinsh. ibi. Theater of great
Brit in end. Howes hiſtorial præf. Cambd. præf. hiſt.
Eliz. &c.) and the occaſion King Henry tooke
to make his reuolt from the Church of Rome,
becauſe the pope would not conſent for his
putting away his wife Queene Katherine, that
holie Ladie of Spayne. For before that time,
king Henry was ſo obedient a childe to the Sea,
and Religion of Rome, that by the pen of the
bleſſed Biſhop Fiſher (whom hee after put to
death, for denyal of his aſſumpted Supreamacy)
in his owne name he defended them againſt the
ſcurrilous bookes of Martin Luther: and was for
that ſtiled by the Pope, *Defenſor fidei, defendor of*

the faith (*Henr. 8. l. cont. Luther*) which his Maieſtie King Iames ſtill vſeth by vertue of that donation.

One of late among the reſt, with greateſt warrant, ſpeaking of this his firſt reuoult, hath theſe wordes (*Hovves hiſtoricall præface to his Hiſt. in Henry 8.*) *This was done after the king was deuorced from* Catherine *of* Spaine, *his firſt wife, with whom he had liued aboue twenty yeares, and by her had fiue children. The cleargie nor parlamēt notwithſtanding the Kings importunitie would neuer yeelde to the diuorce, by reaſon they could not finde any iuſt cauſe. The King made* Cranmar *Archbiſhop of* Canterbury, *who was very apt, and ready to performe the Kings will, and he denounced the ſentence of diuorce. Then the King, contrary to the good liking of all men, marryed* Anne Bulleyne, *by whom he had the Ladie* Elizabeth. *And then by acte of Parlament, made it treaſon againſt all men, that should ſay the marriage was not lawful. And preſently after her birth, he pickt a quarrell againſt* Queene Anne, *and then repealed the former acte, & made a new acte of Parlament, whereby it was enacted, that it ſhould be heigh treaſon, for any to iuſtifie his former marriage to be lawfull, and the next day after her behedding, he marryed her hand-maid,* Iane Seymor, *and then declared the Ladie* Elizabeth *to be illegitimate.* Thus word by word this Proteſtant hiſtorian : Then by this, & ſuch like proceedings, as firſt bringing the cleargie into danger of Premunire, threats, importunities, and
                                                                    ſuch

fuch practifes, as thefe Proteftants tel vs (*Parker, Stow, Hollinshed, Theater, vt fupr.*) procuring the title of Supremacie to himfelfe in matters ecclefiafticall.

This Proteftant antiquarie thus proceedeth in this Kings proceedings: *The king obtained the Ecclefiasticall fupremacie into his particular poffeffion, and therewithal had power giuen him by parlament, to furuey & reforme the abufes of al Religious houfes & parfons. But the King becaufe he would go the next way to worke, ouerthrew them, and razed them. Whereat many the Peeres and common people murmured, becaufe they expected, that the abufes should haue bene onely reformed, and the reft haue still remained. The general plaufible proiect, which caufed the Parlaments confent vnto the reformation, or alteration of the Monafteries, was that the Kings exchequer should for euer be enriched, the Kingdome and nobilitie ftrengthened and encreafed, and the common fubiectes acquitted and freed from all former feruices and taxes: to witte, that the Abbots, Monkes, Friers, and Nunnes being fuppreffed, that then in their places should be created fourty Earles. threefcore Barons, and three thoufand Knights, and fourtie thoufand fouldiers, with skilfull captaines, and competent maintenance for them for euer, out of the antient church-reuenewes, fo as in fo doing, the King and his fucceffors should neuer want of treafure of their owne, nor haue caufe to be beholding to the common fubiect, neither should the people be any more charged with loanes, fubfidies and fifteenes,*
fince

ſince which time there haue bene more ſtatute laws,
ſubſidies, and fifteenes, then in fiue hundred yeares
before, and not long after that, the King had ſubſidies granted, and borrowed great ſommes of money,
and dyed in debt, and the forenamed religious houſes
were vtterly ruinate, whereat the cleargy, peeres,
and comon people, were all fore grieued, but could not
helpe it. He alſo ſuppreſt the knights of the Rhodes,
and many faire hoſpitals. This was done after the
king was diuorced from Catherine of Spaine his
firſt wife. He began his raigne prodigally, reigned
rigorouſly, liued proudly, and dyed diſtemperatly.
Through feare and terrour he obtained an acte of
Parlament, to diſpoſe of the right of ſucceſsiō in the
Crowne, and then by his laſt will and teſtament contrary to the law of God and nature, conueyes it from
the lawful heyres of his eldeſt Siſter, marryed to the
king of Scotland, vnto the heires of Charles Brandon and others, thereby to haue defeated preuented,
and ſuppreſſed the vnqueſtionable, and immediate
right from God, of our gratious Soueraigne king
Iames. At his death he was much perplexed, and
ſpake many things to great purpoſe, but being in-
conſtant in his life, none durſt truſt him at his death.
Thus your Proteſtant hiſtorian hath deſcribed
this firſt proteſtant ſupreame head of the church
in England.

They that deſire more knowledge of him,
may reſort to his owne ſtatutes, the Proteſtant
Theater of Britanie, Sir Walter Raleigh his preface to his hiſtorie of the world: and a booke
of

of the tyrants of the world, publifhed by the Proteftants of Bafile, where they may find him a fupreame head among them (*ſtatut.Henr.8.ab an.Regni 21. Theater of Brit.in Henr.8.Walter Ral̄ biſtor. of the world. pręf.lib.of Tyran. Baſil.*) And his ghoftly father *Cranmer* his chiefe inftrumēt in thoſe mofte execrable finnes, for a Cleargie man was not inferiour vnto him. Hee was as your firft proteftantly ordained Archbifhoppe Parker in his life, with others witneffeth, both the mooued and moouing inftrument of this king, in this, and many other his wicked defignements. Hee was of all the Religions of King Henry the 8. & Edward the 6. He diuers times fwore to the Pope, and was forſworne: Hee fwore to King Henry the 8.and was forſworne, when he fwore otherwife to king Edward his fonne, and was publickly prooued a periured man: he was a chiefe executor of king Henrie the 8. his will, and within 24. houres of his death, a chiefe breaker thereof. He was a continued felon vnto him in his life, married againſt his lawes, making it felony in ſuch men : hee was for chaftitie,to my reading the firft,laft,and onely trigamus, a Bifhoppe, husband of three wiues in the world. He counterfeited the hands and feales of 50. conuocation men, and among the reſt of the bleffed martyr, Bifhop Fifher. He gaue chiefe confent, and fwore, that Edwarde the 6.a childe of nine yeares old, was fupreame head of the Church, had al iurifdiction fpiritual

in

in himſelfe *(Parker antiq.Britan. in Cranmer.Foxe
tom.2. in Cranmer. Stow hiſtor. in Har.8.Holinsh.
Hiſt. of Engl. ibid. Theater of great Britanie in K.
Henr.Godwyne Catalogue of Biſhops in Canterburie in Tho. Cranmer. Stow, Holinſh,Theater, Foxe,
and others in Q .Marie. and Edw.the 6.Harpesfield,
in the life of B. Fiſher)* and all that Cranmar had
he receaued from him, yea your Proteſtants witneſſe, by the Proteſtant Confeſſions themſelues
of *Heluetia,Bohemia,Belgia, Auguſta,Wittenberge,
and Swe,* that boyes could not take or giue ſuch
power.*(Th.Rogers pag. 140. artic.23. Confeſſ.Hel-
uet.Bohem.Belg. Auguſt. Wittenb.&c.)*

If any thing now controuerſied, defended &
ſworne vnto, can make a man an heretike, Cră-
mar profeſſing and ſwearing vnto them all, was
an hereticke and traytor to God: If conſpiracie,
open hoſtilitie , and rebellion to his true and
lawfull prince, Queene Marie,doth make a man
a traytor to his Soueraigne:If to be hiſſed in the
publicke ſchooles of Oxford, in publike diſputation, after all theſe changes doth conuince a
man, vndertaking ſo many matters,to be a man
vnworthie and ignorant: If to recant hereſie, &
fall to it againe, putteth a man in caſe of relapſe
of hereſie , all theſe thinges be written of this
Archbiſhop, Archactor, Architector,Arch-here-
ticke, Arch-traytor, Arch-periured & prophane
wretch of your Religion, by your owne writers
here cited,and were publickly to the eternal in-
famie of that vnhappie and graceleſſe man,and
his

his followers therein, prooued againſt him.
Therefore, although King Henry the eight did
rather differ from the Church of Rome in matter of Iuriſdiction ſpiritual (by his claymed Supremacie) as your proteſtants teſtifie, and his
lawes are witneſſes (*Stow hiſtor. in. Henr.8. Holinſh .and Theator ibid.ſtatut of K.Henrie 8.&c.*)the
any way in matter of doctrine, Catholiks cannot in conſcience by your Proteſtants, ioyne
either with him, or you therein,beeing the firſt
(as they haue aſſured vs) that euer claymed it
in this kingdome; and procuring it in ſo vile &
vnlawful maner, as your hiſtorians haue declared;and practizing it to his wanton and ambitious ende,againſt his owne conſcience.For al the
foundatiõs of ourReligious houſes being *pro re-
medio animarũ,to ſay Maſſe & pray for their poſteritie for euer.For the honor ofGod,the moſt bleſſed Virgin, and other Saints,* as all our antiquities giue
warrant to write:he in all his life time cõtinued
in theſe doctrines, and at his death in his laſt
will and teſtament, proteſted himſelfe to continue in that opinion (*Bed. Henric.Hunt. Guliel.
Malmesb.Roger.Houeden.Matth.Weſt.Flor.Wigor.
Camb.Stow. Holinſq.Theator,&c.*) And for the
ſupremacie it ſelfe (as hath bene prooued in the
time of Queene Elizabeth, and your proteſtant
hiſtorian, hath ſufficiently inſinuated) he recanted it (*Booke intituled, Leſters common wealth*)
your Proteſtants wordes of him theſe be: *At his
death he was much perplexed, & ſpake many things*
to

to great purpoſe, but being vnconſtant in his life,
none durſt truſt him at his death (Howes ſuper.hiſt.
preface in Henry 8.) which relation from a proteſtant writer, can carrie no other conſtruction.
And I take God to witneſſe, I haue heard my
father (then liuing in Courte) often make relation, that this king Henry the 8. at his death, was
ſorie for his taking that title of ſupremacie vppon him, was willing to reiinquiſh it, and laboured to be reconciled to the Church of *Rome,*
promiſing if he liued, ſo far as he could to make
reſtitution. But being demanded of him preſently to take order therein, he was preuented
by death, and dyed with ſuch burthen and horror of côſcience, as chanceth in ſuch caſes: which
this Proteſtant before aymeth at, when he ſaith,
he was much perplexed, and ſpake many thinges to
great purpoſe. Therefore the Catholikes of England, are rather confirmed by this king, then
weakned by him, in profeſſion of their holie
faith.

And though in his life he perſecuted and
put to death many renowned Catholikes, for
deniall of his ſupremacie, and ſacramentary Proteſtants (ſuch as thoſe in England now are) for
heretikes, yet he neuer recalled this ſecond, as
he did the firſt; neither made any new lawe, by
which they were put to death, but left their
triall to the auntient Canons of the Catholike
Church; yet put thoſe Catholikes to death only
by pretence of his new inacted Edict of his ſu-
pre-

premacie, neuer heard of in England before, as Proteftant antiquaries haue tolde vs. Therefore this firft fupreame head of religion in England, in all things confirmeth the religion of Catholikes, and condemneth that of Proteftants: and this the more if we adde from your Proteftant hiftorians, how fraudulently, or rather forcebly he obtained his firft colourable tytle to that his fpirituall fupremacie, by which he kept fuch turbulét fturres in this kingdome. A Proteftant hiftorian and an Efquire by ftate, as he ftileth himfelfe, thus relateth it. *William Martine Efq. in hiftor. of Henr.8 pag. 388.389.*

Cardinal Wolley *being dead, the King by his Councel was informed, that all the cleargie of England was guiltie of premunire: becaufe in al things they fupported and maintained the authoritie, and power legatine of the Cardinal: wherefore to preuent mifchiefe, before it fell vpon them, they gaue to the King for their redemption, and for their pardon, the fomme of one hundreth thoufand pounds, and by a publicke inftrument in writing, fubfcribed and fealed by the Bifhops and fathers of the Church ; they acknowledged the King within his owne kingdomes and dominions, to be fupreame head of the Church.* Thus vniuftly he procured that vnlawful prerogatiue, & more vniuftly as before, made his wicked vfe therof. I neede proceede no further in his proceedings, for they ar dead with him: the prefent proteftant ftate, as his owne childré before, by lawes and Parlaments condemne them; all

Proteftants in the worlde reiect them, and hee
himfelfe before his death (by the moft manerly
fafhion he could) refufed his title of fupremacie, in which he moft differed from the church
of Rome, as I haue brought Proteftant witnef-
fes before: therefore Catholiks are rather confirmed, then weakned in their religion, by the
proceedings of this King.

That English catholikes cannot be perfwaded vnto,
but much diffwaded from Proteftant Religion, by
the Proteftant proceedings in the time of King
Edward the 6.

NOW let vs come to the next temporall
rule, that claymed fupremacie in fpiritual
matters in England: King Edward the 6. he was
but 9.yeares olde, when this charge was layed
vpon him, yet he was elleuen yeares olde, whē
your religion was firft borne in this nation, in
the fecond or third yeare of his raigne, as all
lawes and hiftories of that time giue recorde.
(*Parl.2.& 3. Edw. 6. Stow hift. in Edw.6. Holinfh.*
Theater, and others ibid.) So this childe begot it,
and his fifter Q Elizabeth nurfed it. We knowe
for fhame you will not tye vs, to the cenfure of
an infant king; then you muft appeale to thofe
that inftructed, and directed him in fo great a
bufineffe. Thefe were temporall, and fpirituall,
and chiefly thofe that were of councell, and
had fworne otherwife to King Henry the 8.
during

during his life, liued in his Religion, and after his death continued the same vnder this yong king in his beginning and first Parlament (*Parl. 1. of Edw.6. Stow. Holinsh. & in k. Edw.6*) were executors of the last will and testament of king Henry the eight, in which concerning matters of trust in religion, they truely executed nothing at all: but in the exheredation of his Maiesties holy Mother and himselfe, as much as they could they executed it (*Howes historial preface, supr. Stow, Holinsh. Theater, & in Q. Marie & Edward.6.*

The chiefest of these for spiritual men was Cranmer their Archbishop, and the rest of the Bishops of that time that were not Catholikes, of which we finde but two, onely *Hooper* and *Ferrar* put to death for their Religiō by Queene *Marie*: For *Cranmer, Ridlie,* and *Latimer* were condemned for treason (*Foxe tome.2. Monumen. in Q. Marie. Godwyn Catalogue of Bishops of K. Edwards time.*) and what can we accompt of the religion of these two, changing their profession so often with king Henry and K. Edward? and *Ferrar* (to vse your Bishops wordes) *was thrust out of the Bishoppricke, in the beginning of Queene* Marie, *for being married, and ended his life in the fyer:* more for being desperate how to liue, then for loue of Religion, so far as we can gather. (*Godwyn in S. Daudis 79. Robert Ferrar*) The other, *Hooper* (*Godwyn in Worcester.75. Glocester.2. Iohn Hooper*) a man of such conscience, as your

Bishop

Biſhop writeth, that being made Biſhop by the childe king _anno_ 1550. _Biſhop of Gloceſter held alſo the Biſhopricke of Worceſter in commendam by licence of King Edward the ſixt_ ; this is his commendation. The reſt that fled not the Realme for treaſon (which were not of your Proteſtant religion, but Puritanes in forraine countries) were depriued in England for being married, which by no Religion Biſhops might doe: ſuch were _Buſh_ of Briſtow, _Harley_ of Hereford, _Holgate_ of Yorke and others that became Catholikes (_Godwyn in Briſt. Heref. Yorke, &c._) _Couerdale_ was ſet at libertie by Q. _Marie_, and of ſo ſmall eſteeme with you in the beginning of Q. Elizabeth her raigne , that no Biſhopricke was allowed him.

Now let vs come to your chiefe temporall councellours then , theſe were by their owne creation, the Dukes of Sommerſet and Northumberland, called Protectors to the young king (_Stow and Holinſh. and Theater. K. Edw. 6. and Q. Marie_) the firſt baſely put to death in that time for felonie: the other for treaſon and open rebellion againſt Q. _Marie_ : And after hee had bene thus with Cranmar, the chiefe inſtrument to ouerthrowe Catholike Religion, and ſet vp Proteſtancie in the time of that yong king: hee plainely recanted his new faith, and was reconciled to the Church of Rome. And yet among theſe vnworthie men , vnder that yong king there were but 6. Biſhops, and 6. others that
made

made the Church-bookes of their religion the: (*Statut.An.3.Edw. 6.cap. 12.Foxe, Stowe, and others in Edw.6.*) and for religion it selfe, they had no Canons, articles, or decrees of it in all the time of that king. *Howes* your historian thus writeth of it: Edward, *at nine yeares of age succeeded his father, and then the Church was fleest againe, the Bishoprickes cut and pared, all Chantries supprest, the Bishoppricke of Durrham alienated. By all which, the Kings Exchequer was very litle enriched, neither was the common wealth eased, or benefited; nor the auntient nobilitie any way dignified, onely some few preferred. The Earldome of Northumberland giuen to the* Suttons *, who obtayned the title of the Duke of Northumberland. In the first and second yeare of his raigne, the Maße was wholly supprest, and part of King Dauids Psalmes were turned into english verse, by* Hopkins *and* Sterneholde, *Groomes of the Kings chamber, and set them to seuerall tunes, consisting of galliards and measures. The Duke of Sommerset, vncle to the King by the mothers side, being the Kings Protector, did all things in the Kings name, and inclyned ouer-much to the subtile counsel of his secret enemie, the Duke of Northumberland, who was fully bent to defeat and suppreße the apparant heires of God and nature vnto the Crowne, and to preferre the heires of the Duke of* Suffolke, *according to the iniurious determination of k.Henrie the eight.For the better effecting whereof, they made a combination, which had as good succeße, as so bad a practise deserued. The Protector*

G 3   among

among other things that crossed his greatnesse in po-
pularitie was, the spoyling of churches and chappels,
the defacing of auntient tombes and monuments, &
namely, twelue goodly tombes in Christ-church: *his*
attempting was to pull downe all the Belles in parish
Churches, *and to leaue but one Bell in a steeple,*
whereat the commonalitie were reddie to rebell. Hee
raigned seuen yeares, mette with a tricke of trea-
son. He meaneth that he was poysoned by his
protestant Protector Cranmar , & other protestants of that most wicked combination.

They that desire to know more of that yong
kings times, may resort to your Protestant histories of Foxe, Stowe, Holinshed, Speede (*Foxe*
tom.2. in king Edw. Holinsh. and Theater ibid. In-
iunctions an. 1. Ed. 6.) and the childish Iniunctions in matters of Religion, set out in the name
of that Nouice, and Nouecins supreame head
of your church : where he may finde the chiefe
care of the councell and executors, left by king
Henry the eight, spiritual and temporal, to loade
themselues with new and great titles, and honours of dignitie, grow riche, by the last ruines
of the Church, and to be of no setled religion at
all: For we doe not finde either in histories, or in
confession of Protestants diligently collected
by them, or in any priuate or publike monu-
ment, any forme, fashion, shape, articles, canons
or decrees of Religion, either vnder king Henry
the 8.k. Edward the 6. or Q. Elizabeth, vntill
her

her fourth yeare, anno 1562. when the booke of the artickles of your religion was firft contryued and publifhed to the world. *Booke of Articles of Religion, an. 1562.*

Therefore wee may not ioyne with thefe men in Religion, as neither you doe, efpeciallie with king Henrie the eight, but rather marnaile why you and all that clayme title to religion from them, do not finde great motiues rather to bethinke what wrongs they did vnto vs, then perfift in heaping new and more prefsures, and perfecutions vpon the Catholikes of your owne nation, and kindred. For you haue heard from your Proteftants before, that they obtayned that their power againft the Religeous houfes of England, onely vpon this motiue to reforme abufes, if they could finde them: *To create and maintaine for the perpetual defence and fecuritie of this Kingdome. 40. Earles, 60. Barons, 300. knights, and fourefcore thoufand fouldiers, with skilful captaines, and competent maintenance for them all for euer, out of the auntient Church reuenewes*: and yet to leaue for the maintenance of religious parfons, profeffing and liuing in the perfect way of chriftian Religion, chaftitie, obedience, and pouertie, watchings, faftings, prayers, and aufteritie of life, continued & maintained here from the comming of S. Iofeph of Aramathia into this Iland by our kings, euen the Pagan kings, *Aruiragus, Marius, and Caillus,* and other Chriftian Princes, and

G 4   holy

holy founders after, to these dayes *(antiq.Glaston, apud Lel in assert. Arthur.Capgraue in S. Ioseph. & S.Patric.& protest.histor.)* which neither the Religion of King Henrie the 8. King Edward the 6. Queene Elizabeth, or King Iames, did or doth condemne.

Neither can any of them (as these Protestantes haue before bene witnesses) dissallow of their Masses and prayers for the dead, but acknowledged the contrarie opinion to be hereticall and damnable: yet both to the temporall and spirituall dammage of many thousands, frō that time they still perseuer in that estate of iniustice, so obnoxious to restitution, and are so farre from performing King Henrie the eight his condition, to maintaine so many thousand souldiers & others, and ease their kingdome of taxes and contributions, that they are not now able to performe the first, nor to maintaine their dignities without the other. In all which, the Catholikes of England, are onely innocent, and yet they alone for their innocencie, are condemned, and persecuted.

THAT THE PROCEEDINGS OF Q. *Elizabeth ar noe warrant for protestants to persecute Catholicks, nor noe true conuiction, but rather a confirmation of the Romane Catholicke Religion: by the writings of English protestants themselues.*

All

ALl theſe proteſtant arguments conclude much more ſtrongely againſt the procee-dings of Queene Elizabeth in theſe matters: for if it was publickly addiuged for lawe in the time of kinge Henry the ſeuenth (our lawes remayning the ſame) *That the parlament could not make the king beeing a lay man, to haue ſpiri-tuall Iuriſdiction.* (*temporibus Henrici 7.*) How much more an vnpoſſible thinge is it, to en-title a woman, and ſuch a woman to that dig-nitie by ſuch donation? for firſt euen by our pro-teſtants, it is the Pepuzian hereſie to ſay a wo-man at all is capable of that ſpirituall vocatiõ ſhee ſtooke vppon herſelfe, and preſumed to impart to others. (*Epiphan. & Aug. in hareſ. Pepuzian.*) And thereupon your proteſtants aſ-ſure vs : *The Queens maieſties parſon was neuer capable of any part of ſpirituall power:* (*Ormerod. proteſt. Aſſert. an. 1604. pag. 218.*) Then much leſſe of that ſupreame power. And if ſhee had been a man, yett in that caſe your proteſtant hiſtorians before haue told vs, made illegiti-mate by publicke parlament, the Kinge, Lords ſpirituall, and temporall with the reſt, there muſt haue beene as greate a power to recall yt, which was not in that her firſt parlament, for the Lords ſpirituall, whoe onely haue power in ſuch caſes, did vtterly diſſent to yeeld her any ſuch priuiledge, ſoe that noe man, or com-pany that had power of diſpenſations, in ſuch things, diſpenſed with her, but contrary.

Agayne

Againe, it is a maxime in the Lawes (as you Lord Cooke writeth *(l.4.fol,23.) nemo po-teſt plus iuris in alium transferre qnàm ipſe habet. None can giue more power to an other, then they haue to giue*, and the contrarie is vnpoſſible: Therefore ſeeing no Parlament that euer was in England, when all the Biſhops and Abbots, and chiefe ſpirituall men it euer had were aſ-ſembled, had at any time, either for themſelues, or to giue vnto any other, that ſupreame ſpiri-tuall power, but as your Biſhops haue told vs before, it was wholly in the Pope of Rome euer from our conuerſion, and ſo could neuer be de-riued to King Henry the eight, or Edward the ſixt *(Parker antiquit. Britan. in Cranmer.Polyder. Virg.in Henr.8.l.vlt.hiſtor. &c.)* it is much more ſtronge againſt Q. Elizabeth,both for her ſexe, and the other incapabilitie,as Proteſtants aſſure vs.And for her or any to clayme it, by that Par-lament wherein ſhee tooke it vpon her, is a thing more then to be wondred at: for all men of that Parlament, which had any ſpiritual iu-riſdiction (as the Catholike Biſhops) did by all meanes reſiſt and contradict it: and the words of the ſtatute (as your Proteſtants haue publi-ſhed it) by which ſhee tooke vpon her to exer-ciſe it,and perſecute Catholikes onely by pre-tence of this power there giuen vnto her, are theſe:*Moſt humbly beſeech your moſt excellent Ma-ieſtie,your faithful and obedient ſubiects, the Lordes Spiritual, and Temporal,and the vvhole commons in*
this

this your present Parlament assembled. That the supreame power spirituall, should be in that Queene, when it is euident by all our Protestāt histories, that not one Lord Spirituall, either desired it, or consented vnto it, but all repugned and gaine-said it; and for that cause were committed to prison, or otherwise most grieuously afflicted. (*Stow histor. an.1. Elizab. Holinsh. Theater.an.1. Eliz. Cambd. annal. rerum Anglic. in 1. Elizab. &c.*) And yet there was not any man in that Parlament, that could giue vnto her, if she had bene capable (as she was not) the least spiritual iurisdiction ouer the least parish in England.

And if she had not insisted in her fathers steppes of flatterie, terrors, & dissimulatiō, promises of great matters without performāce, & in some degrees (by the cunning of some about her without conscience) exceeded him, shee might haue founde as little applause, and consent in the Lords temporall and others; For vsing all meanes she could, to further her strange proceedings, (partly to be hereafter from her Protestant writers remembred) yet shee found such and so manifest reasons opposed against her, that the scarres of those wounds then giuen to your religion, will neuer be recouered. A principall antiquarie among you writeth (*Cambden Annal. in Eliz. pag.26.*) that the Lord Vicount Mountague, which a little before had bene Ambassadour at Rome, with Bishop *Thursby* of Ely, for the

the reconciling of England to the Church of
Rome in Queene Maries time, publickly in parlament theſe oppoſed.

*Hic ex Religionis ardore, & honoris ratione acri-
ter inſtabat, magno Angliæ dedecori eſſe, ſi ab Apo-
ſtolica ſede, cui nuper ſe ſubmiſſe reconciliarat, mox
deficeret. Hee out of loue of religion and care of honour, did earneſtly vrge, how great a shame it would
be to England, if it should ſo ſoone reuoult from the
Sea Apoſtolike, to which it had lately ſubmißiuelie
reconciled it ſelfe: and would turne to greater dau-
ger if excommunicated, it by ſuch defeċtion be expo-
ſed, to the rage of neighboring enemies. Hee in the
name of the nobilitie, and all degrees in England, in
their name had done obedience to the Pope of Rome,
and muſt needes performe it. Therefore he vrgently
beſought them, that they would not depart from the
Romane Sea, to which they were indebted, both for
firſt receauing the faith from thence, and from thence
hauing it continually preſerued.*

This was ſufficiently prooued at that time
of the reconciliation of England to the Church
of Rome, in open Parlament alſo by Cardinall
Pole, as your firſt proteſtantly ordeyned Arch-
biſh. in theſe wordes affirmeth (Parker ant. Brit.
in Reginald. Polo) *Hāc inſulæ nobilitatem, atque glo-
riam Dei prouidentiæ, atque beneficientiæ ſoli accep-
ta ferendam, ſed tamen viam ipſam atque rationem
qua hac nobilitas atque gloria parta eſt, ſede Romana nobis prima ſemperque monſtratam, & pateſa-
ċtam fuiſſe. In Romana exinde fidei vnitate nos ſem-*

*per perseuerasse , fuisseque nostram antiquissimam
Romanæ ecclesiæ subiectionem. The noblenes of this
Iland, for being the first of all the Prouinces of the
worlde,that receaued the Christian faith , and the
glorie thereof, is to be acknowledged to haue proceeded from the prouidence and goodnesse of God, yet the
way it selfe and meanes, by which this nobilitie &
glory was wonne vnto it, was first & alwaies shewed and layde open vnto vs from the Sea of Rome: wee
haue alwaies from that time perseuered in the vnity
of the Romane faith, and our subiection to the Romane Church is most auntient.*

And this reconciling of England then to the
Romane Church, was so ioyful and honorable
a thing to this natiō, that to vse your Protestant
Archbiſhops wordes (*Parker antiquit. Britan.in
Polo*) *In Synodo decretum est,vt dies ille quo ponti-
fici Romano authoritas restituta fuerit , quotannis
festus dies celebraretur, atque Anglicanæ ecclesiæ re-
conciliatio diceretur.* It was decreede in a Synode,
that the daye on which authoritie was restored to
the Pope of Rome, should yeerely be kept holie daie,
and called, the Reconciliation of the Church of England. Abbot Fecknham (*in Parlm. Elizab.*) in his
oration to that Parlament of Q. Elizabeth hath
thus : *Damianus and Fugatianus as Ambassadours
from the Sea Apostolike of Rome, did bring into this
Realme* 1400. *yeares past, the very same religion,
whereof wee are now in possession, and that in the
latine tongue, as the auntient historiographer Dominus Gylduas witnesseth , in the prologue and begin-*
                                                    ning

ning of his booke of the Britaine hiſtories, which he would not haue dared to vtter, in that time and place, but that then he could produce that anti-quitie to be his warrant: which with many o-thers condemning the new religion of Prote-ſtants, are by them ſuppreſſed. All the Biſhops (of whom more hereafter)and whom tearmeth your Proteſtant glorious & renowned men, *ob-firmate refragati ſunt. Did ſtoutly giue their voyces againſt this innouation.* They offered publicke defence by diſputation of Catholike Religion, both for doctrine and iuriſdiction. *Cambden An-nal.pag.26. in appart. ad annal.pag.36 Maſon lib. 3. conſecrat.pag.206.cap.5. Stow hiſt. an.1. Eliz. Holinsh.ibid. Godwyn.Catol.*

But the Proteſtants knowing how their chie-feſt champions , had bene before ſo conuinced by them, that they were hiſſed by the auditors, durſt not come to triall. But the Parlament be-ginning on the 23. day of Ianuary, they preſently proceeded to make Queene Elizabeth ſupreme head of the Church, and by that title to make a religion what pleaſed her, and her few fauori-tes, which by ſuch indirect meanes, as is heere teſtified by theſe Proteſtants, they brought to paſſe in the beginning of that Parlament, and in the very firſt acte and ſtatute thereof.(*Theater of great Brittaine. lib.9. cap.24.parag.4.Godwyn Ca-tal.in the Bish. depriu.an.1.Eliz.ab.Parlament.1.an. 1.Eliz.cap.1.* And would neuer hearken to any diſputation whatſoeuer, vntill they had thus
obtey-

obteyned their purpose, and vntill the laſt day of March two moneths after, as all Proteſtant hiſtories giue euidence.

And when they had by onely 6. voyces of laye-men, condemned our learned Biſhops, and their holy religion: the religion of the vniuerſall Church of God, they would not then allow them (though condemned thus vniuſtly) any diſputation at all, except they would accept of that bable and mockerie of diſputation, and all religion; which I haue from theſe Proteſtãts remembred before (*Cambden in Annal. lib. pag. 27.*) Therefore let vs paſſe it ouer in this place, and deſire your inſtructing Proteſtants a little further to inſtruct and informe vs, how ſhee proceeded, and ſo ſtrangely preuailed in this matter. *Orbe Chriſtiano mirante, to the wonder of all the Chriſtian world,* for the prophane proceedings then vſed, as your Proteſtants before haue teſtified (*Camben annal. ſupra.*)

So ſoone as ſhee was proclaimed Queene, & long before her Coronation, *by proclamation ſhe ſilenced the Catholike Biſhops and Cleargie not to preach, and by her Iniunctions, gaue warrant to her laye proteſtant commiſſioners, to giue licence to preach* (Proclamation of *Q. Elizabeth. an. 1. Stowe hiſtor. an. 1. Elizab. Iniunctions of Q. Elizabeth. an.*) *Shee put in practiſe the oathe of Supemacie amongſt many which refuſed that oath, was the Lord Chancellour, D. Heath, Archbiſhop of Yorke, from whom ſhee tooke the priuie ſeale, and remitted it*

to Sr. *Nicholas Bacon* (*Stowe biſtor.* in *Queene*
Elizabeth an. reg. 1.) *shee putt many from the*
coⱳncell, *and tooke* neⱳ coⱳnſaylers : *ſuis adiun-*
xit, ſayth your beſt Antiquary, (*Cambden Annal.*
in *Elizabeth pag.* 18. 19) *pro temporum ratione,*
Gulielmum Parrum , Marchionem Northamptoniæ,
Franciſcum Ruſſellum, comitem Bedford:æ, Thomam
Parrum, Edwardum Rogers , Ambroſium Cauum,
Franciſcum Knolles, & Guilielmum Cecilium, pau-
loque poſt Nicholaum Bacon, ſingulos proteſtantium
doctrinam amplexos, nulloque ſub Maria loco: Quos
vt reliquos, in eorum locum iam inde ſuffectos , ita
temperauit & cohibuit, vt ſibi eſſent deuotiſſimi, &
ipſa ſemper ſui iuris , nulli obnoxij . Shee ioyned
to hyrs for the ſtate of the tyme, William Parr,
Marqueſſe of Northampton, Francis Ruſſell,
Earle of Bedford, Thomas Parr, Edward Rogers, Ambroſe Caue , Francis Knolles , and
William Cecile, and ſoone after Nicholas Bacon, all become proteſtants, in noe office vnder
Q. Mary , which as the reſt which ſhee putt
in for thoſe ſhee diſplaced, ſhee ſoe tempered,
and kept them in awe, that they were moſte
ſeruiceable to her, ſhee allwayes to doe what
pleaſed her, none to contradict her.

Shee concluded *cum paruulis intimis* (*Camb-*
den ſupr. pag. 22.23.) ⱳith *a* feⱳ *moſt* inⱳard ⱳith
her, *de nobilibus à regio conſilio amouendis epiſco-*
pis & eccleſiaſticis de gradu deijciendis , Iudicibus
qui pro tribunalibus ſederunt , & hirenanchis per
ſingulos comitatus, qui regnante Maria re & æſti-
matione

matione magni erant, hos locos deturbandos, & legum seueritate coercendos, nullosque nisi protestantes ad rerum administrationem adhibendos, & in collegia vtriusque academiæ coaptandos censuerunt, simulque pontificios præsides ex academijs, scholarchas ex Wintoniensi, Aetoniensi, cæterisque scholis submouendos. Q. Elizabeth presently after the death of Q. Mary taketh order, with very few of her inward frends how to restore protestant Religion. The plott by them was, that new cōmissions should bee directed to iudges, with prouision, they should not giue any office: new Iustices of peace, and sheriffes should bee made in all countries, the noble men should bee put from the councell, Bishops and ecclesiasticall men displaced, all iudges and iustices of peace that were in estimation in the tyme of Q. Mary, should bee remoued in all shires, and seuerely kept vnder, and none but protestants to bee admitted to gouernment in the comon wealth, and placed in the colledges of both vniuersities, and all popish presidents of howses, and scholemasters to bee renewed from Wincester Eton and other scholes.

And accordinge to this conclusion, this Elizabeth neyther beeing crowned Queene as yet, nor haueinge by any pretence power to meddle with the Title of Supreamacie, because to speake in your protestants words, (*Stowe histor. an. 1. Eliz. ab. statut. in parlam. an. 1. Mariæ*) *Queene Mary restored all thinges according to the*

H *church*

church of Rome, *reduced all eccleſiaſticall iuriſdic-*
tion, vnto the papall obedience : yett to write in
the ſame proteſtants pen and words: (*Stowe*
hiſtor ſupr. an. 1. Eliz.) *The Queene tooke an ex-*
act ſuruey of all her cleargie and officers of eſtate,
and putt in practiſe the oath of ſupreamacie, and
amongſt many which refuſed that oathe, was the
Lord chaunncellor D.Heath Archbiſhop of yorke: ſhee
committed the cuſtody of the greate Seale vnto Sr.
Nicholas Bacon, a man moſte malicious againſt pa-
piſts, whoe from that tyme was called Lord keeper.
Cambden ſupr. annal. pag.27.

Haueing thus diſplaced through the kingdome all catholicke magiſtrates, and diſſolued
the catholicke parlament, continueinge at the
death of her Syſter Queene Mary, and putt new
proteſtant officers in their places, with all
ſpeed ſhee ſommoned a parlament to begyn in
Ianuary followeinge, within twoe moneths
of her ſiſters death. (*Stowe ſupr. Holinſh. hiſtor.*
an. 1. Eliz.ab. Theater of Britan. 16. Cambd.Annal.
ann. 1. Eliz.ab.) And haueing thus prouided for a
fitt company in the lower howſe of parlament,
ſwearers to the ſupremacie, ſhee and her *pauculi*
intimi, were as prouident to packe ſome in the
vpper howſe alſoe. Therefore a fewe dayes before the parlament, to ſpeake as your proteſtant,
(*Stowe an. 1. Elizab. Cambden annal. ſupr.*) *the*
13. of Ianuary, the Queene in the Tower created
Sr. William Parr, ob læſam maieſtatem ſub Maria
gradu deiectum, attainted of treaſon in Q. Maryes
tyme

tyme Lord *marquesse* of Northampton, *Edward Sey-*
mor sonne to the late Duke of Sommer*sett,* attainted, *vicount* Beuchamp, *and* Earle *of* Hertford: Tho.
Howard *second sonne of* Tho. Duke of Norfolke,
vicount Bindon; *Sr.* Oliuer Saint Ihon, *Baron of*
Bletsoe; *and Sr.* Henry Carey, *Lord* Hounsdon. Qui
singuli à pontificia Religione alieni, all which were
alienated from the popes Religion, all which that
Queene and her *pauculi intimi, very* fewe *that con-*
sented vnto her, knew by that meanes would
giue their voyces in parlament to what shee
should desire, and not content with this , proceeded soe in these indirect courses, that as your
protestants haue written: (*Cambden Annall. pag.*
27.) *plures è protestantibus data opera, è comitatibus*
tum è ciuitatibus, & burgis fuisse electos, & Norfol-
cia ducem, Arundeliaque *Comitem, inter proceres*
potentissimos, in suam siue rem, siue spem, Cecilium-
que sua solertia suffragia emendicasse. The papists
complayned, *that more protestants of sett purpose*
were chosen out of Countries, cyties, and burroughts,
and the Duke of Norfolke *and Earle of* Arundell
moste potent amonge the nobilitie , eyther for their
owne good , or hope (by the Queens promises of
marriadge or such things) and Cecyle by his cun-
ninge had begged voyces. And to helpe and further soe bad a cause, the Queene herselfe (your
protestants words) *openly protested at that tyme in*
parlament, that shee would neuer vexe, or trouble
the Romane *Catholicks, concerning any difference*
in Religion.

Ney-

Neyther did this Queene or hir *pauculi intimi*, Cecile and Bacon, take this ſtraunge courſe in hand, for diſlike of catholick Religion : for your Antiquary telleth vs of Q. Elizabeth her-ſelfe: *ad Romanæ Religionis normam ſacra audiret, & ſæpius confiteretur. Miſſam permiſit poſt mortem Mariæ & litanias*. Q. Elizabeth heard maſſe after the Romane order, often went to confeſſion, and after Q. Maryes death allowed maſſe and litanies, (*Cambden in Apparatu pag. 13.*) The like is as well knowne of thoſe her *intimi* at that tyme. But they had other little laudable ends, by proteſtant proceedings now, thus expreſſed by your cheifeſt Antiquary: (*Cambden in Annal. Reẏ. Anglic. in Elizabeth pag. 21. 22.*) *Nonnulli ex intimis Conſiliarẏs in aures aſſiduè inſuſurrarunt molliſsimo ingenio virgini, dum timerent ne animus in dubio facillimè impelleretur, actum de ipſa & amicis eſſe, conclamatum de Anglia, ſi pontificiam authoritatem in diſpenſando, aut alia quacunque re agnoſceret: duos pontifices matrem illegittimè Henrico 8. emptam pronuntiaſſe, & inde in eorum ſententia iam lata Scotorum Reginam ius in Regnum Angliæ ſibi arrogare pontificem ſententiam iſtam nunquam reſciſſurum.* Some of her inward Counſaylors did dayly whiſper into her eares, beeing a mayden of a moſte tractable diſpoſition, while they feared leaſt her minde in doubt might moſt eaſely bee driuen forward (to marry with king Philip of Spayne, and ſoe continue the catholicke Religion, that ſhee and her frendes were vndone,

if

if shee should acknowledge the popes authority in dispenseinge or any other matter. For two popes had allready pronounced, that her mother was vnlawfully marryed to Henry 8. and soe in their sentence denownced the Queene of Scots did challendge right to the kingdome of England. And that the pope would neuer recall this sentence.

And agayne: *Prospexit huiusmodi matrimonium ex dispensatione contrahendo, non posse non agnoscere seipsam iniustis nuptijs natam esse.* Shee thus *perceaued that this marriadge with king Philipp of Spayne her Systers husband, to bee by the popes dispensation, must needs acknowledge that shee was borne in vnlawfull wedlocke.* And they knew alsoe that shee remayning a catholicke must seeke for the popes dispensation of this her birth, not onely made and declared illegitimate, by the pope, but by her father himselfe, and the whole parlament, and Title to the crowne giuen her onely by the will and testament of her father, *parlament Henr. 8. of Illeg. Lady Elizab.*) against which in this case your protestant historian thus exclaymeth: (*Howes histor. preface in Henry 8.) through feare and terror Henry 8. obteyned an Act of parlament to dispose of the right of succession to the crowne, and then by his last will and testament* (K. Henry 8. *in his last will and Testam.) contrary to the law of God, and nature, conuayes it from the lawfull heires of his eldest sister, marryed vnto the kinge of Scotland, vnto the heires of Char-*

H 3   *les*

les Brandon and others, (his daughter Elizabeth
and of theſe others) *thereby to haue defeated, preuented and ſuppreſt the vnqueſtionable, and immediate right from God, of our gratious ſoueraigne,
kinge Iames, as if it had beene in the power of his
will, or of the parlament, to diſenherite, and preuent
the diuine free guiſt, and grace of almightie Goa,
by which the kings of this land doe hold their
crownes.*

Thus your proteſtant and priuiledged hiſtorians: by which is euident that this proceedinge
by ſuch exorbitant courſes concerning Religiō,
was not for loue or likinge of their proteſtant
Religion, further then yt gaue them licence and
libertie to doe and liue as pleaſed their ſenſuall
appetites, which the church and Religion of
Rome would not allowe. And yett all theſe ſi-
niſtre and prophane proceedings not withſtan-
dinge, to inſiſt in your proteſtants words in
chaungeing Religion in that her parlament.
(*Howes hiſtorial.preface. in Q. Elizabeth.*) *In this
parlament notwithſtandinge the preſence of the
Queene* (to countenance their bad cauſe) *with
the apparant likelyhood of hir longe life, and hope
of iſſue to ſucceede her, yett the maior part exceeded
the minor but in ſixe voyces, at which time* (to
wringe out conſents) *the Queene openly pronounced, that ſhee would neuer vexe, or trouble the Romane Catholicks, concerninge any difference in Religion.* Which promiſe of hirs was as well performed, as that condition of her fathers before,
of

of beſtoweinge the church reuenewes, for as
your proteſtants haue related, her perſecutions
which ſoe vnprincely and vnchriſtianely in her
name and power of that ſtraunge claymed ſupreamacie in a woman, and ſuch a woman, e-
qualed, or exceeded thoſe of Nero, and Diocle-
ſian, infenſiue tyrants and enemyes of Chriſtianitie. *Syr Edwyn Sandes in Relation of the ſtate of
Religion.*

And in that parlament yt ſelfe, where ſhee
ſpake theſe words, and proceeded to cruell inflicted penalties, againſt thoſe Romane Catholicks, as all our holy Biſhops were depriued, impriſoned, or exiled, ſoe were all other ecclefia-
ſticall parſons that would not doe as pleaſed her.
(*Stowe hiſtor. an. 1. Elizab. Holinſhed Theater ibid.
Cambd. in Annalib. Rerum Anglicarum in Elizab.
Parlament. 1. Elizabeth.*) greate forfaictures and
puniſhments impoſed vppon all, that ſhould
heare maſſe, or not bee preſent at her new deuiſed ſeruice, premunire, loſſe of lands goods, and
perpetuall impriſonment, and loſſe of life alſoe
with note of Treaſon, to them that would not
acknowledge that ſpirituall ſupreame power in
her, of which ſhee was ſoe far vncapable in the
iudgment of her owne proteſtants, that diuers
of them wrote, and publiſhed to the world, that
a woman could not bee a ſupreame gouernor in
things temporall; (*Knoxe, Godman and other proteſt. againſt the Regim. of women.*) and they were
ſoe violent herein, both in England and Scot-

H 4   land,

land, against those two blessed Queene Maryes: that Q. Mary of England was inforced to make a statute in parlamēt, to suppresse yt: the Abridgement thereof is thus. (*parlament 2. an. 1. Mar. 20. die April. 1554. cap. 2.*) *The Regall and kingely power of this realme, and all the dignities, and prerogatiues of the same, shall bee as wel in a Queene, as in a kinge.*

How the protestants in England vpon such good doctrine rebelled against that Q. Mary, all knowe; And in Scotland they rather chosed to crowne our Soueraigne in his cradle, then the true Queene his mother should raigne, & haue any power spirituall, or temporall at all, in her owne hereditary kingdome, (*Holinsh. histor. of Scotland. Stowe hist. an. 1. Iacob.*)but by the violence of those Scottish protestants, to bee driuert from thence. And landeinge in this kingdome of England.(*Cambden in Annal. in the life of Q. Mary of Scotland.*) Where by these protestants before shee had such iust right of succession, as they haue declared, & left that most vndeniable Title, and interest, by which moste truely, lawfully and vndoubtedly , her sonne our soueraigne kinge Iames now enioyeth both this whole kingdome of Britanie, Ireland, and all the adiacent Ilands by hereditary right from her, shee fownde noe further fauour here of the English protestants, but to bee a perpetual prisoner in her life, and to her eternall glory , and english protestants soe longe endureinge shame,

mur-

murthered and martyred at her death . *Stowe*
Holinsh. Theater of Britanie in Q . Eliz. &c.

Moreouer in this foe termed parlament, befides the takeinge of this greate and fupreame
fpirituall chardge and office vnto a woman (neuer heard of in the world before) and fuppref-
finge of the holy facrifice of the maffe, euer
fince Saint Peters tyme (as before is proued)ex-
cepting three yeares of kinge Edward the 6. a
child, and in place thereof admittinge a forme
of communion and common prayer neuer vfed
by any people catholicks or proteftants , but in
that fhorte tyme alfoe of that yonge kinge in
England, not any one Article of proteftant Religion eyther againft the 7. Sacraments of the
church, inuocatiō of Saints, prayer for the dead,
purgatorie, validitie of good workes, merit, iuftification or whatfoeuer els now contradicted
by thefe proteftáts, was thé, or vntil the fourth
yeare of Q. Elizabeth,concluded by any parlament proteftant Authoritie in England, but left
arbitrary for euery man to beleeue and practize
as his fantafie ferued , without any rule at all.
Booke of Articles and Conuocation an. 1562.

And for the communion Booke yt felfe,it had
not any approbation of any one parlament má,
diuine or other , as your proteftants affure vs,
but the chardge of making or mareing that was
onely committed fayth your prime proteftant
Antiquary with others, *Cambden annal. pag.* 23.
Parkero, Billo, Maio, Copo, Grindallo whitheado &
Pil-

*Pilkingtono Theologis, Thomæque Smitho Equiti: To
Parker, Bill, May, Cope, Grindall Whithead and Pil-
kington diuines, and Thomas Smyth a knight.* The
firſt and cheifeſt of theſe ſeuen beeing Mathew
Parker, had beene of ſeuen Religions vnder
kinge Henry 8. Edward 6. Q. Mary and Q. Elizabeth, chaunging in euery one of thoſe chaun-
ges, as before is proued, (*Godwyne Catalog. of
Bish. in Canterbury Matth. Parkr. Foxe to. 2. in k.
Henr. 8. Edw. 6. Q. Mar. &c.*) and al Q. Maries
tyme profeſſinge the catholicke Romane Religion in England, both before and after his de-
priuation of his liuings, in the ſecond yeare of
Q. Mary for being marryed.

For the reſt of theſe proteſtant diuines, they
were fugitiues for mariadge againſt the canons
of the church, and conſpiracy againſt Q. Mary,
before which time they were in the ſame diſeaſe
of chaungeing Religion with the former princes, and after their going forth of England, profeſſed the religion, & diſcipline alſo of the puritane churches where they liued, namely to ex-
emplyſie in the liturgie or common booke of
prayer of the proteſtants of Franckfort, publiſhed an. 1554. in Q. Maryes tyme, denyinge both
the ſupreamacy of temporall princes, and other
matters of engliſh proteſtant Religion : this is
the ſubſcription of the engliſh proteſtants then
in all their names. (*Liturgia ſeu ritus miniſterij
in Eccleſia peregrinorum Francofordiæ an. 1544 per
Petrum Brubachium in fine in ſubſcript.*) *Subſcri-
bunt*

bunt Angli ob Euangelium profugi totius Ecclesiæ
suæ nomine. Iohannes Mackbræus &c. The protestants of England that were fled for the Ghospell,
subscribe in the name of their whole church. Ihon
Mackbree minister, Ihon Stanton, William Hamon,
Ihon Bendall, William Whithingham, and to assure
vs that these men in particular before named,
bee Authors or correctors of yt, & neyther did,
nor in their owne iudgment could allowe
yt, it is euident: first both because they were of
this protestant Franckford congregation, se-
condly because: *The first protestants of this king-*
dome (your protestants words. *Couel in examin.*
pag. 72.) *in a letter subscribed with eleuen of their*
hands, whereof Knoxe, Gilby, Whithinghame and
Godman were foure, moste of them hauing iudge-
ment and learninge, vtterly condemned yt. (*Couel a-*
gainst Burges pag. 69.122.47.185.) Soe did Cal-
uine at Geneua, Ridley your protestant Bishopp
and supposed martyr in a letter to Grindal himselfe a cheife agent in it: all the Caluinists in the
world abrode in their publick confessions, and
at home haue likewise euer, and doe still condemne it, as alsoe all Lutherans that euer were,
and all those writers or correctors of it them-
selus, and all the protestants in that first parlament in all probable iudgment, except fowre
new cownsaylers of Q. Elizabeth, the Marquesse of Northampton, Earle of Bedford, Ihon
Grey of Pyrge, and Cecile her *pauculi intimi,* to
whome onely (as sayth your historian. *Cābden*
                                              supr.

ſupr. in Annal. in Eliz.ab.) this matter was com-
muhicated vnto: *re nemini communicata, niſi Mar-*
chioni Northamptonia Comiti Bedfordia , Iohanni
Greio de Pyrgo, & Cecilio.

And this matter was ſufficiently proued by
ſome of your late Biſhops in the Conference at
Hampton Court, publickly betweene the proteſtant Biſhops and puritans, before our kinge
himſemſelfe; where Barlowe your Biſhop in re-
lating of that diſputation, *(Barlowe Conference at*
Hampton Court pag. 14. 15.) bringeth in Babing-
ton, a proteſtant Biſhop of yours openly to acknowledge, that in the beginninge, *your proteſ-*
tants religion, and communion booke thereof , was
propoſed and approued in that firſt parlament by am-
biguous and indirect dealeinge of the compoſers of
that communion booke, and citeth the Archbiſhop
of yorke to that purpoſe. And if wee may beleeue your proteſtant Relations of that diſpute
printed with priuiledge, (*Their proteſtant Rela-*
tions of that Confer. printed by Ihon windet cap. 1.
2. 3. *all annexed to Barlows Relation.*) wee ar told,
that your proteſtant Archbiſhop of Canterbury,
Biſhop of London, & Biſhop of Wyncheſter did
here vpon their knees before his maieſty confeſſe
as much of the errors of that booke, and their
Religion: thus wee haue from them in three ſe-
uerall relations , and from the fourth by your
Biſhop Barlowe as before

Finallie thus wee pore catholicke preiſts and
catholicks haue toyled ourſelues in ſearching,
seeking

seeking and preaching all proteftants proceedings, parlaments, lawes writings, liues & dea-
leings of thefe pretended reformers , and the
further wee wade ,the deeper wee ar in error, if
Catholick Religion could poffibly bee error;
for as is euident before, wee can finde nothing
in any of thefe proteftant patterns and examples, but fuch as confirme vs in that faith wee
profeffe with the catholicke chriftian world in
all ages. To which God of his mercy conuert
them that bee in error. And foe much for this
firft part of this *proteftant Plea and petition.*

But feeing wee cannot finde any comforte
by your owne writers and relators of thefe
thinges to ioyne with you in your New Religion: wee will next proue vnto you by your
owne doctors and Antiquaries, that holy Religion which wee embrace(& for which you perfecute vs)to be the fame which was firft preached here by Saint Peter and his holy difciples,
and foe confequently deliuered by Chrift himfelfe, and continued in this nation in all ages
euen fince then, vntill thefe tymes.

FINIS.

APPROBATIO.

Ego infrascriptus legi libellum Angli-
canum cui Titulus præfigitur, *Proteſtants
plea and petition for Prieſts and Papiſts*,
& nihil in eo reperi fidei Catholicæ vel
bonis moribus aduerſum, quin potius eun-
dem vtilem futurum iudico, & dignum
qui in lucem prodeat. Datum Duaci 19.
Septemb. 1 6 2 1.

MATTHAEVS
KELLISONVS.

WILLIAM BELL
The Testament of
William Bel
1632

THE TESTAMENT

OF

WILLIAM BEL.

GENTLEMAN.

LEFT WRITTEN IN HIS OWNE
HAND.

*SETT OVT ABOVE 33. YEARES
AFTER HIS DEATH.*

With annotations at the end, and Sentences, out
of the H. Scripture, Fathers, &c.

By his sonne FRANCIS BEL, *of the Order of
Freers Minors, Definitor of the Province of
England: Guardian of* S. BONAVENTVRES
*Colledge in Dovvay: and Professor of the sa-
cred Hebrevv tongue, in the same.*

Electo meo   fædus   excidi

לבחידי   בריח   כרתי

Vulgat.
Psalm. 88.   *Disposui testamentum electis meis.*

Permissu Superiorum.

AT DOWAY,

By BALTHAZAR BELLERVS

at the golden Compass. Anno 1632.

TO THE RIGHT

WORSHIPFVLL

M.ʳ EDWARD

SHELDON

of Beoley, &c.

SIR.

Anciently,
when after the
rihgt of natu-
re, the earth
was Cõmon,
and all the gooddes therof:
that a man Could say to his

A 2   neigh-

Genef.
13.9.

neighbour הלא כל הארץ לפנך haſt
thou not all the earth before
thee? ſeparate thy ſelfe from
mee , if thou go to the left
hand I will keep the right, if
thou go to the Right hand I
will howld the left, Men gaue
in theyr teſtaments to theyr
children only cœleſtiall doctrines , that to whom they
had given being, they might
alſo giue well-being. By thees
meanes wee haue heard and
knowne ſo manie things: declared to vs by our fathers,
which in the next generatiō
were not hid from theyr
children, declaring the prayſes

Pſalm.
77,

fes of our Lord , his virtues, and mervailes done by him, that reifed vp teftimonie in Iacob : and gaue a lawe to Ifraël. how manie things did hee commande our fathers to make knowne to their fonnes to the end that the next generatiõ might know them, that the children that should arife and bee borne of them, might tell them againe to theyr children , and all, that they might fett theyr hope in God, not forget his worckes , and fearch out his Commands . Moyfes. Re- ^{Deut.} member the dayes of oulde

Deut. 32.

A 3   thinck

thincke vpon everie severall generation, aske thy father & hee will declare, thy elders and they will tell thee . Men gaue , I say , from hand to hand the lawe of God , his feare, & loue: with benediction to the keepers, malediction to the breakers of it, Commending vertue, condemning vice : foretelling payne and glorie the rewards *Epist.* of both . Such testament , *Iud. ca.* *1.14.* the seaventh man from A- *Gen.48* dam, Enoch made. Such was *49.* the Patriarch Iacobs testament disposed to his 12. sonnes: such also those, of these 12. Pa-

12. Patriarches themselues. *A most ancient Hebrew booke, called, the testamēt of the 12. Patriarchs* But of that new & euerlasting testament of IESVS-CHRIST the sonne of God what shall I say? therin is all knowledge of the heauenly kingdome: the eternall beatitude and fœlicitie of man. After this incomparable Testament, in which are all the treasures of the riches and wisedome of God, I may bring in that godly testamēt of my holy Father S. Francis, which after he was signed with the sacred stigmats of our Sauiour IESVS CHRIST, full with feruour, and the

A 4   holy

holy ghoſt], neer the end of his life , he left to vs his children, that more ſincerely and catholickly we might keep his Evangelicall rule.

Divers pious teſtaments haue been by ſundrie devout perſons, at ſeverall times ordained : And not among the laſt doe I accoumpt this teſtament of my father, a man knowne and eſteemed of your worship no leſs then of M.ʳ Raphe your father of happie memorie . It hath been kept in his owne manuſcript theeſ 44. yeares and more. By divine providence,

it

it hath at laſt come to my
hands: who hauing been
aboue 18. yeares out of my
countrie in forraine lands,
neither ſought for , nor
thought of anie ſuch thing
(although ſeing it now, I remember that in my younger
yeares I haue ſeen it before)
when a graue father of our
ſeraphicall order venerable
for his well ſpent , yeares
from his infancie till 67. (ſo
owld he is at this day) and no
leſs for his profownde iudgement and eloquence both in
ſpeach and ſtyle , lighting
vpon it ſent it out of Eng-
A 5   land

land to mee, with no small
commendations therof. His
censure animated me to put
it in print. And for a patrone
to whom I might dedicate it I
had not farre to seeke : your
Constant Christianitie and
professing of the Catholike
Religion : who like the great
Patriarch Abraham , to follow God , haue gone out of
land and Countrie and fa-
thers house and friends and
kinred, and familiars, or like
Saint Peeter out of all, doth
Chalenge so christianlike a
testament: especially from
mee who, as appeareth in the

34. §.

34. ſ. of it, am ſeverely charged to bee ſerviceable towards
you and yours

That ſervice together with
my ſelfe I offer here to your
worſhip, for vs all that haue
the charge there layde vpon
vs : that we be not chalenged
with the vile vice of ingratitude : or breach of the dead
mannes will. my ſelfe haue
had part of my education frō
M.ʳ Frācis Daniel, my vncle,
of whom mention is made in
the 32. ſ. who now liveth not
on earth. Of the Throckmar-
tōs of Coughton or Fekenhā
mentioned in the 33. ſ. I
haue

haue yet no knowledge,
nor of Sir Ihon Littletons
houſe, ſpoken of in the end
of the 34.ſ.I may liue to doe
them ſervice. your ſelfe only
remaines the man that moſt
extended his godnes towards
vs in accomplishing this wil:
in bringing vp my brother
Edmund together with your
owne ſonnes to learning to
muſicke, & to the vniverſitie
of Oxforde, as was required.
your ſiſter alſo the Religious
Ladie Ruſſell gaue educatiõ
ſucceſſiuely to two of my ſiſters Margarit & Dorothe.

Receiue therfore from me
this

this laſt will of my father as
my firſt will to ſerue you,
which with my life ſhall laſt,
and bee my laſt. ſo ſhall I
fulfill that iterated precept of
the holy ghoſt

שמע בני מוסר אביך

hear o my ſonne the inſtru-
ction of thy father.

Pro-
verb.
1.8.

נצר בני מצות אביך

keep o my ſonne the precept
of thy father.

Pro-
verb.
6.20.

God preſerue your worſhip
long to his higheſt glorie, the
good of our familie, and
chiefly of our ſeraphicall order to which you haue alwaies
ſhewed a charitable affectiõ :

and

and finally chosen in our
Convent at Namur Abra-
hams double caue for buriall
to your happilie decessed
wife and you. From our celle
in S. Bonaventures Colledge
in Doway this 7. of Ianuarie.
1 6 3 2.

Your worships obliged.

Br. FRANCIS BEL.

I N T H E N A M E

of God. Amen.

HE twentith day of
October in the year of
our Lord one thou-
sand fiue hundred fo-
werscore and seaven:
and in the nine and
twentith year of the
reigne of our sove-
reigne Ladie Elizabeth. I Williā Bell, alias,
Bellne , of Temple - Broughton in the
Coun-

Countie of Wigorne, Gentleman : being in good health of bodie, & of foūd & perfect memorie, (our Lord be bleſſed & thanked therfore) calling to my remembrance that all fleshe is graſſe, according to the ſaying of the Prophet Eſaia , and borne to die, and that in this decaying age of the world and triumphing time of ſinne ; beſides the courſe of nature , manie new and dange-rouſe diſeaſes doe ariſe : & manie malitious complottes and practiſes of Sathan and his miniſters are taken in hand; wherby our life is continually endangered and ſodeinly ta-ken away wherof there be infinite naturall: & ſome ruefull & tragicall examples. And having reſpect and regard of my fraile ſub-ſtance : of my short pilgrimage in this worlde , and long account I haue to make to my Maker in the worlde to come . And deſirous to make knowne to my poſteritie the ſtate of my ſoule and bodie. I doe now declare, ordaine, and publish, my will and teſtament: as a farewell to the vaine and diſ-ſembling world: and doe therby giue, and bequeath, deniſe, and declare, in manner & forme following.

§. 1.

§. 1.

In primis. I giue, and as a true Chriſtian Catholike man, bequeathe my ſoule into the hands and mercie of Almightie God; by faith confeſſing and in hope repoſing my ſalvation to bee in the only merites death, and Paſſion of Christ Iesvs, truſting to raigne with him in glorie, that for the redemption of mee and all mankinde raigned and triumphed over ſinne, death, and hell it ſelfe, in the Altar of the Croſſe. Wherunto I implore, and beſeech the aſſiſtance by prayer of the bleſſed and immaculate Virgin Marie, and of all the holy companie of heaven, who being now in glorie, members of the triumphant Church, haue in Chriſt compaſſion of the members of the militant Church. And I will that my bodie, when it ſhall bee diſſolued into his firſt ſubſtance, bee decently buried in the pariſh Church of Handburie, or whereſoever elſe it ſhall pleaſe God to appoint.

§. 2.

And, for as much as in this ruefull decay of the Catholike religion, and in this moſt iniurious and troubleſome time, I as a true Chriſtian, and carefull father, haue a zeal-

B   ouſe

ouſe care to leaue to all the world, and eſpecially to my Children, for their imitation, a
Confeſsion of my faith.

§. 3.

Bee it knowne to them, and to all the
world, that I profeſſe, and from my heart
proteſt to liue, and die a member of Chriſts
true Catholike and Apoſtolike Church
out of the vnitie and fellowship wherof,
there never was, nor is, nor can bee, ſalvation, what plauſible perſwaſions or pleaſing
pretences ſoever now bee, or by the divels
drift may hereafter bee deviſed, to the
contrarie. In which faith, and vnitie of
which Church, I acknowledge God the Father my maker, God the Son my Redeemer,
and God the holy Ghoſt my Sanctifier:
three perſons, and one very and eternall
God.

§. 4.

I beleeue and hold the twelue Articles of
the Chriſtian faith, as the Catholike
Church teacheth them : The Nicene
Creed, and Athanaſius Creed. I hold and
acknowledge the ten commandements, as
God declared them to Moyſes, to be the
ſub-

substance of the Law. I beleeue there be in
Christs Church , seauen Sacraments or
fountaines of grace wherby the holy Ghost
doth by our receiving and vse of the same
worke in our soules grace, that is to say,
Baptisme , Confirmation, Matrimonie ,
Confession, Orders, Supper of our Lord,
and Extreame Vnction, and that to be de-
prived of the vse of these, is an impediment
and stopping of Gods grace in vs; wherof
many a Christian soule doth in this time of
sinne feele a ruefull losse.

§. 5.

I beleeue that in the Sacrament of the
Lords Supper ; otherwise called the Sacrament of the Altar, after the words of Consecration, in the sacrifice of the Masse, done
by the Priest duely ordained, there remaineth the very Real presece of Christs Bodie,
and Bloud, without any other substance of
creatures, and that all figurative speeches, all
spirituall meanings, all glosses of words, all
surmises of false spirits, that suppose or teach
the contrarie, are derogatorie to the power
of God and injuriouse to the salvation of
Christian soules, the words of the Gospell
saying . Take eate, this is my Bodie , and
take and drinke, this is my Bloud;
B 2

§. 6.

§. 6.

I beleeue that the examination of conscience and Confessiō of sinnes to a ghostly father, is a worke necessarie to saluation, as the Church of God doth require it: and that it is the most comfortable meane to stirre vp the soule, sunke into sinne, vnto repentance and amendment that can bee: and that by the often vse therof Gods grace doth wonderfully worke in our mindes, and that by the neglecting of the same Satan worketh his will.

§. 7.

I beleeue that the doctrine of the Catholike Church concerning invocation of saints, prayer for the dead, and holding of the place for purgation of soules dying in the state of grace, and of christian workes to be effect of christian faith, is a most sound and wholsome doctrine, and that the new found Doctrine of sole faith is the fine force of Satan to deceiue the world.

§. 8.

§. 8.

I beleeue, and firmely avow, that the holy Ghost, since Chrifts afcension, hath bin and continued with this Catholike and Apoftolike Church, teaching her all truth, and fo shall continue to the end of the world; and that the gates of Hell shall never prevaile againft her, according to Chrifts promife: And that the pretended reformers of Religion are Divels, transformed into the shape of Angels of light, fallne into the delicacie of wordly mens delights, in this latter age of the world . And that this is true may be proued by a fenfible confe-quent. Firft of the new pretéded reformed Religion there was never, publike profef-sion in the Chriftian world before thefe fortie or fiftie yeares laft paft, or there-abouts; then, it being fifteene húdred yeares fince Chrift eftablished his Church, either it is to be confeffed, that the Church and Religion that had beginning and continu-ance from Chrifts time vntill thefe preten-ded reformed dayes, is the true Church, and true Religion, and that the contrarie is falfe, or elfe, that Chrift hath not kept pro-mife when he afcended, faying, that he would fend to his difciples the comforter, which should teach them all truth, and

con-

cōtinue with them to the end of the world:
but to say so were blasphemie , as I trust e-
very Christian heart will affirme . And
Christs Church is no hidden thing , for in
the scriptures shee is cōpared to a Citie set
vpon an hill , that every one may see ; to a
Candle set vpon a cādlesticke, to lighten al
that come into the house: And a most ruefull and lamentable thing,my deare infants,
it is , that we should now condemne that
Religion which we received first into this
Realme , aboue thirteene hundred yeares
past , and continued in vntill about fiftie
yeares past , and then altered into such a libertie of life , a discharging of the conscience, a carnalitie of pleasures,a securitie
of salvation , a rash beleeving of spirits, a
condemning of the Fathers,a pride af opinions,a setting vp of sects, a pretending of
pietie , a performing of impietie , a dissol-
ving of obedience, and generally into such
a pleasant safetie of sinning,as I can not but
(in the charitie towards all Christians,and
especially of you my deare children, that
may haply liue to see and feele the truth of
these things) with an inward sorrow of
heart remember .

§. 9.

§. 9.

For conclusion , I holde and beleeue all that the Catholike and Apostolik. Church holdeth and beleeveth , in the summe and substance of faith,and in the godly ceremoniall rights of teaching therof, and I protest to hold it , and affirme it in the passage of my soule: And I desire the eternall God for Christs sake to grant you my children his grace to doe the same , without the which you can never possesse the ioyes of heaven. And I beseech you , in the mercies of CHRIST IESVS, and charge you all,as a father,vpon my blessing, that with continuall prayer you call vnto God to direct you this way,to bring you to this faith,and then no doubt but he will also bring you into life everlasting : which CHRIST IESVS graunt you, and me , and all people . Amen .

§. 10.

And from a resolute heart , and settled Faith,I doe now here make protestatiõ,that if hereafter,either by weakenesse, or debilitie of bodie, by meanes of sicknesse, or for

B 4   the

the shunning of any worldly dangers, loſſes, or perſecutions , wherof no part of the world ever knew halfe ſo many and ſo great as we now doe, or for any torment or trouble ; wherof there be tragicall , and wonderfull inventions : or for any carnall affection of wife or children : or by any temptation, ſubtilty, or shift of the adverſarie whatſoever , I shall bee of any other minde , or my ſenſes abuſed to offend againſt this faith , which God for Chriſts ſake forbid , that then I doe now in perfect minde , by the aſsiſtance of God his ſpirit vtterly denie, deteſt , and renounce, the ſame , as wicked, and doe adhere and abide, in life, and in death, to the former declaration of my faith. Which proteſtation and reſolution, I will you my children and all men to witneſſe with mee , before God and his Angels in the dreadfull iudgement. And I beſeech our Lord I may then ſee the ſame found in you and all other men.

§. II.

Thus having briefly made knowne vnto you the faith and religion wherwith and wherin I meane to paſſe (by Gods grace) out of this world : For as much as I may

leaue

leaue you young and tender , and your
deere mother and I by countrie farr divided , and yet laftly conioyned by God in
mariage , wherby you may be ignorant of
fome things not impertinent for you , in
worldly refpects,to know : I haue thought
good , before I difpofe of other things , to
acquaint you with what you are by me . I
may, I hope , commend you by defcent of
honeft parentage , as the world knoweth :
whofe predeceffors haue tafted of fuch in-
fortune as in the world is not ftrange , and
for more . Albeit true generofitie confift in
virtue , and is lawfull for euery one to obtaine , and not tyed to the only defcent of
flesh and bloud : yet are you not ignoble
that way. Which I leaue you,not by way of
a vaine vaunt,but rather to excite you therby to endeauour the obtayning and continuing of true generofitie.

§. 12.

The firft of mine Anceftours by name,
within this Countie of Worcefter , was
Hugo de Belne,a Gentleman; who, (as by
tradition it hath continued in our familie)
was advanced , as I take it , in the time of
Edward the firft : for feruice to him done
by

by the long Bowe; being an excellent Ar-
*Et hæ-
redibus
masculis* as it
is said.
cher. This King gaue vnto the said Hugo de
Belne, and his heyres, the fee-farme of diverse lands and teniments in Kingsnorton,
within the Countie of Worcester: Which
fee-farme cometh every yeare in charge
to the Sheriffe of Worcester-shiere out of
the Exchequour, to this day, vnder the title,
*De terris & tenimentis quondam Hugonis de
Belne, &c.* the lands are called Blacke greue,
and Bells, in value better then an hundred
markes by yeare.

§. 13.

From him the lands descended, from one
to another of the heyres males, by lineall
descent, wherof the Court Rolles of the
manours of Bromesgroue, and Kingsnort-
ton, remayning in the steeple at Bromesgroue, can witnesse and all in the title of
gentilitie; vntill the time of my great grandfather, in the dayes of King *Henrie* the eight,
whose name was *VVilliam Bel*, or *VVilliam
de Belne*, who marying to a second wife,
the bace daughter of Sir *Arthoure Planta-
gener*, was, for the maintenance of her dis-
solute life, forced to sell all his patrimonie:
part wherof he solde vnto Sir *Edvvard
Lit-*

Littleton of Staffordshiere , and part to
M.r *Sheldon* of Spettesley , whose heyre
Philipp Sheldon , at this day enioyeth the
same , by means wherof my grandfather
Iohn Bel , his heyre by the first wife , was
disinherited .

§. 14.

My father , whose name was also *Iohn* : in
his lifetime vnderstanding that the lands
were entayled to the heyre male , with re-
mainder in the Crowne, made entrie into a
messuage , and lands called Blackgreue, but
being not able to proceede in the tryall, for
want of abilitie , was forced to giue over ;
which moved him to extend his abilitie for
my maintenance in learning, hoping thereby to procure a recoverie of our inheritance, for that the commune report of him
was , that the lands were but mortgaged,
with condition of redemption at any
time .

§. 15.

At schoole I continued in the Countie
of Warwicke vntill I was 18. yeares
of

of age. From thence I went to the vniuersitie of Orford, where, with good allowance
of my good father (whose soule our Lord
blesse) I continued 7. yeares, proceeded ba-
chelour of art, and was fellow of *Ballioll*
Celledge there, and being readie to proceede Maister of Arte by time of yeares, I
was enuied by some vngratefull, God forgiue them, accused of discontentation in
Religion, and called to answere the same:
But declyning the malice of time, I retyred
my selfe by fauour of my Colledge with a
cause allowed for on yeare. And after re-
turning and finding the malice continuing,
for the quiet of my conscience I was forced
to leaue my societie, and to commit my
selfe to the fauour of God in the world: by
whose direction, and vpon earnest request
to me made, I came then to a right worthy
Magistrate, and worshipfull Gentleman,
Sir *Iohn Throkmarton*, Knight, chiefe Iustice
of the Marches of Wales, with whom I
continued in especiall good fauour, and
credit, and in entertainement as a dëare
friend of his, by the space of 12. yeares: in
so great contentation euerie way, and such
liking both in minde and bodie, as, respec-
ting the securitie, I found not elfe where to
bee hoped for, at that time. But perceiuing
my yeares increasing and mine habilitie as
yet

yet nothing, I was in part perſwaded by the said Sir *Iohn Throkmarton* to vndertake the ſtudie of the common lawes of the Realme, at the Innes of court. Wherupon admitting my ſelfe a Fellow of Clements Inne, in chamber and bed with that Worshipfull Gentleman M.ʳ *George Sherley*, I fell to the ſtudie of the Lawes. Where finding, vpon two yeares experience, that the ayre of the cittie did vtterly ouerthrow my heath, being never well in health one whole month together, I was forced to returne into the countrie : where was willingly afforced me, by Sir *Iohn Littleton* knight, the execution of rhe Office of the Clercke of the Peace, of the Countie of Wigorne : which with the good favour of Sir *Iohn Throkmarton* I accepted, and executed with ſuch liking and favour of my countrie as I leaue in modeſtie to ſpeake off.

ſ. 16.

Shortly after dyed Sir *Iohn Throkmarton* : a man whoſe vertues and rare guifts were worthy a longer time, for one ſo wiſe and politick in governement, in counſell, ſo graue and prouident ; in iuſtice ſo ſound; in learning, (for one of his calling) ſo rare; in companie, ſo affable and pleaſant; in his diſports,

ports, so gentlemanlike; so pitifull to the
poore; so plentifull in hospitalitie; to good
men such a patrone;to offenders such a terror; and generally so compleate a man everie way , as lived not his like in England.
The losse of him, to me a principall friend,
moved me eftsoones to returne to the Innes of Court , determining to haue gone
through with the studie of the Lawes: but
still finding the decay of my health. I was
eftsoones forced to retire into the countrie,
to my house at Templebroughton , which
Sir *Iohn Throkmarton* had graunted me.
During mine aboade in the Innes of Court
many crosses and troubles befel me,putting
me to long trouble and charges.

§. 17.

In this time I resolved to marrie:wherein
commending my happe to the good direction of God, he so guided me, as I became
acquainted with the Worshipful Gētlewo-
man your grandmother *Daniel*,who for her
vertue, pietie , and liberall house-keeping,
was not then in many places matchable.
Among her daughters I made choice of
your mother for a wife, and shee,with the
good liking of her friends, content to become

come mine, wherin I can not account my
selfe so happie with the best fortune of the
world, as in hauing her to me a wife, and
to you a mother. A woman I assure you
towards God so Religiouse, in loue and
affection towards me so liberall, in faith
and vowed chastitie so sound and inuiola-
ble, in patience so perfect, in obedience
so humble and readie, in housewifely care,
and discreete governement of her house-
hould, so wise and provident, to you,
my children, so loving and naturally affected, to all my friends so kinde and
gentle, and generally towards all so mo-
dest and courteouse, as her match is not
easily found : And therefore both you and
I owe much to God in such a blessing :
which for my part, as I am resolved to
be thanckefull for whilest I liue, so I
require you, my children all, that
you doe the like . And if it shall please
God shee doe surviue me in this world,
I require and charge you vpon my
blessing, and vpon all the dutie that
by the lawes of God or nature you
owe me, that during your life you loue,
honour, and obey her, in word and
deede, that you cherish and comfort her,
that you bee serviceable and dutiefull
vnto

vnto her : that you never murmure , nor
grudge againſt her,that by any meanes you
prouoke her not to anger , or diſpleaſure,
that for any vaine pleaſure you never doe,
nor conſent to the thing that may offend
her , that you be ever readie to releeue her
in all diſtreſſes , with all the abilitie of your
bodies , and with all that God ſhall giue
you in this world , that you continually
pray for her and me , and in ſo doing,
be right well aſſured , that Almightie
God will bleſſe you , he will multiply and
encreaſe you, and you ſhall ſee in this your
poſteritie bleſſed vpon the earth,and all that
you take in hand ſhall proſper , and goe
well with you; yea,the dewe of heauen will
fructifie all that you ſhall haue ; God hath
ſo promiſſed , who will never faile you if
you faile not your ſelues. Remember it is he
that in the commandement hath promiſſed
long life to them that honour their parents :
The wiſe man hath ſaid , that the fathers
bleſsing buildeth vp the roofe of the houſe,
but the mothers curſe rooteth vp the foundation. Behold all the hiſtories,both divine
and profane,from the creation of the world
to this day : and you ſhall never finde but
the obedient childe was fauoured of God
and man: and contrariwiſe,the diſobedient
was hated, and never failed of his iuſt pu-
nish-

nishment in this world, either in him selfe,
or in his succession.

§. 18.

And to the intent you may the better
performe this, and all other good actions
you take in hand, for as much as nothing
is, nor can possibly be profitable vnto man
in this world, without the grace of God,
and assistance of his holy spirit, and that he
is our God, and we his creatures, and the
worke of his will: who hath commanded
to knocke and it shall be opened vnto vs,
to seeke and we shall finde, and to aske,
and we shall haue, I now most instantly,
and before all things, require and charge
you, that with continuall prayer you call
vpon God that he may indue you with his
grace, that he will in this time of the Provinciall darkenesse of England, wherein
you are borne, open vnto you the knowledge and light of the true Catholike and
Apostolike Faith, that he will confirme
and fasten you therein, that you never
swarue from the same, nor stagger to your
liues end. What greater ioy or comfort can
any worldly man haue, then if he were in
want or necessitie of any thing, to haue his

C   Prince,

Prince, or some great man that were of a-
bilitie and power, to say vnto him: aske me a
lordship, a farme, an office, or great store of
treasure and thou shalt haue it, and might
thereupon in deede haue it; were not such
an one that would loose all this for want of
asking worthie to want and abide in most
miserable beggarie? it cannot be denyed
but he were. And then, what an injurie
were it to your selues, and what an ingratitude to so mercifull a God, that hath
heaven and earth and all the rich contents
therof to dispose of at his pleasure, and
that so freely and willingly offereth to them
that seeke, aske, and knocke, not to pray to
him in our necessities, and for our reliefe,
who can haue nothing in this world but of
his free mercie. The mindes of worldly
men are mutable, who oftentimes promise
and pay not, though we never so much intreate them: but God is so iust as he will not
alonely performe all promise, but giue with
encrease of measure and in abundance: for
a full demonstration wherof, looke, among
many, vnto the Prophet *David*, who in all
his distresses, persecutions, adversities, and
crosses, ever humbled himselfe to God by
prayer, and was heard and delivered.

§. 19.

§. 19.

This prayer of yours muſt haue faith
and truſt in God, charitie and the feruencie
of zeale, ſuch as was in the Prophet when
he ſaid. *Exaudi me Domine quoniam clamavi
ad te*, and againe. *Dominus mihi adjutor, non
timebo quid faciat mihi homo*. *Dominus protector vitæ meæ, à quo formidabo?* and infinite
other places, whereby he euer obtayned of
God comforr, and deliverance.

You are, my children, as *Dauid* ſaid of
himſelfe : *In te proiectus ſum ex vtero :* So
from your mothers wombe were you caſt
vpon God, where our Lord graunt that
you may faſten your ſelues for euer.

§. 20.

Of the effect of prayer, and the moſt
ſweete comfotts therof, no man can ſpeake
more effectually then I your father, and
herein I proteſt before the ſacred Majeſtie
of Almightie God, to whom I muſt yeeld
account of all my words, deedes, and
thoughts, that I will ſpeake no more then
truth: That from the time of my infancie,

wherin

wherin I was taught to pray, to this prefent day, as I haue many and fundry times in my life felt ficknefle, neede of many worldly things, forrowes, loffe of friends, falfe ac-cufations, the fting of envie, as a matter that did ever oppreffe me, cloafe imprifon-ment in an innocent caufe, houfeholde troubles, falfe friends, and infinite others, and aboue all, the lacke of the higheft my-fteries, and fweeteft comforts to both foule and bodie: fo ever in all my necefsities re-payring vnto God by prayer, I haue ever found reliefe, comfort, and deliverance therby. Wherof no creature vnder heaven could shew you more rare and notable examples then I; which in this place I omit. Onely crying vnto you from my whole heart, to be earneft, zealous, & perfeverant in prayer, and if you had nothing in the world to releeue you, yea, all the world op-pofed againft you, yet shall you prevaile and receiue the blefsing from God by faith-full prayer.

§. 21.

Hitherto having made knowne vnto you the Confefsion of my faith, my worldly courfe, and my counfels in the fame : I am now to make my purpofed legacies, and bequefts among you: wherin I firft giue, &
com-

eommend you all to the mercifull care and protection of God the Father , God the Sonne, and God the holie Ghoſt,& to the aſſiſtant prayers of all the bleſſed compa-nie of heaven: beſeeching CHRIST IESVS, that bought vs all with his pretious bloud, to bleſſe you,ſaue you, & make you heires of his Kingdome . And I deſire Almigh-tie God ſo to diſpoſe of you in your ſeveral callings,in this world,as may be moſt to his glorie , and your owne ſoules health , and that it may pleaſe him to powre downe the dew of heauen vpon you , bleſſe you , in-creaſe you, and all your labours , and all things that you ſhall take in hand,and ever-more deliver you from the power and evill purpoſes of your enemies. Amen.

§. 22.

Concerning my worldly goods , as I re-ceived nothing in this world from my pa-rents but mine education,to them(conſide-ring the courſe of my life) both carefull and coſtly , ſo hauing not much,in reſpect of the tyme(an enemie to the thrift of a di-ſtreſſed conſcience) I can not much be-ſtow,and yet , (bleſſed bee God for his in-creaſe) ſhall leaue you ſomething.

C 3

§. 23.

§. 23.

" The worldly goods I haue, I giue, and
" bequeathe to *Dorothe* my deare & louing
" wife : therewith charging and requiring
" her, in the faith shee beareth me, and in
" the loue shee beareth my children, to see
" them vertuousely brought vp, and instru-
" cted in learning, the more readily to pre -
" pare them to the seruice, of God, and true
" knowledge of him.

§. 24.

The chiefest thing I doe desire therein,
is, to haue *Edmund* and *William* trayned in
schoole to learning, as their capacities will
admit, and so to goe to the vniuersitie of
Oxford, if by any meanes they may obtaine that preferment : and there to *Balliol*
Colledge, of which house I was fellow,
and where Doctor *Bel* founded two schol-
lerships for Worcestershiere men : or else
wheras it may be obtayned.

§. 25.

§. 25.

After they are entred in their learning,
and are 7. or 8. yeares of age, I would they
should be taught plainesong, and pricksong
skilfully, and to play vpon the lute, and vir-
ginales: a shill not alonly comfortable in it
selfe to the haver, but a verie good meane
of preferment, or a gratefull entertainement with the best, and to such of them as
shall best affect the same, I bequeathe my
best lute, sythorne, and gittorne. Item, if
either *Edmund* or *VVilliam* shall be enabled,
and haue a desire to studie the common
lawes of the Realme, which I greatly desire, then to him so affected, and enabled, and
doing the same, I giue and bequeathe al my
law-bookes, which I wish should be duely
preserved together for that purpose.

§. 26.

" Item if *Francis* my sonne doe here-
" after recover speech, then I will that he
" be, according to his birthright, mine
" heyre, and to haue all my lands, tene-
" ments, and hereditaments, to him and his
" heyres males for ever, and not otherwise:
yeelding

" yeelding & paying to my sonne *Edmund*
" out of the same , after my said sonne
" *Edmund* shall accomplish the age of 21.
" yeares * * * by yeare, during his naturall
" life, at two tearmes in every yeare, that is
" to say, at the feast of *S. Michael* the Arch-
" angell and the Annunciation of our blef-
" sed Ladie the vergin by equall portions.
" But if *Francis* my sonne doe not recover
" speech and good discretion , then I doe
" now giue and bequeathe to *Edmund* my
" sonne to be mine heyre, and he to haue
" all my manour of Templebroughton and
" lands, tenements, and hereditaments, to
" him and to the heyres males of his bodie
" lawfully begotten, and not otherwise.

§. 27.

" Item I giue and bequeathe to *Marguerite*
" my daughter , to her preferment in ma-
" riage, when shee shall accomplish the age
" of 18. yeares * * * and if I haue no issue
" male, then I giue vnto the said *Marguerite*
" all my lands , tenements , and heredita-
" ments, to haue to the said *Marguerite* and
" her heyres for ever.

§. 28.

§. 28.

" Item, albeit I haue formerly giuen all
" my goods and chattels to *Dorothey* my
" wife , yet is there in the same gift an im-
" ployed trust which shee hath promised
" me , and which I doe most certainely af-
" sure my selfe shee will never breake nor
" violate towards me and those that are
" hers and mine.

§. 29.

Item, I would that every one of my children should haue a ring of fine gold weigh-
ing 3,[1] wherin should be written this sentence well enameled : *Iacta super Dominum
curam tuam & ipse te enutriet* . Which may
be engraven in two roūds, because it is too
much for one , and these rings to be made
presently after my decease, and to be delivered them at 18. yeares of age . Which
rings I charge them on my blessing,never to
depart withall to their dying day . And
which of them soever wilfully breaketh
this charge , it will goe worse with him, be
he well assured.

C 5 §. 30.

§. 30.

" Item if my wife be now with childe,
" such care as I haue had of my other
" children, I would should be had of it, be
" it man or woman, which care I must
" commend to my deare wife : and shee
" with that God hath lent vs, to provide
" for it, and the rest, as God shall enable vs,
" and my will is, and I doe giue to *Dorothey*
" my wife, the issues, and profits of all my
" lands, teniments, and hereditaments, till
" my sonnes come to 18. yeares of age,
" & then so to allow *Edmund* * * * yearely
" during her life and shee to haue the rest
" of the profits of my lands during her
" life.

§. 31.

" Item I would that *Marguerite* my
" daughter should, so soone as thee is able
" to goe to schoole, and be applyed in her
" booke, and with her neelde, so farre forth
" as shee shall be of capacitie, and if it may
" be, that shee be also taught her pricksong,
" and plainesong, and to play on the vir-
" ginalls, and if we cannot preferre her far-
" ther,

"ther, this will be (with Gods grace to
"guide the same) a competent preferment
"in the world. Item I will that *Dorothey* my
"wife shall fully possesse my goods to the
"vse of my children: as I am assured shee
"will doe no lesse then if shee were my
"sole Executrix, but Executors or Execu-
"trix, I will (for some private respects)
"make none : and so to doe concerning
"my will, so farre forth as shee shall be
"able, to execute the same, in all points,
"according to the conference, and pro-
"mise betweene vs made and agreed,
"and that doe assure my selfe shee will
"doe. Notwithstanding, for as much as we
"are all mortall, my will is, that if *Doro-*
"*they* my wife doe die before shee per-
"forme my will, and deliver my children
"their portions, or for any other respect
"doe refuse to doe the same, then I doe
"constitute and appoint all my children
"iointly to bee my Executors, and they
"to doe the same, as by the sound advice
"of their friends (whereunto I ever ad-
"vise them to giue eare) they shall be di-
"rected.

§. 32.

§. 32.

Item, I will that *VVilliam* my third sonne, shall haue * * * by yeare, payed him during his life, after he cometh to 21.yeares of age, by *Edmund*. Item, for as much as the greatest perill of infants is in their education, if the same be not wisely governed and provided for, if God call me away leaving my Children young and tender; and that if God continue their mother, they shall ever be assured of an especiall comfort by her, so farre forth as shee shall be able: yet for as much as many accidents in the world may hinder her good endeavour, I doe instantly desire my very especiall good mother M.rs *Marguerite Daniell*, and my good bretheren M.r *Iohn Daniell* Esquier, and M.r *Francis Daniell*, the Right Worshipfull my verie good friend, M.r *Ralphe Sheldon*, and all the friends I haue in alliance to mee by my wife, and in consanguinitie to my children, that they will assist my wife in the care and regard of her children, and for their education in vertue and learning; wherin they shall doe a worke of merite, and worthy their profession towards God, and affection to me.

§. 33.

§. 33.

" Item, in respect of the great favours I
" haue found, and the many obligations of
" friendship wherin I am bound to be
" gratefull: I doe now commēd to my chil-
" dren, and their posteritie : that they ever
" shew themselves inwardly affectionate,
" and, as may concerne them in duetie, fer-
" viceable, to the Worshipful family of the
" *Throkmartons* of Coughton, and among
" those, in especiall to the posteritie of my
" deerest friend Sir *Iohn Throkmarton* of
" Fekenham, wherof there is in the eldest
" lyne but onely one young Gentleman,
" *Iohn Throkmarton*, the sonne of *Frācis*, the
" sonne of Sir *Iohn* : this yong *Iohn Throk-*
" *marton* is my Godsonne : I humbly be-
" seech our Lord to blesse him , defend
" him, and increase and multiply him with
" his grace , that he may , in the fauour of
" God , repaire the ruines and worldly ac-
" cidents that vnfortunately and ....
" fell on his father and grandfather. Whose
" rare and wonderfull gifts both of body
" and minde God graunt may, in dutifull
" obedience to his Prince , descend vpon
" him, and he vse them to his glorie.

§. 34.

§. 34.

☞ In most ample merite , and for greatest favour , I require , and charge all my children, with all that euer they shall be able, in bodie and minde , to be gratefull , serviceable , and loving, to the right Worshipfull M.ᵣ *Ralphe Sheldon* of Beoley, Esquier, and to all that familie , by whose great and inward affection borne me, after the decease of Sir *Iohn Throkmarton*, I was not alonly comforted and favoured, but releeved and holpen with all that I haue in effect , as my wife by particularitie of knowledge can well witnesse. They are a fortunate familie, and haue relieved and bred vp moe men of account, than all the gentlemen of Worcestershiere . And I would that all mine should serue and follow them, before any " other familie whatsoever . With these I " require them , to be both gratefull, and " dutifull, to Sir *Iohn Littleton*, Knight, and " that house, of whose good fauour I did " also tast .

§. 35.

§. 35.

And now to bid farewell , and conclude
with mine advice,to you my children,after
you haue refolved , and indeede become
the fervants of God,and ever to vfe prayer,
as the meanes to make God mindefull and
carefull of you . Refolue with your felves
to vfe truth , in word and deede, never to
lye , nor diffemble with any man , for any
caufe: for albeit the fame be counted now
(the more is the pittie) with many vn-
godly , but a worldly pollicie , yet affure
yourfelves , that thofe fubtill shifts haue in
conclufion a shamefull detection : and
leaue behinde them a ftarre of difcredit ,
that will not be blotted out . feeke to pleafe
good men,and pray for the evill.

§. 36.

Delight not in ribawdrie , fcurrilitie, nor
vncleane communication, for fuch ftuffe as
men vtter with a pleafing tongue, wife men
will iudge there is ftore therof in the heart.

§. 37.

§. 37.

Among all the vertues , make choice of humilitie, and abandon pride, for it is such a horse as will sure giue his maister a fal, sit he neuer so fast : you shall find moe men exalted from meane estate by being humble, courteouse, and affable to all, than by any other worldly occasion.

§. 38.

Entertaine all men with gentle speeches; and be not daintie to put off your cappes to the poorest creature : for, let me your father be beleeued, that there is nothing that winneth the hearts of so many with so little cost .

§. 39.

Accompanie your selues with the best, with all humilitie , and euer desire to be among wise men ; with them rather the meanest, then to be Captaine of an vnruly rabbell of Roysters , for with whom men flocke most , of such shall they be iudged to be .

§. 40.

§. 40.

Be not rash, and haftie in iudgement of any thing : nor prone to anger, for the one is a short madneffe and the other the mother of error.

§. 41.

Vfe few words, and thofe with difcretion, efpecially among your betters: where it is ever more feemly to be a hearer then fpeaker, without you bee required.

§. 42.

Be not curious medlers with other mens matters : nor bufie lookers into other mens liues; but amend your owne, and pray for them that doe amiffe.

§. 43.

Be fecret and filent in all things committed to your credit, for the blab is not liked, though he haue never fo many other ornaments.

D   §. 44.

§. 44.

Aboue all other things, in worldly respects, I warne you my children not to medle with matters of estate; but to looke to your calling; liue in obedience, and leaue Kings, and their causes to God : for the busie intermedling with Gods counsell (which I take the affaires of Princes to be) hath destroyed moe rare over-reaching wits, then any one thing else.

§. 45.

Vse temperance in dyet, and beware of drunkennesse, for besides that it is a thing displeasant vnto God, no man will trust the Drunkard.

§. 46.

Beware of suddaine passion, either in disport, or otherwise, for the rash man neuer wanteth woe: and no man will willingly haue friendship, with such an one.

§. 47.

§. 47.

Be conſtant , and reſolute, in all honeſt
offices ; and faſt in friendship, for a turner
with the wind is worthie the reward of a
wethercocke ; and that is , ſtill to be fed
with the wind.

§. 48.

Vſe patience , and in any wiſe forbeare
revenge, as a propertie peculiar vnto God:
for I can by experience aſſure you, that to
be patient , and pray for them that offend
you , will kill more enemies, and winne
more friends, then the ſword, had you the
power of a Prince.

§. 49.

Be not too liberall in expences, but learne
to vſe frugalitie , proportionating your
charge, according to your ſtore.

§. 50.

Be not overhaſtie to beleeue the faire
words of everie ſeeming friend, & truſt not
with

without triall . Be thanckfull for euerie
courtesie, and requite it as you may; but let
time breed the friends you commit secrets
vnto. *Quia defecit veritas à filijs hominum.*

§. 51.

Let the familiaritie you haue with your
Superiours, if they therunto admitt you, be
euer with due reuerence , and not sawcie :
for though lyons play , yet haue they long
nayles, to scratch at their pleasure.

§. 52.

Be readie to releeue all that are distressed,
as it shall fall to your abilitie , for he shall
neuer want a friend that hath beene a
friend.

§. 53.

Haue charitie with all men, and pittie the
poore, forward theyr suites , and releeue
them for you may be assured that God will
giue an abundant blessing therfore.
Quod tacitum velis nemini dixeris.

§. 54.

§. 54.

Embrace chaſtitie , as a ſweet ornament
of the ſoule, and beware of the allurements
of the harlot : for they deſtroy the bodie
here , and after draw ſoule and bodie into
hell .

§. 55.

Beware of ſuertieſhip , as a meanes of
the vndoing of manie : neither be buſie
borrowers aboue abilitie to pay, which will
either with the canker of vſurie conſume
your ſubſtance, to the very ſynders of beg-
gerie: or driue you into exile, from countrie
to countrie , or leaue you conſuming in
priſon .

§. 56.

Apply your ſelues in companie to a mo-
deſt mirth, agreable to the delights of ſuch
as you are with : for ſir Sulen, and ſir So-
lemne, are ſeldome welcome to any place.

D 3   §. 57.

§. 57.

One thing is my meaning, and full purpose, and I charge and adjure you, *Edmond*, and *VVilliam*; to performe it. That albeit I haue made a graunt to each of you by leafe of my lands in poffeffion, yet I require you before the majeftie ef God, that you never prefume to take one foote therof from your mother, fo long as fhee liveth, nor to trouble her in the occupation therof, otherwife then fhee fhall freely giue you; as before I haue appointed ; and if you doe, looke for a fharpe revenge at the hands of almightie God, who will feverely punifh contempt to parents, and breach of the dead mans will.

HERE

HERE FOLLOVV

certaine fragments of the same Teſtament , that vvere left vvritten in the same coppie, but out of their order.

I Tem , I doe giue to *VVilliam Turner* my black ſilke raſh dublet , a coate and cloake.

Item , to the intent my wife may make *VVilliam Turner* beholding to her: I requier her to beſtow on him , as it may appeare I did loue him as a friend.

Item , I doe giue to *Arthur* my ſonne my gaſſell bowe, my beſt lute, and gitterne: and my will is, that every of my foure children ſhall haue a ioyned bedſteed, with a fetherbed, and the furniture: and looke what portion I did aſſigne vnto *Francis,* whoſe ſoule God pardon, I would ſhould be aſſigned betweene *VVilliam* and *Arthur,* and to *Marguerite* my beſt virginalles.

Item , to every of my children a ſilver cup, and two ſilver ſpoones: the choice, as they are in age.

Item, to whom ſoe ever my lands deſcend , I will he or ſhee to haue my greateſt clocke.

Item,

Item, I giue to *VVilliam* my fonne, my guilded watch, which coft 3.pounds twelue shillings : which I commonly carrie about me : it was made the fame yeare that *VVilliam* was borne 1589. which yeare is grauen by the name of the maker, on the watch : by the fly : and my gold ring with a crapon ftone.

Item, I giue to *Edmond* my fonne, my round guilded watch, which is the larger of the two : and my ring of gold with the red fealing ftone but I will my wife shall haue the vfe of my round watch during her life.

Item, I giue to euerie childe two olde ftarre-Riolles.

Item, I doe giue to *Edmund* my fonne my croffe-bowe, hand-gunne, and short dagge.

Item, I giue to *VVilliam* my fonne my ftone bowe and my longer dagge.

A N-

ANNOTATIONS VPON
the precedent Testament.

And first of the reason of them.

SEeing the Author to call the Sacramēt of Penance, by the name of Confessiõ, and the Sacrament of our Saviour IESVS CHRISTS Bodie and Bloud, the Lords Supper: and fearing the weake might take occasion of offence where none was iustly giuen: I vndertooke to note those places, and all others, if any of like sort were found different from the vsuall maner of speaking in these times; yet not so as I would make any great treatise, or discusse matters in controversie, so much handled and rehandled now a dayes: but only with reason to shew, by the practice of good men, that in such vse of speech there is no other thing than may well become a Christian man.

This I thought to haue done by way of marginall notes, but perceiving it encrease

to more then could with conveniencie enter in the margents, I dilated my selfe and
adioyned it to the end of the Testament,
adding withall, some sentences of the saints,
and renowned men, vpon severall passages
therof applyed.

THE TESTAMENT.] The originall
had no title prefixed, but thus I thought
good to style it, rather then to call it a last
will, or codicill, or donation for cause of
death, &c. Because although, generally
speaking, a last will doe comprehend a Testament, yet every last will is not a Testament : in a codicill there cannot be given
inheritance. *c. de codicill. in l. si idem.* And donation for cause of death, is but as it were
a last will.

A Testament, speaking properly, doth
not comprehend every last will, for a Testament is the iust sentence of our will,
concerning that which one will haue to be
done after his death, with institution of an
heyre. *l. iuncta glossa. ff. e.* therfore without
institution of an heyre there is no Testamēt.
insti. de leg. in § . ante hæredis. And consequētly
a Testament comprehendeth not a codicil.

This, whether we respect the spirituall
doctrines, or temporall distributions, may
haue the name of a Testament, of the first
all, of the latter each one respectiuely are
in-

inftituted heyres : the Author, with full
power of teftation : for everie man may
make a Teftament that is not fpecially prohibited. *no. glo. & Bart. in l. fi quæramus. ff. e. &*
fpe. in ti. de inftru. edic. in §. compendiofe.

Facultie of making Teftaments is a
thing gracioufly graunted men : be aufe
the teftatour difpofeth of that time, wherin
he is not to be Lord of any thing , for a
Teftament is confirmed in death . *Vt in c.
cum Martha. de cele. miß.* That is, after his
death when he ceafeth to be Lord or haue
any dominion. Whence, although the dif-
pofition be made when he is Lord and at
fu h time as he is able, yet the effect is be-
ftowed at fuch time as he is vnable: which
of meere right , or law , should not be
la full . *l. quod fponfa. c. de dona. ante
nup.*

Teftamentum, according to the etymolo-
gie of the word is *teftatio mentis,* a teftifica-
tion or witneffing of a mans minde . the
Hebrewes call it בְּרִית , a compact, or co-
venant betweene the dead and the living,
which as the dead cannot , fo the living
may not change, *Paul ad Heb.* 9 16. Where
there is a Teftament of necefsitie the death
of the teftatour muft come in ; for a Teftament is confirmed in the dead, otherwife it is of no force , while he liveth
                                        that

that made the Testament. God Almightie, in the death of CHRIST IESVS disposed the new Testament to his elected, the sonnes of adoption,

Aug. Epist. ad Gal. circa medium expositi. lib. 1. Tom. 4. A humane Testament is much more infirme then the divine, and yet the confirmed Testament of a man, none dare make voide, nor ordaine any thing a new vpon it:for when the testatour changeth his Testament, he changeth an vnconfirmed Testament, because it is confirmed by the testatours death. And looke of what value is the death of the testatour to confirme his Testament, because he can now no more change his counsell: of the same value is the incommutabilitie of Gods promise to confirme the inheritance of *Abraham,* whose faith is reputed for iustice.

The Author of this Testament confirmed the same in his death 11. yeares after the making of it, dying in the same profession of the Christian faith, with all the rites of the holy Catholike Church: leaving the Testament whole and entire in all, except the disposition of his goods; which by reason of the death of some, and birth of other children, encrease of his goods and other occurrences, he left crossed in some places; and in others vnperfect; all which places

goe

goe noted in the margent with femicircles,
and with afterifes, or interpunctions in the
middle of the line.

In the name of God] A Chriftian
forme of beginning, not only Teftaments,
but every good worke : and with great
reafon doth he call vpon God in all his
works that cannot be, much leffe worke of
himfelfe : man that is by the will of God
muft doe all things in the name of God.

Enofch the fonne of *Seth* , the fonne of A- Gen. 4.
dam, being borne, then was the name of our 26.
Lord firft begunne to be invocated, that is,
with more |expreffe forme of words, and
rites then before.

Every one that invocateth the name of Ioël. 2.
our Lord fhall be fafe : not that everie one 5.
that fayeth Lord, Lord, fhall goe to heaven: vulgata,
but that there is no falvation for any, vpon 2. 32.
whom the name of the true God is not invocated .

Hieremias 14.9. And thou Lord art moft
inward to vs: and thy name is invocated of
vs, forfake vs not.

1. *Reg.* 18. *vulgat.* 3. *Reg.* All nations doe
invocate the names of their Gods.

Elias . Yee fhall call vpon the names of
your gods, and I will invocate in the name
of the Lord.

Coloff. 3. 17. All things whatfoever yee doe

in

in word or worke, doe al in the name of our
Lord IESVS CHRIST.

Pfalm. 123. Our aide is in the name of
the Lord that made the heaven and earth.
When others haue confidence, fome in
their chariots, and others in their horfes, we
will invocate the name of the Lord our
God. *Pfalm.* 19.

Iudic. 11. Invocate the gods that yee haue
cholen. *Ionas* 1. Arife & invocate thy God.

Many invocate not but in fwearing, cur-
fing, or blafpheming, contrarie to that
Exod. 20. Thou shalt not affume the name
of thy God in vaine; and *Levit.* 19. Thou
shalt not periure the name of God. Thou
shalt not pollute the name of God.

Efaia 4. Let only thy name be invocated
of vs, &c. To thofe that invocate him, our
Lord is of much mercie. *Pfalm.* 85. To all
that invocate him in veritie. And therfore
is alwaies adioyned Amen [ಠಠ] Veritie, a
particle of one affenting, and yeelding
truft; as if it were faid, let it be firme, be it
ratified, be it truely fo, be it done indeed,
truly, certainly, in verie deed, conftantly;
which if it be redoubled becommeth fu-
perlatiue after the vfe of the Hebrew tongue, Amen, Amen, moft truly, moft certainely.

Efaias 65. 16. He that bleffeth himfelf

on

on earth, shal bleſſe himſelfe in God Amen. אֵֽלֹהֵי אֵֽלֹהֵי. Who is this God Amen, de-mandeth *Rabbi Racanat* vpon the 15. of *Exodus*. Whereto the Cabaliſts anſwere by the rule of Notariacon, where a letter ſtan-deth for a word. א For אֲדוֹנָי *Adonai*. Our Lord. מ. For מֶלֶךְ. *Melech*. A King. ן. For נֶאֱמָן. *Neeman*. Faithfull, true: Which is no whit diſſonant from the faith and confi-dēce which he that prayeth ought to haue, but rather much confirmeth it, when at the end of euerie prayer he addeth Amen, that is *Dominus, Rex, Fidelis*: Our Lord is a faith-full King: Our Lord is Potent and of good will to graunt vs our Petitions made in his name.

Greg. Nazianz. in Apologetica. The beſt order of every word or worke, is, that we take our beginning from God and referre the conſummatiõ thereof vnto him againe.

OVR SOVERAIGNE LADIE ELIZABETH] Shee was proclaimed Queene the 17. of November 1558. the ſame day that Queene Marie dyed.

TEMPLEBROVGHTON] This Ma-nour belonged in former times to the order of the Templars.

HEALTH OF BODIE: AND OF SOVND AND PERFECT MEMO-RIE.] The firſt is neceſſarie, in as much

as it conduceth to the latter, which is absolutely necessarie . For whatsoever is by a
man done without it , although it be the
action of a man (as the action of a brute
beast is the action of a brute beast) yet is it
not a humane action . Which proceedeth
from a deliberate will , hauing free facultie
to worke,or not to worke,and also sufficient
light in the vnderstanding to consult and
deliberate vpon the things that are to be
done , and to discerne betweene morall
good and evill . Which actions alone, and
no others, doe merite or demerite,serue to
the end of a man, and beare away reward.
Want of health, and olde age, doe oftentimes diminish, & oftentimes quite abolish
the necessarie vse of reason in a man at that
time when most of all he should haue it: at
his end, when he is to dispose of his house,
his earthly inhabitation, & leaue the same,
Ecclesi-
astes.
12.1. קהלת. Remember thy creator in the dayes
of thy elections : before the evill dayes doe
come , and the yeares lay hold on thee of
which thou mayest say I haue no will in
them . The dayes of elections, the vulgate
calleth the dayes of youth, as wherin a man
hath most vigor to extend his hand to fire
or water and choose good or evill; and the
dayes in which we haue no will,is the time
of dotage when a mans actions are scarcely
                                            hu-

humane, or the dayes of infirmitie & sicknesse which the vulgate calleth the dayes
that please vs not.

Greater madnesse can not be, then to deferre the thing that most concerneth, and
that of necessitie we must doe, vntill such
time as we be most vnable to doe it: as if a
man that were to carrie an hundred
weight, should let it alone when he were
strong, with purpose to beare it when he
were fainting through feeblenesse: yet such
is the want of reason in many men as they
deferre and putt off, not onely the disposing of worldly goods, but even the profession of their faith, or conversion to God by
pennance & good life, vntill they be hardly
able to exercise any act of life.

Let vs not, saith *S. Augustine*, so secure our
selues of Gods mercie, as to heape sinne
vpon sinne, nor say, while we be in the vi-
gour of our age, let vs exercise our concupiscences, and at last in old age we will
doe pennance for our evils, because our
Lord is pious, and mercifull, and will no
more remember our crimes. Let vs not, I
beeseech you, thinke so; for, thus to thinke
is follie in the highest degree, being it is impious for any man to will to haue such licence from God, whereof the very beginning, is, to separate vs from God : therfore,

E   I say,

Aug. l.
de salu-
tarib.
docu-
mentis
cap. 39.
Tom. 4,

I say , let vs not thinke of such things , being we know not what day we are to die: for no man living knoweth the day of his departure . All die not in ould age, but in diverse ages they depart out of this world; and in what acts soever a man is found , in the same shall he be iudged, when the soule goeth out of the bodie : for the Psalmist saith,no man shall confesse thee in hell. Let vs therfore make haste to be converted to pennance, &c.

Come hither mad man; the disposing of soule and bodie which thou hast at thine owne will , is it a worke to be done in time of sicknesse , which time yet thou art not sure to haue, or in ould age,of which thou hast as little certaintie , or rather a worke that requireth health , and strength of bodie, with perfect vse of all the powers of thy soule ? Age and sicknesse, thou saiest, will force a man,to looke about him. How Alas, shall then that habit come vpon thee of which there hath beene no precedent, act ? thou art habituated in deferring, and that habit will still follow thee: thou wilt yet deferre , and if for euer thou couldest deferre , for euer thou wouldest not serue God : of whom it is yet doubtfull whether he will accept of this thy last will, which was , never to giue God but

the

the laſt, and that is now rather neceſſitie then will, and in it thou ſeekeſt not God, but thy ſelfe, becauſe thou feareſt to be loſt for ever. How miſerable a thing it is not to know to die! how goodly a thing it is before death to conſummate life, and then ſecure to expect the reſt of our time! Being in agonie thou wilt doe, as commonly the afflicted vſe, repute it the higheſt felicitie to be exempted from thoſe moleſtations, and iudge it the greateſt beatitude to want that miſerie; wheras that temporall moleſtation ought rather to admoniſh vs how we ſhould thinke of that life, wherin we may liue without anie labour: eſcaping, not the turmoiling anguiſh of a little time, but the horrible paines of everlaſting fire: for, if we now deale with ſo much care, ſo great intention, and ſuch labour, that we fall into no tranſitorie vexation; how much more ſolicitous ſhould we be to avoide everlaſting miſeries? And if death that finiſheth temporall labour be ſo feared, how is that to be feared that caſteth vs into neverending ſorrowes; and if the foule and ſhort delights of this life be ſo loued; how much more vehemently are

[marginal notes:] Senecæ in Agamennone. Seneca epiſt. 32 Bernardus ſermo. 10. in pſal. qui habitat. Aug. epiſt. 131.

E 2   the

68

the pure and infinite ioyes of the world to come, to be fought after ? then in the time of youth and health , and not of crazie old age . Sicknesse comming on , a man seeketh only how to get eafe, which had, he is then as farre to seeke as before, in that conversion which before he pretended. While we haue time , faith the Apostle, let vs doe good, he that deferreth, finneth ever, in as much as if he should never leaue to liue, he would never leaue to sinne, and perchance that is the sinne to death , wherof S. *Iohn.* I fay not that any man pray for such an one. Among the fentences of S. *Augustine* is this: The remedies of conversion to God are not with any delayes to be deferred, left the time of correction perish by our sloth : for he that to the penitent hath promised indulgence, hath not to the dissembler promised to morrowes day . Life is not much worth , if a man liue to no other end , but that in the few yeares of this life , which with a short end is to be cut off, he heape vp to himselfe eternall paines to last without end. But left any one become too secure or wax remisse by the felicitie of such newe credulitie, left perchance any one doe fay in his heart , let not my guilty conscience fo farre gripe and trouble me, nor my culpable life fo farre contristate me, I fee in a momēt,

I fee

Epist. 1.
c. 5.
Tom. 3.
cap. 71.

Aug. de
Temp.
Serm.
120.

I see in a small space of time the good theefs
crimes forgiven him, &c. First in that
theefe is to be considered, not only the
compendiousnesse of his credulitie, but his
devotion, but the occasion of that time
wherin those things were done, in which
even the perfection of the iust is said to
haue beene shaken. Then shew me first the
theefs faith, and after promise thy selfe the
theefs beatitude; the divell casteth in securitie that he may draw on perdition. It cannot be numbred how many this shadow of
vaine hope hath deceived. Let, I beseech
you, the innumerable companie of people,
vnder colour of such securitie taken out of
this life, voide of all good, full of all evill,
deterre vs from this persuasion. By daily
fearing the vncertaintie of our passage and
departure hence, which even now are
vnlooked for, and yet at hand, and are to
want all remedie for ever, the day must be
prevented which is wont to prevent vs. He
seduceth himselfe and playeth with his
death that thinketh thus, the indulgence of
the last houre may helpe me; securitie promissed at the last day is most perilous. Then
againe, it is a most foolish thing to commit
vnto the vnprofitable extremitie of the
now faliing life, that cause which treateth
of eternall necessities. It is odious before
E 3   God,

God , when a man finneth more freely
through confidence of pennance that he
will doe in oulde age . Beleeue me, my
deareft, it is a difficult thing for craftie
diffimulation of ordering a mans end , to
be found worthie to obtaine perdon: with
that interpreter of the heart , there will
be admitted no arte to falvation. But that
bleffed theefe of whom we haue fpoken,
did neither wittingly deferre the time of his
falvation , nor with vnluckie fraude put
the remedies of his ftate in the laft moments , nor referue the hope of his redemption , to the laft of defperation ; Before that time he neither knew Chrift nor
Religion ; which if he had knowne he
had beene perchance amongft the Apoftles,
not the laft in the number who became the
firft in the kingdome . In this therfore he
pleafed God at the laft, becaufe to the
obtayning of the faith, that was not the
laft houre , but the firft. Neceffarie therfore it is that by daily acts a man provide
for himfelfe , and procure his confumma-
tion, it is neceffarie that all our life be fuch
in converfation, as we may deferue to be
free in the end . Thincking inceffantly
vpon the day of our paffage, and the time
of iudgement.

Ad-

Admit thou haſt at laſt both health and
memorie, thou art not ſure the grace ſhall
then be offered, which often offered thou
haſt refuſed. Thou that deſpiſeſt, ſhalt thou Iſaiae
33.
not alſo be deſpiſed? Remember in all thy Eccleſ.
words, thy laſt things and thou wilt not 7.40.
ſinne for ever. He will contemne all things Hieron.
with eaſe that alwaies thinketh how he is Epiſt. ad
Paulin.
to die. in fine.

If men would alwaies beare their day of tom. 3.
Aug.
death in minde, they would reſtraine the ſerm. 10
ſame from all covetouſneſſe or malice. But de San-
ctis
that which wholſomly now they will not tom. 10.
thinke vpon, neceſſarily hereafter, & without all remedie they ſhall ſuſtaine : For the
laſt day will come vpon them, the day of
iudgement will come, when neither it ſhall
be lawfull for them to doe pennance, nor
can they by good works redeeme themſelves from everlaſting death : then with
ſuch deepe thought the ſinner is ſtrooken,
as dying he forgets himſelfe, who whileſt
he lived did forget his God.

They that were hired to the vineyard, Aug. de
verb.
when the father of the familie went out Domini
and hired ; for examples ſake, thoſe that ſerm. 59.
tom. 10.
he found the third houre ; did they ſay
vnto him, expect, we will not goe thither till the ſixth, or thoſe that hee
found the ſixt houre, did they ſay, we
E 4　　　　will

will not goe till the ninth ; or those that he
found the ninth houre,did they say,we will
not goe till the eleventh ? for he will giue all
alike and wherfore shall we wearie our
selves more then the rest? What he is to giue,
and what he wil doe,is in his owne power,
the counsell is to himselfe , doe thou come
when thou art called : for equall reward is
promised to all,but about the houre of working there is a great question: for if they,
for examples sake , that were called at the
sixth houre constitute in that age of bodie
when the youthfull yeares are fervent, as at
the sixt houre it is hot; if those young men
called should say, expect for we haue heard
in the Gospell that all shall receiue one reward,we will come at eleven, when wee be
old , being to receiue alike wherfore shall
we labour? it would be answered them and
said; wilt thou not labour that knowest not
whether thou shalt liue to be old ? thou art
called at the sixth houre;come,the father of
the familie indeed hath promised thee thy
pennie if thou come, even at eleven ; but
whether thou shalt liue till the seventh
houre no bodie hath promissed thee . I do
not say till the eleventh,but till the seventh.
Wherfore then doest thou put off, and deferre him that calleth thee being certaine of
thy wages and vncertaine of the day? Looke

to

to it, lest perhaps what by promise he is to
giue thee, thou by deferring take frō thy self.

If a man doe pennance when he hath
power to sinne, and while he liueth, correct
his life from all crime; there is no doubt but
that dying he passeth vnto euerlasting rest.
But he that living wickedly doth pennance
only in perill of death; as his damnation is
vncertaine, so is his remission doubtfull. He
therfore that in death desireth to be certaine of indulgence, let him doe pennance
while he is sound, let him sound, and in
health, bewaile his passed heinous facts.
Isidorus lib. 2. de summo bono. cap. 13.

If any one being now in the last extremitie of sicknesse will and doth accept of
pennance: and immediatly is reconciled,
and departeth hence; I confesse to you,
we denie him not what he asketh, but we
presume not that he departeth hence well.
I do not presume, I deceiue you not, I de
not presume. The faithfull living well, departeth hence secure, he that was baptizeð
but an houre before, departeth hence secure: he that doth pennance and is reconciled
while he is in health, and after liueth well,
departeth hence secure: he that doth pennance at the last and is reconciled, whether
he depart hence secure, I am not secure.
Aug. lib. 50. hom. 41.

In vaine doth he powre out his prayers before the tribunall of Chrift, who negle-cteth the time of pennance given him. *Aug.ſerm.7 1.ad fratres in eremo.*

Integritie of the mind, and not health of bodie, is required in the teſtatour, at that time when he maketh his teſtament. *Digeſt. lib. 28. tit. 1.*

Gen.47 9. SHORT PILGRIMAGE] *Iacob* ſaid to *Pharao*, The dayes of the yeares of my Pilgrimage, are 130. yeares: short and bad haue the dayes of the yeares of my life beene, and they haue not reached to the dayes of the the yeares of my anceſtours liues, in the dayes of their Pilgrimages.

By way of malediction was mans life firſt cut from the ordinarie length of 500. or in ſome 900. and ſtinted to 120. *Gen. 6. 3.*

Pſal.89 The dayes of our yeares in themſelves are 70. yeares: And if in able men they bee 80. yeares: what is aboue that is labour and griefe.

Pſal.38 Behould thou haſt ſet my dayes meaſurable: how short is our life that is to be meaſured, not the dayes of it only, but the houres, but the moments: not by the divine, or Angelicall ſcience alone, but by everie man that hath but a little taſted of Arithmetike?

Well

Well may his dayes be meafured, whofe verie fubftance is as nothing in the fight of God.

Long accovnt] Long and ftrict, when of every idle word which men haue fpoken, they fhall render an account therof in the day of iudgement. _{Mat.12: 36.}

Every one of vs fhall render to God an account for himfelfe. _{Rom.14 12.}

§. 1. Pag. 17. A trve Christian Catholike man] By this title did *S. Augu-ftine* ftile himfelfe : *Sed de me quid dicam, qui iam Catholicus Chriftianus eram ?* But of my felfe what fhall I fay who was now a Catholike Chriftian? _{Lib. de vtilitate credēdi.}

The name of Chriftian was given to the Difciples firft at Antioch in the very beginning of the Apoftles preaching of Chrifts Gofpell. _{Act. 11: 26.}

The Apoftles themfelves in their fymbole called the Church Catholike, and the members therof Catholiks.

As many as being baptized haue put on Chrift are called Chriftians; this the vfe of the name hath obtained ; although with fome nations he is not holden, in common vnderftanding, for a true Chriftian that is not alfo a Catholike, and the one name comprehendeth as much as the other, and they be convertible.

Befides

Besides these so ancient names wherby ever since Christs time those of the true Religion haue beene knowne, whosoever bringeth in another, doth iniurie to the catholike cause, which the Hereticks of our times haue laboured much in , to haue vs called Roman Catholikes, that cōsequently themselves might also be called catholikes of other particular Churches, suppose, of Amstelrodam, Geneua, or the like. This they doe pricked on by the sting of envie seing vs alone to beare away from thē that most ancient and glorious name: while they therby shut out of the whole, must of necessitie remaine sects, and by one name, whatsoever they be, be called Heretikes. This fraude, and the poyson of their malicious intention some Catholikes not perceiving, take vpon them the addition of Roman: Which although it be good in it selfe becaufe the Roman Church is the Catholike Church, yet more glorious it were for vs, and more confusion to our adversaries to stand fast to that our first name of Catholike which we haue prescribed from them and never suffered to goe out of our hands.

Taking Catholike in the true sense, it signifieth a man that professeth the only true Religion wherin one God is worshipped and

Aug. de vera Religione, Tom. 1.

and with moſt purified pietie knowne, and acknowledged for the beginning of all nature, by whom all the vniverſe is both begunne, and perfected, and conteined, in the one, onely, and vniverſall Church which is called Catholike, and not tyed to one place, but diffuſed into all places and all times.

We, ſaith *S. Auguſtine*, muſt hold the Chriſtian Religion, and the communicatiō of that Church, which is Catholike, & called Catholike, not only of thoſe that are her owne, but alſo of all her enemies. For whether they will or noe, the verie Hereticks themſelves, and nourtured in ſchiſmes, when they ſpeake not with their owne cōpagnions, but with ſtrangers, they call Catholike, nothing elſe but Catholike, for otherwiſe they can not be vnderſtood, vnleſſe they diſcerne her by this name, by which ſhee is called of all the vniverſall world. *Aug. de vera Religione, c. 7.*

Of vniverſall ſaith *S. Auguſtine*, Catholike tooke the name: our Lord himſelfe ſaying: It is not for you to know the times which my Father hath kept in his owne power: but you ſhall receiue the vertue of the holy Ghoſt comming vpon you, and ye ſhall be witneſſes for me in Hieruſalem, & all Iudea, & Samaria and through all the earth. Behold frō whēce Catholike is called. *Aug. contra litteras Petiliani. c. 38. Tom. 7. Act. 1.*

A Chri-

A Chriſtian I am, and a Catholike I am of the ſame Chriſtian faith that the Diſciples were at Antioch and the ſame Catholike faith that was founded vpon ſaint *Peter* and continueth in his ſucceſſours the vicars of Chriſt at Rome: which is to be a Chriſtian Catholike man ſimplie, and abſolutely. He that calleth himſelfe a Roman Catholike doth like him that calleth a man a riſible reaſonable man, giving no more diſtinction, in the laſt then at the firſt: for all that they will haue a Roman Catholike to ſignifie, is but the ſame that is ſignified by a Catholike.

A Roman Catholike, ſoundeth in ſome ſenſe as if one ſhould ſay a particular vniverſall. *Auguſtine*. Marke a little what Church Cyprian called Catholike when he defended the vnitie therof, the Church, ſayth he, ſpread through with the light of our Lord ſtreacheth out her beames through the whole world. Yet it is one light which is everie where diffuſed, and the vnitie of the bodie is not ſeparated. Shee extendeth her branches over the vniverſall earth with copious plentie: her large ſpread ſtreames more broad ſhee layeth forth: yet the head is one and the origin one: and one mother copious in ſucceſſions

Aug. contra Gaudét. lib. 5. tom. 7.

fions of fecunditie ...... if yours be
the Catholike Church shew her ftretching
her beames over the whole world : Shew
that shee extends her branches with copious fertilitie over the vniverfall earth :
For hence is Catholike of the Greeke
word καθοληκῶς named . and ὁλον *holon* in
Greeke maketh in English the whole , or
vniverfall, fo that through the whole , or
according to the whole is καζα ὁλον or
καθολον *Catholon*, from whence Catholike
is called .

To be a Chriftian is glorious, and may
fuffice vs in as much as he that is a good
Chriftian muft neceffariely be a good Catholike, for he is a Chriftian that being baptized profeffeth the whole doctrine of
I E S V S C H R I S T in his Church, and the
fame is alfo a Catholike , which name was
given to diftinguish betweene fome and
others of the baptized that not profefsing
the whole doctrine, of Chrift did fticke to
parts and making a doctrine of their
owne , leaving the whole , are therfore
Heretikes: which only name is condiftin-
guisht againft Catholikes , that whofoever is not a Catholike is by the fame an
Heretike : and not a Luthers Catholike
as , the Germans call it , nor a Calvins
Catholike , nor no Catholike : for no
                                    other

other fort of Catholike is there,or can bee then a Chriftian Catholike, *S.Peeter Maui-men* dyed a Martyr at *Damafcus* about the yeare of our Lord 742. Slaine by the Ara-bians,for faying:Everie one that embraceth not the Chriftian Catholike faith, is dam-ned , like as Mahomet your falfe prophet is. *Mart. Rom.* 9.*Kal. Mart. Theophan.in hift. Mifcell.lib.* 22. Anno 2.Conftant.6.Imp.

Aug.l.1 Quæft. ex Mat. Good Catholikes and evill Catholikes *S.Auguftin* admitteth . Calling thofe evill Catholikes, who, although they beleeue thofe things to bee true which appertaine to the true doctrine of faith ; and if there be any thing that they doe not know they thinke it is to be fought out , and without breach of pietie doe difcuffe it , without any preiudice to the truth it felfe , and in as much as they can , doe loue and honour thofe that are good,and whom they thinke to bee good ; yet they liue wickedly and full of heinous crimes,otherwaies then they beleeue that they ought to liue . And good Catholikes are thofe which follow both entire faith and good manners.

Aug. de Civitate Dei.l.10 c.32. What is the vniverfall way , but that which everie nation hath, not proper only to it felfe : but is given from God , that it may be common to the vniverfitie , of na-tions , to all people : this is our pietie , which

which therfore is called Catholike, because
it is not delivered to any certaine people, as
to the Iewes, but to all humane kinde, and
excludeth not any one; by this all may be
saved, and without it none; and in this
every nation hath not his owne religion,
like as with the Gentils; for with the Ro-
mans other Gods were, and worshipped after another manner then with the Greekes;
others with them then with the French,
Spanish, Scythians, Indians, Persians: all
nations that haue professed Christ doe
worship the same God, and with the same
kind of sacrifice; and *Augustine* calleth the Aug.
Breui-
culi cõt.
Church Catholike not alone for the pleni-
tude of sacraments therin, but also for the
vniuersitie of nations, and people that
therin communicate.

    S. Athanasius, in his dispute against *Ar-* Lue.
rius, giveth the reason of the Disciples Act. 11.
26.
being called Christians, thus: All that be- Mart.
leeued in our Lord IESVS CHRIST, were Rom. 8.
Kal.
not called Christians, but only Disciples: mart.
And because there arose many Authors of
new opinions, contrarie to the Apostolicall
doctrine, they called all their followers Disciples; and there was no difference in name
betweene true and false Disciples, whether
they were Christs, or *Dositbees*, or the followers of one *Iudas*, or of *Iohn*, that confes-

           F   sed

sed themselves, as it were, of Chrifts Church,
but all were called by that one name of Difciples . Then the Apoftles cōming together
(as by *S. Lukes* narratiō the Aɗs beare witneffe) called all the Difciples by one name
Chriftians , differencing them from the
common name of Difciples; and that the
faying of the divine Oracle pronounced by
Ifaias 62.2. might be accomplished, which
hath ; And thou shalt be called by a new
name which the mouth of our Lord shall
declare, &c.

Epipha.
hæret.
27.

Not long after the Heretikes had emula-
tion to this name , and the Carpocratians
firft vſurped it, whom others followed, reproaching ſo great a name with falſe do-
ɗrine, & evill manners, as now they would
doe with the name of Catholike.

Rom.
10.

Pag. 17. §. 1. lin. 4. BY FAITH CONFES-
SING] With the heart we beleeue, to iuſtice , & with mouth Confeffion is made to
ſalvation . Faith in the heart, confefsion in
the mouth. This is the word of faith which
we preach (faith the Apoftle) that if thou
confeffe our Lord IESVS in thy mouth, and
beleeue in thy heart that God hath raiſed
Aug. de
fide ad
Petrum,
Tom. 3. him from death, thou shalt be ſafe. *S. Auguſtin* to *Peter* the Deacon. I am glad indeed
that thou haſt ſo much ſolicitude for the
keeping of the true faith, without any vice
of

of perfidiousnesse without which faith no
conversion can profit, nor yet be at all : for
the Apostolicall authoritie saith; that without faith it is impossible to please God : because faith is the foundation of all good
things : faith is the beginning of humane
salvation ; without this faith no man can
come to the number of the Sōnes of God :
because without it neither in this world
doth any one obtaine the grace of iustifi-
cation , nor in the world to come shall he
possesse life everlasting. And if any one doe
not walke here by faith, he shall not come
to the vision. Without faith all mans labour
is in vaine, for such it is, as without the true
faith whosoever will please God by contempt of the world: as if one bending toward the countrie in which he knoweth he
shall liue blessedly , should leaue the right
way and improvidently follow errour , by
which he cannot come to the blessed Citie, but fall into precipice, where will be no
ioy giuen to him that cometh , but destru-
ction brought in to him that falleth.

IN HOPE REPOSING MY SALVATION]
A right order first to beleeue and confesse,
then to hope. I haue beleeved and therfore
haue I spoaken , and am over much humbled; saith the Psalmist, as it were betwixt
hope and feare.

An-

Auguſtin. Encheridion ad Laurentium.
Tom. 3. What can be hoped for which is not beleeved : and yet ſomething may be beleeved which is not hoped for. As, which of the faithfull beleeveth not the paines of the damned, and yet he doth not hope for them? and whoſoever beleeveth that they be now at hand, hanging over his head, and with a flying motion of his minde doth abhorre them, is better ſaid to feare then to hope. Which *Lucan* diſtinguiſhing, hath ſet downe thus : Lett him that feareth hope. Faith is both of evill things and good: for both good and evill things are beleeved and that with good, and not with evill faith. Faith is alſo of things paſt, and preſent, and to come, for we beleeue that Chriſt dyed, which now is paſſed: We beleeue that he ſitteth at the right hand of the Father, which now is : We beleeue that he ſhall come to iudge, which is to be. Faith is alſo of a mans owne things, and of other mens, for everie man beleeveth of himſelfe that he had a beginning, and that he was not ever, and ſuch other things : nor only of other men but alſo of the Angels we beleeue many things that appertaine to Religion . But hope is only of good things, and thoſe to come, and belonging to him that is ſaid to hope for them. All which being ſo, for theſe
cau-

causes faith is to be distinguished from hope , as well in reasonable difference as in the name. For in that belongeth to the not seeing either those things that are beleeved or hoped for , it is common to faith and hope. In the Epistle to the Hebrewes , the testimonie wherof the illustrious defenders of the Catholike rule haue vsed ; faith is said to be a convincing of those things which are not seene. Although when any one saith himselfe to haue beleeved , not words, nor witnesses, nor any arguments, but the evidence of the present things, that is, to haue given credit to them, it seemeth not so absurd , that he might rightly be reprehended in word , and it should be said vnto him , thou hast seene and therfore thou hast not beleeved ; whence it may be thought not to be consequent that whatsoever thing is beleeved must not be seene, but better we call that faith which is taught by the divine word, of those things,to witt which are not seene.

And of hope the Apostle saith , hope which is seene is not hope ; for that which one seeth,what doth he hope for? but if we hope for the things that we see not, we expect with patience . When therfore future good things be beleeved of vs , they are no other thing then hoped for.

Now

Now what shall I say of loue without
the which faith profiteth nothing? and hope
without loue cannot be: To conclude, as
S. Iames faith, the diuelles beleeue and tremble, and yet they doe not hope, or loue, but
rather that which beleeving wee hope for
and loue, they feare shall come vpon them.
Wherfore the Apoftle *Paul* approoveth &
commendeth the faith which worcketh by
loue, which verily cannot be without hope,
nor hope without loue, nor both without
faith.

D. Thom. 2.2. quaft. 17. Eternall beatitude
is the proper obiect of hope. For we may
not hope for leffe of God then himfelfe, in
enioying of whom confifteth life euerla-
fting. And suppofing our vnion to our
neighbour by loue, a man may by the vertue of Theologicall hope, hope for beatitude for him as well as for himfelfe: but to
confide in Princes or the fonnes of men,
concerning falvation, or to fet our hope in
man, the holy Ghoft forbiddeth and giues
a curfe to him that doth it. That faith being
old will I keep in which a childe I was
borne. *Hieronymus ad Pammachium & Ocea-*
num, paulo ante finem. Tom. 2. Now doth
faith fwimme in many mens lippes, when
in their heart there is either none at all, or
that

that that is doth vehemently languish. For who doth not professe that which we reade in the Deuteronomie. Heare Israel, thy Lord thy God is one Lord? And, thou shalt adore thy God and serue him alone? Who doth not daily recite with mouth, I beleeue in God the father Almightie? notwithstanding he beleeueth not in God, that doth not place in him alone all the trust of his felicitie: neither hath he one God and Lord that by harlottrie, by riotte, and auarice, doth the commands of Sathan: nor doth he serue him alone, that serueth his bellie, that is giuen to this world which is set all vpon wickednesse. The heathens thinke there be many Gods, and dost thou seeme to thy selfe a perfect Christian, because thou art persuaded that there is but one God? What great matter doest thou? the Iewes doe the same, who daily blaspheme the Sonne of God in their Synagogues; the same doe the diuells beleeue and tremble at it. If truly thou beleeuest in God beleeue him to be iust and true. Iust in rewarding the good, and punishing the euill: true in his promises: beleeue that there is no hope of saluation but only in his Sonne whome he deliuered to the crosse for all of vs, and to death,

Deut. 6. & 10.

F 4 beleeue

beleeve that no evill can fall to them that
deliver themfelues wholly over vnto his
will; and doe perfever in the fame, this is to
beleeue in God the Father, this is to beleeue
in his Sonne, this is to beleeue in the holy
Ghoft. *Cyprian. de duplici martyrio longe an-*
te finem. Tomo 4. Vnexercifed faith foone
languisheth, and idle is tempted with frequent difcommodities : the craftie enemie
breakes in vpon remiffe fentinels : but ex-
terne fraude inftructs the man thats exerci-
fed in warre and beares him glorioufly to
the palme of victorie. Peace therfore to the
faithfull is matter of corruption . *Ambrof.*
ferm. 11. in Pfal. 118. longius ante fine. Tom. 4.

Pfalm.
141.

I haue cryed to thee O Lord, I haue faid
thou art my hope, my portion in the land of
the living .

Pfal. 26

Abide our Lord, deale manfully, and thy
heart shall be comforted, and fuftaine our
Lord. Becaufe the world, what it promifeth
feemeth here to giue in the land of the
dying; and our Lord, what he promifeth is
to giue in the land of the living, many are
wearie of expecting the true ioy and are
not ashamed to loue the deceitfull; of fuch

Eccle. 2

the Scripture faith. Woe to them that haue
loft their patient fuftayning , and diverted
into wicked wayes. *Aug. de verbis Apcft. ferm.*
25. Tom. 10.

Spe

Spe salvi facti sumus. Spes non confundit. by hope we are saved, hope confoundeth not. How hope should be without faith I doe not finde, for no man hopeth that he can attaine that which he doth not beleeue to be. It behooveth therfore that al three be in the minde, faith, hope, and charitie : that both a man beleeue the things be true to which he is called , and hope that he may attaine to them, and that he loue them. *Aug. lib.* 21. *sententiarum, sent.* 8.

One hope is of the eternall rewards, another of comfort in the humilitie of tribulation. *Aug. enarr. in Psalm.* 118. *super, Memor esto verbi tui servo tuo in quo mihi spem dedisti. Tomo* 8.

Because the man that is converted to God hath his delight changed ; the things that he delights in are also changed , and not taken quite away; for all our delights in this life , are not yet in deede: but the hope it selfe is so certaine as it is to be preferred before all the delights of this world. *Aug. enarr. in Psalm.* 74. *Tomo* 8.

Pag. 17. §. 1. lin. 5. IN THE ONELY MERITS] All our merits are founded in the merits of Christs incarnation, life, and passion: which ground worke taken away, no man hath , or ever had, or could haue since *Adam* any merits towards life everla-

F 5   sting,

iting, which by his demerits he loſt and merited damnation. Whoſoever reckeneth vp
his merits to thee, what doth he but recken
vp thy free guifts.

Aug.
Côfeſſ.
cap, 13.
tom. 1.
Et de
Trinit.
l. 13. c.
10. tom.
8.

What was ſo neceſſarie to erect our
hope, and deliver mortall mindes, deiected
with the very condition of mortalitie,
from deſpairing of immortalitie, as that it
should be demonſtrated vnto vs how much
God weighed vs and how much he loved
vs? And what token of this more manifeſt
and more excellent, then that the Sonne of
God, immutably good, remaining in himſelfe what he was, and taking of vs, and
for vs, what he was not, without detriment of his ſoules nature, vouchſafing to
enter into our fellowship, firſt without
any evill merit of his owne, he would
beare our evils: and ſo now beleeving how
much God loveth vs, and hoping for that
which before we deſpaired of, with
bountie no way due, he would beſtow his
gifts vpon vs without any good merits of
ours, yea, with many precedent euill merits; for even thoſe things that are called
our merits, are his gifts: for that faith may
worke by loue, the charitie of God is diffuſed in our hearts by the holy Ghoſt given
vs. *Aug. enarr. in Pſalm. 144. tom. 8. Gratia
ſalvi facti eſtis.* Where thou heareſt grace,
vn-

vnderſtand gratis , if therfore gratis ,
then thou haſt brought nothing , thou
haſt merited nothing : For if any thing be
rendred for merits, it is wages and not
grace : by grace, ſaith he , you are ſaved
through faith. Expound that more cleere-
ly for the arrogant., for thoſe that pleaſe
themſelves, for thoſe that are ignorant of
Gods iuſtice and will conſtitute their
owne . And this ſelfe ſame thing more o-
penly . And this, quoth he , that you are
made ſafe by grace is not of your ſelves, but
the gift of God . But we perhaps haue
done ſomething to merit the gift of God .
What then ? doe not we worke well ?
yes, we worke, but how? he working in vs
becauſe by faith we giue place in our heart
to him who in vs and by vs worketh good
things . . . . Hearken to the
ſame thing; what diddeſt thou merit ſinner?
Contemner of God , what diddeſt thou
merit ? ſee if thou canſt meete with any
thing but puniſhment , ſee if thou canſt
meete with any thing but paine: thou ſeeſt
then what was due to thee, & what he gaue
thee that gaue thee gratis. Perdō is given to
the ſinner, the ſpirit of iuſtification is given,
charitie and dilection is given , wherin
thou mayeſt doe all good things: and aboue
all this , he will giue both life everlaſting
                                                        and

and the focietie of the Angels: all of mercie , boaſt no where of thy merits becauſe
thy merits themſelves are his gifts . *Domi-*
num Deum tuum adorabis & illi ſoli ſeruies :
Thou ſhalt adore thy Lord thy God and
ſerue him alone, and thy neighbours erring
and labouring thou muſt help as much as
is lawfull and commanded ; ſo as this very
thing when it is well done , we doe vnderſtand God to doe it by vs , and deceived
with vaine glorie chalenge nothing to our
ſelves,by which one vice we be from height
drowned in the deep. *Aug.De quantitate a-*
nimæ,lib.1.cap.34.tom.1. & de libero arbitrio
lib. 1. cap.14. Of our merit that it is volun-
rarie . For this that eternall law hath with
immutable ſtabilitie confirmed,that merite
be in the will , reward and puniſhment in
beatitude and miſerie . When therfore we
ſay that men are voluntarily wretched, we
ſpeake not as if they had a will to be wret-
ched:but that they be in ſuch will, as whether they will or no , miſerie muſt neceſſarily follow : and therfore it repugneth not
in the ſuperiour reaſon that all have a will to
be bleſſed and yet cannot : for all will not
liue vprightly , to which only will, bleſſed
life is due . And againe. *De morib. Eccleſiæ*
Cath.lib.1.cap.25. tom.1. Life everlaſting is
the whole reward , in whoſe promiſe we
haue

haue ioy: and the reward cannot goe before
the merits and be given a man before he be
worthie of it? for what is more vniuſt then
this; and what more iuſt then God ? we
muſt not therfore demand reward before
we haue merited to receiue it.

*Aug.lib.de Beata vita.Meritis matris ſe vivere
credit*. *Auguſtine* thought he lived through
his mothers merits; and *lib.* **1**. *Soliloquiorum*.
He diſprooveth the error of thoſe that
thinke the ſoules to haue no merit with
God : of merit,ſee. *Aug*.moſt copiouſly in
many places . *Impreſſione Baſileæ* **1543**.
Tom.2.col. 161.*a*. 163.*a*. 161.*c*. 464.*c*. *Tom.3.
col.*204.B. *Tom.*7.*col.*770.*a. & Tom.*2.*Epiſt.*
105. What merits then of his owne, ſhall
he that is delivered boaſt of, who if he had
according to his merits, ſhould be nothing
but damned ? Are then the merits of the
iuſt none ? they are verily, becauſe they are
iuſt, but that they might become iuſt there
were no merits ; for they were made iuſt,
when they were iuſtified : but as the Apoſtle ſaith,iuſtified by his grace gratis . *Multa
ibi vide. Tom.*2. *col.* 466.*a*. 486.B. *Tom.*7.
col. 1306.B. *Tom.*8.*col.*1104.B. *Tom.*9.*col.*
26.*a. Tom.*4.*col.*1014.*a.*1234.*a. Tom.* 10.
406. *a. Tom.*3.191.*a.*162.B. 189.*d.*190.B.
437.*a.*584.*c.d.*186.*d. Tom.*4384. B. 169.*d.*
171.*d.*1305.*c.*876.*c.d.*919.*d.*

I i m-

I IMPLORE THE ASSISTANCE BY
PRAYER OF THE B. AND IMMA-
CVLATE VIRGIN MARIE AND OF
ALL THE HOLY COMPANIE OF
HEAVEN] Concerning Prayer to Saints
it is in vaine to aske of what opinion he
was that thus actually prayeth to our bleffed Ladie and all the Saints . So prayed
S. Augustine to the Saints. You therfore that
haue merited to become companions of
the heavenly citizens and enioy the claritie
of eternall glorie, pray for me to our Lord,
that he will take me out of this prison
wherin I am holden bound and cap-
tiue, &c. *Tom. 3. l. de spiritu & anima, col.* 898.
And *de ecclesiasticis dogmatibus* , *cap.* 73. The
fame S. faith, the bodies , and chiefly the
reliques of the bleffed Martyrs are moft
fyncerely to be honored, as if they were the
members of Chrift , and Churches called
by their names, as holy places dedicated to
the Divine worship, with moft pious affection and devotion to be moft faithfully
frequented we beleue : and of the maner
how the Saints ought to be honoured; at
large. *Lib.* 8. *De Civitate Dei : cap.* 27. &
Tom. 6. *contra Fauftum Manichaum, lib.* 20.
cap. 21. The Chriftian people celebrateth
the Martyrs memorie with religious fo-
lemnitie, both to excite themfelves to imi-
ta-

tation , and that they may be cuppled in
fellowship to their merits, and holpen by
their prayers : yet fo,as to none of the
Martyrs , but to the God himfelfe of the
Martyrs we conftitute Altars , although in
memorie of the Martyrs . For which of
the Bishops affifting at the Altars in places
of the holy bodies, hath at any time faid:
we offer to thee *Peter*, or *Paul* , or *Cyprian* :
but that which is offered , is offered to
God who crowned the Martyrs , at the
memories of them whom he crowned :
that by the admonition of the very places
greater affect arife to whet charitie , both
towards them , whom we can imitate,
and towards him by whofe helpe we be
able to imitate . We therfore worship the
Martyrs , with that worship of loue and
focietie , wherewith alfo in this life holy
men of God are worshipped whofe hearts
we perceiue to be prepared to the like
paffion for the Euangelicall truth . But
thofe by fo much more devoutly , as more
fecurely after all vncertaine things overcome, and with how much more confident
praife we preach them now victours in a
more happie life,then as yet fighting in this
life. But with that worship which in Greeke
is called *latria*,and cannot be fpoken in one
word

word in latine , being a certaine seruitude properly due to the Diuinitie , we neither worship nor teach to be worshipped , but one God, &c. *Aug. in Psalm. 85. prope finem. Tom. 8.* Our Lord IESVS CHRIST doth yet intercede for vs : All the Martyrs that are with him make intercession for vs, their interpellings doe not passe vntill our sighs haue passed, &c. *Lege de Ciuitate Dei lib. 21. Tom. 5 & in Psalm. 105. Tom. 8. versu, Si nō Moyses electus eius stetisset in confractione in conspectu eius. Aug. serm. 2. de anuntiatione in fine. Tom. 10. serm. de Sanctis.* O Blessed MARIE who is able worthily to repay thee iust thankes and preachings of thy prayses, who by thy singular assent diddest succour the lost world ? what prayses can humane frailtie pay thee , which in thy only commerce hath found an entrie to recouerie ? Receiue therfore how small soever , howsoever to thy merits vnequall thancks - giuings , and when thou hast received our vowes, by prayer, excuse our falts. Admit our prayers within the sacrarie of thy hearing. & bring vs backe an antidote of reconciliation : be it by thee excusable which by thee we intrude , let that become impetrable which with faithfull minde we aske, receiue what we offer, giue againe, what we aske, excuse that we feare, because thou art

the

the only hope of finners, by thee we hope for perdon of our finnes, and in thee moft bleffed is the expectation of our rewards: Holy Marie fuccour the wretches, helpe the pufillanimous, refresh the forrowfull, pray for the people, ftand for the clerecie, make intercefsion for the deuout woman kinde, lett all feele thy helpe that celebrate thy memorie. Afsift readily to the vowes of thofe that aske, and to all, repay the wished effect. Let thy dayly ftudies be to pray for the people of God, who bleffed haft merited to beare the Redeemer of the world that liveth and reigneth world without end.

Very worthy and iuft is it to glorifie Chry-fott. in liturg. thee mother of our God ever moft bleffed and vndefiled, more honorable then Cherubins, more glorious farre then Seraphins, vvho vvithout all corruption haft brought forth God, vve magnifie thee the true mother of God, haile Marie full of grace our Lord is vvith thee, bleffed thou among vvomen, & bleffed the fruit of thy vvombe, becaufe thou haft brought forth the Saviour of our foules.

To thee vve call moft holy virgin, be Athan. in Eväg. de S. Maria Deipara mindfull of vs thou vvho even after thy deliverie diddeft remaine a virgin. Haile Marie full of grace our Lord is with thee,

G   the

the orders of Angels and all men doe call thee blessed . Blessed art thou aboue all woemen,& blessed the fruit of thy wombe. Make intercession for vs O Mistresse , O Ladie, O Queene,and Mother of God.

Greg. Nazian. Traged. Christi. Thrice blessed mother,light of virgins, that dost inhabit the bright temples of heaven,free from filth of mortalitie , adorned now with immortalities stole , yeeld a benigne eare to my words from on high, and receiue I beseech thee O virgin my prayers .

Bernar. serm. 1. de Advent. O blessed inventor of grace , bringer forth of life,and mother of health,let vs by thee haue accesse to thy sonne that by thee he may receive vs, who by thee was given to vs .

I m m a c v l a t e] This is the proper epithete of the Conception of our blessed Ladie.Others there are appropriated to her virginitie, as most entire, most pure,vndefiled, not corrupted, not stayned , vntouched, &c. Whence may be gathered the authors opinion of the immaculate Conception to be the same that our Seraphicall Order hath even from the beginning raised and maintained both in Quire & schooles; that the B.Virgin was alwayes Immaculate even in the first instant of her Conception, as becomed the Maiestie of God, that was

to

tó be borne of her vnſpotted fleſh. Cāt. 4. 7.
Thou art all immaculate, &c.

Pag. 17. §. 1. lin. 15. MEMBERS
OF THE TRIVMPHANT CHVRCH
HAVE IN CHRIST COMPASSION
ON THE MEMBERS OF THE MI-
LITANT CHVRCH] By reaſon of
their vnion . For we beleeue in the holy
Catholike Church the cōmunion of Saints.
The right order of confeſſion required, Aug. in
that after the Trinitie the Church should Enchē-
be adioyned as a houſe to the dweller, ridio.
and to God his Temple, and to the builder c. 56.
his Citie . The which is here to be taken
whole, not only in that part in which it is a
pilgrim here on earth, from the Sunne ri-
ſing to the ſetting of the ſame prayſing the
name of our Lord, and after the captivi-
tie of oldneſſe ſinging a new ſong ; but
alſo in that part which alwayes hath adhe-
red to God in heaven from the time that it
was firſt created, and hath experienced
no evill of his fall : this ſtands faſt, bleſſed
in the holy Angels, and helpeth as it ought,
to doe his part that is in pilgrimage : becauſe both ſhall be one by companie of e-
ternitie, and now is one by the band of
charitie, which whole is inſtituted to
worſhip one God.

G 2   D4-

Pfalm.
118.63.
David said, while he was yet living: I am partaker, with all that feare thee and keepe thy commandements.

1. Cor.
12.12.
As the bodie is but one and yet hath many members and all the members are but one bodie, so also Chrift, for in one fpirit we were baptized into one . The eye cannot fay to the hand I need not thy helpe, nor the head to the feet you are not neceffarie for me . God hath tempered the bodie, giving to it that wanted the more a-boundant honour, that there might be no fchifme in the bodie, but that the members together might be carefull one for another, and if one member feele any fmart, all the members doe condole with it, or if any one member receiue any comfort , all the members doe congratulate with it , and you are the bodie of Chrift and members of his members, &c.

S. Ma-
ximus,
ferm. de
SS. Oc-
tavio,
Adveri-
tio &
Salvato-
re mar-
tyribus
Tauri-
nẽtibus.
All martyrs are moft devoutly to be worshipped but efpecially thofe are to be honoured of vs whofe reliques we haue in poffeffion , for thofe helpe vs with their prayers, but thefe with their pafsion; with thefe we haue familiaritie for they be alwaies with vs, they dwell with vs, that is, they keepe vs whileft we liue and receiue vs when we dye; here, left vvee offend, there left the horrour of hell invade vs. To that

end

end it vvas ordayned by our forefathers,
that our bodies should be laid by the
Saints boanes that vvhileft hell feareth
them, paine may not come at vs , vvhileft
Chrift illuminateth them, our darckneffe
may fly away : Refting vvith the holy Martyrs vve efcape hell by their merits, but not
vnleffe vve be fellowes vvith them in their
fanctitie .

Pag. 17. §. 1. lin. 18. INTO HIS In opi-
FIRST SVBSTANCE] This can not Doct.
be phyfically vnderftood ; but is morally fubtilis.
taken for death; He dyed the 29. of Iune
1598. of a confumption, vvherof he lay
ficke almoft a yeare at his manour houfe of
Temple broughton, and was,according to
his will, buried in S. Maries , the parifh
Church of Handburie, in the place vvhere
the high Altar ftood in the time of Catholike Religion .

Of vvhat age he died I know not but
gather that he could not vvant much of 60.
It is evident in the Teftament that he lived
40. yeares and vpward vnmaried ; after-
vvard he had 12. children borne him by
one vvife at 12. feverall births. Howfoever,
the life vvas fhort for a man of his
vvorth , and yet long by reafon of the
vvorth of it : As it is faid. *Sap.* 4. He that
is confummate and perfected in fhort
time.

time, hath accomplished many times and ages.

De fato sane intellige.

Seneca Epist. 4. *de breviori vita non curandum.* Our care muft not be to liue long, but to liue fufficiently. To liue long wee haue need of fate : to liue fufficiently, a minde. Life is long if it be full : and it is full when the mind hath gotten the maifterie of good, and into its owne hands power over it felfe. What auaile a man 80. yeares paffed in fluggishneffe ? Such a man hath not liued, but made a ftay in life, nor is he late dead but long.

He hath lived 80. yeares; all the matter is from what day you count his death. He hath lived 80. yeares, rather he hath beene 80. yeares: vnleffe you meane he hath lived, fo as trees are faid to liue. Let vs not meafure our life by time but facts. As in little ftature a perfect man may be, fo in a little terme of time a perfect life may be. Age is an externall thing : how long I am, is anothers : but how long I am good, is mine. To liue vnto wifedome is the fpace of moft ample life. *Idem, lib.* 1. *de tranquilitate vitæ. cap.*10. There is no viler thing then an aged ould man that hath no other argument but yeares to proue that he hath lived long.

Lin. 21. I T S H A L L P L E A S E G O D T O A P P O I N T] Man pur-

purposeth and God disposeth. Therfore saith *S. Iames* the Apostle. *Epist. cap.* 4. Say if our Lord will, or if we liue, we will doe this or that, because we know not what shall be to morrow.

So the soule bee safe, it is no great matter where the bodie lye : many a holy bodie lyeth in the sea , many burned to askes, many devoured by wild beasts, &c. Yet every man ought so much to esteeme of Christian buriall, as he ought to seeke for it by all lawfull meanes , and is bound to ordaine as providently as he can ; and a good reason why is giuen in the leafe here before, out of *S. Maximus.*

Pag. 17. §. 2. RVFVLL DECAY OF THE CATHOLIKE. RELIGION] Begunne in England by *Henrie* 8. breaking obedience with the sea of Rome by act of Parlament, 1533. and made more full by *Q. Elizabeth.*

AS A TRVE FATHER] A true father is he that, according to the law of nature , provideth for those whom he hath gotten into the world, not only bodily, but spiritually: which law is so firmely engraffed in nature, as it needs no expresse law writté, to command it: as the children haue to honours their parents : the care of providing corporally for childré is in some parêts over

G 4   much,

much , and the provision for their soules (the chief part) too little.

These are not true fathers, that care not to leaue to their children a true inheritance: but false fathers, leaving inheritāce of false riches ; such as vvhen they haue slept their sleepe, they shall find nothing in their hands. The true father hath his principall care to instruct his children in the law of God : that as, not only the earthly goods, but celestiall doctrines vvere by his forefathers delivered to him; so he, keeping them in the customes and maners of his life, deliver the same to his posteritie at his death. The sonnes , most commonly follow the steps of their fathers, and thinke all lawful to doe that they see them vse . Great is the obligation of parents in the education of their children .

Ioan. 5. 19.

The sonne can doe nothing of himselfe, but vvhat he seeth his father doe; for vvhatsoever he doth, the sonne likevvise doth.

Isaias 38.
Mat. 10. 32.
Marck 8. 38.
Luc. 9. 26. & 12 8.

Pag. 18. §. 3. BE IT KNOWNE TO THEM AND TO ALL THE WORLD] The father to his children shall notifie thy truth . Every one that shall confesse me before men , I vvill also confesse him before my Father vvhich is in heaven . And he that shall denie me before men : I vvill also denie him

him before my Father vvhich is in heaven.

S. *Aug. ferm.* 181. *de tempore*, **Tom.** 10. Vide fu-
Heb. 11. *Sine fide.* Without faith it is impof- pra §.
fible to pleafe God, this faith he acknow- by faith confef-
ledgeth in our hearts, that fearcheth reines fing.
and hearts,but for conferving of the Churches vnitie ; for the difpenfation of this
time, with faith of heart, is alfo neceffarie
confeffion of mouth ; becaufe vvith the
heart vve beleeue to iuftice , and vvith
mouth vve make confeffion to falvation,
not only of preachers,but alfo of thofe that
are inftructed : Otherwife one brother of
another could not have notice , nor the
Churches peace be conferved , nor one
teach another,nor learne of another,neceffarie things to falvation , vnleffe vvhat he
hath in his heart, with fignes of voice, as it
were , with certaine chariots he fent to the
hearts of others. Faith is therfore both to
be kept in the heart , and brought forth
with the mouth: for faith is the foundation
of all good things , and beginning of humane falvation : without this no man can
come to the number of the fonnes of God,
and without it, neither doth he obtaine the
grace of iuftification in this world , nor
shall he poffeffe life everlafting in the world
to come. And if one walke not by faith,he
G 5   shall

shall not come to vifion. The holy Apoftles, having regard to this, delivered a certaine rule of faith, which, according to the Apoftolicall number, comprehended in 12. fentences, they called the fymbole, by which the beleevers might hould the Catholike vnitie and by which they might convince hereticall pravi ie, &c.

A MEMBER OF CHRISTS TRVE, CATHOLIKE, AND APOSTOLIKE CHVRCH] Signes of the true Church are, that it is one, holy, Catholike, and Apoftolike, therfore he adioyneth [OVT OF THE VNITIE AND FELLOWSHIP WHEROF THERE NEVER WAS, NOR IS, NOR CAN BE SALVATION] No more then was for thofe that were without the arke of *Noe*. The true Church can be but one, in as much as truth is one, and can be but one: errour manifold, and in a manner infinite. A man that going a iourney, bent to one place if he leaue the right way, which can be but one, it is no more matter which way he take, of fo many wayes as lie round about him, for in all he erreth, and shall not come to the place intended, be-

Aug. ferm. 181. de tēpore, prope fi- nem, Tom.10

caufe he hath left the way that only leades therunto. *Symbol. Apoft. The holy Catholike Church*. It is to be knowne that we muft beleeue the Church, and not beleeue in the Church,

Church, because the Church is not God, but the house of God. Catholike, he saith, diffu-sed over all the whole world , because the Churches of diverse Heretiks are therfore not called Catholike, because they be con-tained in places, & every one in their owne Provinces, but this, even frō the Sun rising, to the setting of the same , is diffused with the splendour of one faith . There are no greater riches, no treasures, no honours, no greater substance of this world , then is the Catholike faith: which saveth men sinners, illuminateth the blind, cureth the infirme, baptizeth Cathecumēs, iustifieth the faith-full , repayreth penitents, augmenteth the iust, crowneth, martyrs, ordeyneth clerks, consecrateth Priests, prepareth for the king-dome of heaven, and in the everlasting in-heritance communicateth with the holy Angels . Whosoever he be, and of what condition soever he be , he is no Christian that is not in the Church of Christ.

Our Lord IESVS CHRIST like a whole perfect man, both head & bodie: the head wo acknowledge in that man which was borne of the Virgin MARIE, suffered vnder *Pontius Pilate,* was buried, arose, ascended in to heaven , sitteth at the right hand of the Father , from thence we expect him, iudge of the living and the dead : this is the

Aug. in
Psal. 90.
Cōcio. 2
Tom. 8.

head

head of the Church; the bodie of this head
is the Church, not which is in this place;but
which is in this place, and over all the
world : nor that which is in this time, but
even from *Abel* vnto thofe which are to be
borne, and to beleeue in Chrift even till
the end, all the people of Saints,pertayning
to one citie, which citie is the bodie of
Chrift; whofe head is Chrift.

Whofoever feparated from the Church
is conioyned to an adultereffe; is feparated
from the things promiffed to the Church;
neither doth he appertaine to the rewards
of Chrift, that leaueth the Church of
Chrift, he is an Alien,he is prophane,he is
an enemie; he cannot now haue God his father, which hath not the Church his mother. If hee could efcape that was without
the arke of *Noe*, then he fhall efcape that is
without the church. *Cyprianus tract. de fim-
plicitate Prælat.five de vnitate Ecclefiæ.*

I following no firft but Chrift, am con-
fociated to thy beatitude, that is, to the
chayre of *Peeter:* I know the Church was
built vpon the Rocke, whofoever out of
this houfe eateth the lambe, is profane. If
any one be out of the arke of *Noe* while
the floud rageth, he fhall perish. *Hieronymus,epift. 1.ad Damafum,tomo 2.*

The Roman Church in all I feeke to
fol-

follow. *Ambrof.lib.3.de Sacramentis,cap. 1.poft medium, parte 1.* No man blotteth out of heaven the conftitution of God : no man blotteth out of earth the Church of God. *Aug. epift.162. in fine.*

That is the holy Church , the one Church , the Catholike Church , the true Church, fighting againft all herefies : fight it may , bee vanquished it cannot . All herefies haue gone out therof, as vnprofitable fprigs cut from the vine,but shee remaineth vpon her roote , vpon her vine , vpon her charitie, the gates of hell shall not overcome her. *Aug. lib. 1. de fymb. ad cathecum. cap. 5. in fine.*

The funne is eafier extinguished , then the Church obfcured. *Chryfoft.hom.4.in 6. Efaia.*

Theodofius the great , gloried more that he was a member of the Catholike Church, then that he reigned vpon the earth. _{Aug. de Civitate lib. 5. cap.26.}

What is more honorable then the Emperour to be called a child of the Church, this is that *Moyfes* preferred before the Ægyptian treafures , denying himfelf to be *Pharaos* fonne,and choofing rather to be afflicted with Gods people then to haue the pleafure of temporall finne . For before God there is nothing fo magnificent and illuftrious, as pure doctrine, and a foule inftru- _{Ambrof de Eccl. nõ trad. Hæreticis. Heb.11.}

_{Gregor. Naz. epift. ad 150. Epifc .}

110

structed and made perfect with divine o-
pinions.

    Pag. 28. §. 3. lin. 11. *I acknovvledge God
the Father my maker, God the Sonne my redeemer, &c. Matth.28.19.* Going teach all nations baptizing them in the name of the
Father and of the Sonne and of the holy
Ghost. The faith of the Trinitie. In what
place soever thou beest constitute, because,
according to the Rule promulgated by the
command of our Saviour, thou knowest thy
selfe to be baptized in one name of the Father,& Sonne,and holy Ghost;principally,
and without doubt,retaine with thy whole
heart, that the Father is God. the Sonne
God,and the holy Ghost God ; that is,the
holy and ineffable Trinitie, to be naturally
one God ; of whom in *Deuteronomie* it is
said: Heare Israel,thy Lord thy God is one
God:And thou shalt adore thy Lord God,
and serue him alone : Yet because this one
God, who only is naturally the true God,
we haue said to be neither Father alone,
nor Sonne alone, nor holy Ghost alone,but
together Father,Sonne,and holy Ghost,we
must beware, lest as we truly say the Father
and Sonne & holy Ghost,in that belongeth
to their naturall vnitie, to'be one God ; so
we dare say,or beleeue, (which is altogether vnlawfull) that he which is Father is
                        the

Aug.l.1
de fide
ad Pe-
trū,c.1.
Tom.3.

Deut.6.
Mat.4.

the fame that the Sonne, or holy Ghoft; Or
he that is Sonne , either Father or holy
Ghoft; Or he that is holy Ghoft, called properly, in the confeffion of this Trinitie, to
fay or beleeue , that he is perfonally the Father or the Sonne. For that faith which the
holy Patriarchs and Prophets , received
from God before the incarnation of the
Sonne of God; which alfo the holy Apoftles heard from our Lord him felfe in
flesh ; and , by the magifterie of the holy
Ghoft inftructed , not only preached in
word, but alfo to the healthfull inftruction
of pofteritie left in their writings , prea-
cheth the Trinitie to be one God : that is,
Father, Sonne, and holy Ghoft. But it were
no true Trinitie , if one and the fame perfon were called Father, and Sonne, and
holy Ghoft : For if, as the fubftance of
the Father, and Sonne , and holy Ghoft,
is one , fo the perfon were one; there
were nothing wherin it might be truly called a Trinitie. Againe , it were indeed a
true Trinitie, but that Trinitie should not
be one God, if as the Father and Sonne,
and holy Ghoft , are in proprietie of perfons diftinct from one another , fo they
were diftinguished in diverfitie of na-
tures .

But

But becaufe in that one true God Trinitie, not only that it is one God, but alfo that it is a Trinitie , is naturally true ; therfore that true God is in perfons a Trinitie , and in nature one. By this naturall vnitie, all the Father is in the Sonne and holy Ghoft ; all the Sonne in the Father and holy Ghoft; all the holy Ghoft in the Father and Sonne; none of thefe is without any one of them, becaufe none is before another in eternitie, or exceedeth in greatneffe, or furpaffeth in power; becaufe,in as much as perteineth to the vnitie of the divine nature, the Father is neither before nor greater then the Sōne, nor holy Ghoft : nor the eternitie and immenfitie of the Sonne, as it were before, or greater , can naturally precede or exceed, the eternitie and immenfitie of the holy Ghoft .

Aug. de Trin. cap. 4. Tom. 3. All that ever I could reade of, that before me wrote of the Trinitie , which is God , the Catholike handlers of the divine bookes both new and old, haue intended to teach this out of the Scriptures: that the Father, and Sonne, and holy Ghoft , of one and the fame fubftance, with infeparable equalitie, doe infinuate the divine vnitie : therfore they be not three Gods, but one God : Although the Father haue begotten the Sonne , and ther-

therfore the Sonne is not, whom the Father is: and the Sonne is begotten of the Father, and for that he is not Father which is Sonne : and the holy Ghoſt is neither Father, nor Sonne, but only the ſpirit of the Father and Sonne: himſelfe alſo coequal to the Father and Sonne, and pertayning to the vnitie of the Trinitie : And y et not the ſame Trinitie borne of the Virgin MARIE; vnder *Pontius Pilate* crucified, and buried; to haue riſen the third day and aſcended into heauen; but only the Sonne. Nor the ſame Trinitie to haue deſcēded in likeneſſe of a doue vpon IESVS baptized : or on the day of Pentecoſt after the Aſcenſion of our Lord with ſound made from heauen as if a vehement blaſte were carried along, and in divided tongues like fire, to haue ſitten vpon every one of them, but only the holy Ghoſt. Nor the ſame Trinitie to haue ſaid from heaven: thou art my Sonne: when either he was baptized by *Iohn*, or vpon the mount, when the three diſciples were with him, or when the voice ſounded, ſaying : I haue both clarified & againe wil clarify: but only the Fathers voice to haue beene made to the Sonne; although the Father, & Son and holy Ghoſt, as they are inſeparable, ſo do they inſeparably worke. This is alſo my faith, becauſe this is the Catholike faith.

Pag.18.§.4.lin.1. I BELEEVE AND HOVLD] The Apoſtles Creed, the Nicene Creed, *Athanaſius* Creed, the 10. Commandements, the 7. Sacraments : and in a word, all that the Catholike Church teacheth and holdeth; for, to beleeue profiteth nothing vnleſſe we alſo hold and keepe in worke, what we beleeue; and that wholly, and entirely. Whoſoever keepeth otherwiſe the whole law and offendeth in one point: becommeth guiltie of the whole, as if he had tranſgreſſed in all. That the Sacraments are the conducts wherby the grace of God is derived vnto mankinde : Their number, order, names, &c.

Epiſt.
Iacobi.
c.2.10.

1. BAPTISME] He rekoneth the Sacraments in ſuch order as they occurred at the preſent to memorie. Whoſe right order is, firſt baptiſme : wherby we are, regenerate, and borne a new in Chriſt to ſpirituall, and everlaſting life; who before were borne of our parents in the world, to corporall, and, without this Sacrament, to everlaſting death.

Matth.
vlt.

Confirmation; wherby we be ſpiritually ſtrengthened and grow, as in our infancie we be lapped and bound corporally vntill our ioynts be knit and we made able to ſtand by our naturall forces.

Ioã.20.
Act.2.

Eu-

Euchariſtie , wherby we be nourished and fed in ſoule , as by corporall foode we be fed in bodie.

Ioan. 8.
prædi-
catur
Euch.

Penance ; wherby the wounds of ſinne that we receiue in our ſoules after baptiſme. are cured.

Mat. 26.
Iacob. 5
Ioã. 20.
Mat. 16.

Extreame vnction: which ſtrengtheneth vs in our paſſage out of this life, when of our ſelves we be too weake to reſiſt the aſſaults of the divell, who then moſt of all rageth; *tendens inſidias calcaneo noſtro.* Of theſe fiue; ſee *Scotus in 4. D. 2. Q. 1. Concluſione 1.* Whoſe words are theſe: Like as in the naturall life firſt is generation , after followeth nutrition, and corroboration, and reparation of the health loſt, and theſe 4. appertaine to every ſingular perſon: and yet beſides theſe , ſomething is requiſite pertayning to the communitie, by which a man is conſtitute in neceſſarie degree toward ſome act neceſſarie for the communitie. So ſpiritually , to complete perfection outwardly , there muſt be ſome helpe pertayning to ſpirituall generation: and ſecondly, ſomething pertayning to nutrition: thirdly, pertayning to roboration or ſtrengthning: fourthly, to reparation after falling: and fiftly, beſides theſe things is required ſome being, wherby he that departeth be finally

Iacob. 5
Marc. 6.

H 2

pre-

prepared: For this spirituall life is a certaine way, ordaining that he who liveth well in the same, may without impediment passe out of it to the other, for which he is prepared. These things therfore are required as necessarie helps to every person for himselfe.

Of the other 2. Order, and Matrimonie. Scotus ibi.

And for the good of the communitie observing this law, is required also carnall multiplication; because the same is presupposed to the spirituall good, as nature to grace: and spirituall multiplication of others in the same law. So therfore it was congruent to haue seven helpes bestowed vpon the observers of the Evangelicall law; wherin might be both intensiue and extensiue perfection, and sufficient for all things necessarie to the obseruance of this law; and these are, as the Maister of Sentences hath in his text: Baptisme, appertaining to spirituall generation: Eucharist, necessarie to nourishment: Confirmation, for strengthening: Penance, to the reparation of those that are falne: Extreme vnction, to the finall reparation: Matrimonie, to multiplication in the being of nature, or carnall being: and Order, to multiplication in the being of grace, or spirituall being.

Mat.19.
ex 1. &
2.Gene-
fis.
Mat.26.
Ioā.20.

Con-

CONFESSION] By this name the Author calleth the sacrament of Penance, as by the part of that Sacrament which then was, and allwaies hath beene by the divell, and his ministers the Heretiques, most opposed. The first part of the Sacrament of Penance is contrition, or inward sorrow of heart through consideration of Gods goodnesse and our owne wickednesse. No Heretikes are so barbarous, nor any people in the world, that acknowledgeth any God, but they hold this part necessarie, as indeed it is, and hath alwaies beene, to salvation. This they call repentance, and not improperly, if rightly vnderstood. But wheras they hold this to be sufficient to blot out sinnes committed after baptisme, it is false: for since the cōming of our Saviour Christ and preaching the law of grace (which taketh not away, but accomplisheth the former law) sinne is not remitted by only contrition, but confession of it to a Priest is also required: and moreover Satisfactiō must follow: that the partie wronged, whether God, or our neighbour, may againe be appeased, and satisfied: yea, even before the time of our Saviour Christ these seeme to haue beene in vse: *David* confessed his sinne to *Nathan* the Prophet, and did satisfaction by penall worke,

2. Reg. 12.13.

H 3   ad-

adiudging also him that had wronged the poore man, by taking his sheepe, and sparing his owne, to fourefould reſtitution .

Luc. 3. 10. The people of all eſtates that came confeſſing their ſinnes to S. *Iohn* the Baptiſt , demanded, and were by him enioyned what Luc. 19 8. they ſhould doe. The rich *Zachæus* offered our Saviour to giue the halfe of his goods to the poore , and reſtore foure times as much , to any man that he might hap to haue defrauded. In confeſſion is the greateſt humilitie , a man will eaſier part with his goods, or paine his bodie, to ſatisfie, or be contrite in heart, than in Confeſſion to accuſe himſelfe ; which kind of Pride we inherited from our firſt parents : *Adam* Aug. de Civis. l. 13.c.11. in fine. would not confeſſe his ſinne to God that knew it, but caſt the fault vpon the woman: nor ſhee confeſſe, but caſt the fault vpon the ſerpent : deceived in this, that to God rebuking and chaſtizing , he eſteemed he ſhould bring a iuſt excuſe, and ſuch as eaſily he would admit , if he ſhould ſay he did it, to gratifie his companion; and that companiō, not which he had aſſumed to himſelfe, but which our Lord had given him.

How many hard labours , and painefull pilgrimages haue ſome men vndergone to expiate their ſinne : which never the leſſe they could never disburden their conſciece of of vntill they confessed . So much availeth confession,as when it can be had,without it no contrition doth suffice; and when it cannot be had, to make contrition valuable to saluation, we must haue confession at least in desire and will.

Aug. lib. 50. *hom. Tom.* 10. *hom.* 12. Dearely beloved brothers , in all the divine Scriptures we be profitably,& healthfully admonished , that we ought to confesse our sinnes,continually,and humbly , not only to God, but also to holy men; and those that feare God: For God will not therfore haue vs to confesse our sinnes becaufe he cannot otherwise know them, but becaufe this the divell desireth , that he may finde what to obiect against vs before the tribunall of the everlasting Iudge ; therfore he had rather we would defend than accufe our sinnes. On the contrarie side, our God,becaufe he is pious and mercifull, will that we confesse them in the world, that we be not confounded for them in the world to come . The divell therfore knowing the vertue of pure confession, with all his forces endeavoreth to hinder a man that he doe not confesse, and as at first he suggested to make man fall, fo after the fall he hindreth vs from rifing, becaufe he knoweth we cannot rife without confession.

It

It is worse that a man will not confesse, then to contemne the law. That a man will not by satisfaction appease the offense of God, is worse then by sinning to offend the goodnesse of God : for although sinne be forgiven by contrition, yet vocall confessiō is necessarie, either in deede, when opportunitie is had, or in purpose, when the article of necessitie excludeth the same , and not contempt of Religion ; and so, the necessitie of confessing after contrition , is not in such case, for necessitie of the remedie, but for the obligation of the precept.

Conveniently was confession instituted, that he who being in his owne power had departed from God , put vnder the power of an other, with humilitie, and deuotion, may returne. *Chrysost.hom. 3.op.imperfect. de Confessionis vtil.* Confession of our sinnes is a signe of a good minde, and the testimonie of a conscience that feareth God. Perfect feare breaketh through all shame, and there only is the turpitude of confession scene, where the paine of the future iudgement is not beleeved. And because the very shame is a grievous paine , therfore God commandeth vs to confesse our sinnes, that we may suffer the blushing for paine : for this verie thing is part of the divine iudgement . He is worthy of perdon that

seeketh

seeketh not to excuse his sinne, for where
confession is, there is remission, because
shamefaced confession holdeth the next
place to innocencie.

Aug. de pœnitentiæ vtilitate. Because it is a
great shaming to confesse ones sinnes, he
that vndergoeth this shame for Christ, is
worthie of mercie.

Greg. lib. 12. moral. c. 14. Let those that will
mervail at, in everie iust man, the continence
of chastitie, let them mervail at the integritie of iustice, let them admire the bowels
of pietie, I doe no lesse admire at the most
humble confession of sinnes, then so many
sublime deedes of virtue.

Aug. vbi supra. O foole, why art thou
ashamed to tell to a man, that which thou
wert not ashamed to doe in the sight of
God? Remoue from thee shame, runne to
the Priest, reveale thy secret, confesse thy
sinne, otherwise contrition of heart will nothing profit thee, vnlesse confession of the
mouth, if thou cannest, doe follow it. Confession is the health of soules, dissipatour of
vices, restorer of vertues, oppugnatour of
the divels: what will you more? it stoppeth
the gates of Hell, and openeth the gates of
Paradise.

Pag. 19. §. 5. SACRAMENT OF THE
LORDS SVPPER] Although, not only
H 5   in

in many other places, but even in the immediatly enfuing words the mind of the author he fufficiently declared , yet becaufe the wife (that few are) muft fpeake with the multitude , and accommodate themfelves to wife and vnwife, to whom we are debters, with the Apoftle : It is here to be noted , concerning this maner of fpeaking. Everie word abfolutely fet downe ftandeth firft for his principal, and more general fignification . So that *Dominus*, vnleffe it be limited, and drawne to more particularitie of fignification , by fome terme of reftriction , muft after his generall fignification be called, A Lord : or, The Lord : and not our Lord , more then your Lord , or my Lord, or his Lord, or their Lord; which fignification it muft take from fome of thefe adioyned expreffely, our, their, his, mine, &c. Which of it felfe it hath not, but a more noble, becaufe leffe limited. Far more it is to be The Lord, by which we vnderftand The Lord of all, then Our Lord : which, according to the very letter, doth not found Lord of all, but rather excluding others, would feeme to be ours, & not theirs. In fome places, as where it is faid, *Ego Dominus*: it cã haue none other fenfe but, I The Lord: for fenceleffe it were to fay, I our Lord, and not much better to fay I your Lord: the true is, I The Lord. The

The Lord, and Our Lord neither kind
of ſpeech is to be reproved but according
to the occurrent matter both vſed indifferently.

Dominicam Cœnam, ſaith *S. Paul,* 1. *Cor.*
11. 20. The Lords Supper, and *verſ.* 26.
Moriem Domini , the Lords death : which
is better expreſſed in the other ſacred
tongues as ὁ κυριΘ יהוה את eth Adonai
θάνατον τȣ κυριȣ ; the death of the
Lord .

When this ſpeech, Our Lord, is vſed out
of a more feruent deuotion towards God,
it is to be applauded, becauſe we will ſhew
therin a particular relation that we haue to
him more then all other creatures haue: and
that he is Our Lord, with dominion over vs
that are after his likeneſſe, more then over
other creatures, that are leſſe, or nothing
after his likeneſſe: which is inſinuated to vs
in the booke of Geneſis , where God is
never called The Lord , before the creation of man , but 35. times אלהים God,
and after *Gen.* 2. 4. יהוה The Lord. What
dominion hath a man vnleſſe over men ,
that are of his likeneſſe and vſing reaſon ? Over the brute beaſts he vſeth no
ſpeciall act of lordſhip or dominion ,
but as he ſerueth himſelfe with them, ſo
alſo he ſerueth them . Over inſenſible
more

more improperly is man said to haue do-
minion:becaufe they cannot obey his command, but are difpofed of by the labour of
his hands . Thofe things we are moft properly faid to be Lords of, which doe moft
immediately obey the power of our will.
Mans will is immediately fubiect to Gods
will , and not as other creatures are, by the
gouernement of Angels , or influence of
the heauens : And man ought to call Our
Lord, and not The Lord,when the matter
fpoaken of is directly belonging to his will
fubiect only to God and to no creature
whatfoeuer . Which freedome he hath
giuen vs, becaufe he will shew himfelfe a
louing,and not a tyrannicall Lord.In thefe
places as of the Lords fupper,&c. There is
no fpeciall mention of our fubiection, but
of his voluntarie gift, &c. Therfore it may
well be called , The Lords fupper , The
Lords death,&c.

Pag.19.§.5.lin.3. Of the Altar] The
Heretikes of thefe times haue none: only
Catholikes haue an Altar. *Heb.*13,10.*Mala.*1.10.

Lin. 3. Words of conse-
cration] How can that which
is bread be the Bodie of Chrift ? *Ambrof.
de Sacramentis. lib.* 4. *cap.* 4. By confecration . Confecration then with what
words,and by whofe fpeeches is it ? by the
words

words and speeches of our Lord I e s v s:
for, by all other things that are said, praise is
given to God, prayer is made for the people, for Kings, for others, when they come
once to make the venerable Sacrament, the
Priest vseth not his owne words, but the
words of Christ. The speech of Christ
therfore maketh this Sacrament. What
speech of Christ? verily that by which all
things are made. Our Lord commanded
and the heavens were made: Our Lord
commanded and the earth was made: Our
Lord commanded and the seas were
made: Our Lord commanded and every
creature was engendred: you see of what
operation the word of Christ is. If therfore
there be so much force in the speech of our
Lord I e s v s, as that which was not, beginneth therby to be, of how much greater
operation is it, to let the things be which
were, and change them into other things?
the heaven was not, the sea was not, the
earth was not, but harken to him that saith:
He said the word, and they are made, he
commanded, and they are created. That
therfore I may answere thee; there was not
the bodie of Christ before the consecration, but after the consecration, I say to
thee, that now it is the bodie of Christ: He
hath said, and it is made; he hath commanded, and it is created,   S A-

SACRI-
FICE.
MASSE.

} *Malach*.1.11.In every place is ſacrifized and offered to my name a pure oblation which none haue but the Catholike Church.

FIGVRATIVE SPEECHES] By connexion of one place with another, by comparing the antecedent with the conſequent words of Scripture:*Scotus in* 4.*D*.10. *Q*.1. *num*.3. Will haue vs to gather whether things be ſpoken figuratiuely or not: and argueth that here they be not figuratiue, out of the words following ; for when Chriſt had ſaid ; Take and eat this is my bodie, to declare that he meant his verie bodie, and no myſticall bodie, he ſaid immediately, which ſhall be delivered for you; and his bodie was the ſame night delivered to death for all mankind, betrayed by the falſe Apoſtle *Iudas*.

Pag.20. §.6.lin.1. EXAMINATION OF CONSCIENCE] Wherof the Apoſtle. 1.*Cor*.11. 28. Let a man proue himſelfe : and 31. if we would iudge our ſelves we ſhould not be iudged.

No paine is more grievous then a wicked conſcience. An evill conſcience is toſſed with his owne prickings : if publike fame condemne thee not, thy owne conſcience

con-

condemneth thee, becaufe no man can fly
from himfelfe . Wilt thou be never fad ?
Liue well : good life hath alwaies ioy, the
confcience of the guilty is alwayes in
paine . *Bernard. Tract. De interiori domo .
cap. 45.*

Among the manifold tribulations , and
innumerable moleftious afflictions of a
mans foule , there is no greater affliction
then confcience of finne. *Greg. in feptimum
Pfalm. pœnitent. verf. penult.* And, on the contrarie, there is no greater confolation, then
a confcience adorned with vertues. *Vide
Aug. ferm. 10. ad frat. in eremo, Tom. 10. &
ferm. 45.*

How beautifull is the brighteneffe of
the foule ! How happie the confcience full
of good works ! If he be potent , that
commands the world , how happie is he
that in his confcience beareth God ? *Aug.
ferm. 7. de Tempore.*

By good life a good confcience is
gained , that by the good confcience no
paine may be feared : let him therfore
learne to feare that will not feare, let him
learne for a time to be folicitous that will
alwaies be fecure. *Aug. ferm. 214. De
tempore .*

No man reioyceth in God, that liveth in vice. *Aug. lib.50. Hom. hom.33. in medio.& serm.215.* No man hath vniust gaine without iust dammage: where gaine is, there is dammage.gaine in the coffers, dammage in the conscience,

There is no better pleasure then the grace of a corrected conscience, *Amb.lib.2. de Abraham, cap.11.Tom.4.*

REPENTANCE, AND AMENDMENT] Confession maketh contrition or repentance more intense, and as it selfe is caused by them, so it doth againe cherish and encrease them, and of them both proceedeth amendment: for he that with contrition confesseth, submitteth himselfe also to make amends, and doe satisfaction according to the iudgement of him to whom he confesseth : and not only to amend by leading a new life, but as well by satisfiyng for that is past. Of satisfaction.or penance for sinnes. *Daniel.4.24. Matth.3.8.Luc.3.8.* Wherupon see. *Greg. hom.20. in Evangel. Bernard. serm.66.in Cant.Chrysost.hom.10.in Matth. Aug. aut pœnitendum, aut ardendum.* Looke to doe penance,or to burne.

Pag. 20. §.7. lin.2. INVOCATION OF SAINTS] Who being like the Angels of God, can both attend to our need & the visiō of God. *Mat.22.30.18,10. Luc.15,10.*

PRAYER

PRAYER FOR THE DEAD] Saint *Peeter* instructed vs , to haue a gard over the acts of our life every houre: he instructed vs also to burie the dead , and to performe their exequies diligently , and to pray for them, and to giue almes. *Clemens*, *epist.* 1. *ad Iacobum fratrem Domini.*

Dionyſ. de Eccl. Hierarch. cap. 7. Then comming the venerable Prelate readeth a moſt holy prayer over him , that the divine clemencie will forgiue the dead all his ſinnes committed through humane infirmitie, and place him in the light and region of the living, in the boſome of *Abraham, Iſaac,* and *Iacob* , in the place whence is baniſhed all ſighes, ſorrow, and ſadneſſe.

Chryſoſt. hom. 69. *ad populum.* It was not raſhly ordained by the Apoſtles, that in the dreadfull myſteries , there ſhould be commemoration made of the dead.

They that loue their friends , dead in bodie, and not in ſoule, with ſpirituall loue, and not carnall alone ; let them carefully, and inſtantly , exerciſe thoſe things that helpe the ſoules of the dead : as offerings, prayers, and almes. *Aug.*

Lin.4. PVRGATION OF SOVLES] *Matth.* 5. 25. 26. & 12. 32. *Luc.* 16. 22. 1. *Cor.* 3. 13,

CHRISTIAN WORKS] The iuſt

I   man

man is iudged by his works. *Iacob.* 2. 22.
2. *Petri* 1.10. *Apoc.* 22.11. Which places make
alſo againſt ſole faith. 1. *Cor.* 15.58.

Pag. 21. §. 8. lin. 4, TEACHING HER
ALL TRVTH] *Ioannes* 14.16. & 16.13.

Lin. 6. GATES OF HELL] *Mat.* 16.18.

Lin. 10. ANGELS OF LIGHT] *Ad*
Gal. 1.8. But although we, or an Angel from
heaven, euangelize to you another thing
beſides that we haue euangelized to you.
Anathema. *Idem* 2. *Cor.* 11.13.

Lin. 11, DELICACIE OF WORLDLY
MENS DELIGHTS] Contrarie to the
delights of good men, who, renouncing the
world, haue fixed their delight in God. Of
ſuch the Apoſtle warned his Diſciple,
2. *Tim.* 3, Know that in the laſt dayes there
ſhall be dangerous times, and there shall be
men louing themſelues, couetous, loftie,
proude, blaſphemous, diſobeying Parents,
vngratefull, wicked, without affection,
without peace, laying crimes vpon others,
incontinent, rude, without benignitie, traitours, ſawcie, puffed vp, and louers of plea-
ſures more then of God, hauing the appea-
rance of pietie, but denying the vertue
therof. Avoide theſe.

Lin. 17. FORTIE OR FIFTIE
YEARES] *Luther* fell from the Catholike
Church anno 1517. Yet there was no pub-
like

like profession of Lutheranisme , or libertie, so soone.

Pag. 22. lin. 5. A CITIE SET VPON
AN HILL] *Mat.* 5. 14. 15. Where also of
the light of it : and, *Marc.* 4. 21. *Luc.* 11.
33.

Pag. 22. lin. 12. THIRTEENE
HVNDRED YEARES] England first
received the Christian religion from *Ioseph
ab Arimathia*, that buried Christ and came
after into England , preached there the
Gospell, and baptized them that beleeued,
as *Gildas Sapiens*, wrighteth, *Venerable Bede,
Polydore, Vergill,* and others: And *Baronius, at
the yeare of our Lord* 35. *num.* 3.

But more fully it was converted 180.
yeares after Christ in the reigne of King
Lucius , by *S. Fugatius* and *S. Damian* , sent
thither from *Rome* by *Eleutherius Pope.*

And also 400. yeares after that, by *S. Augustine* and his fellowes , sent thither by
S. Gregorie the great, about the yeare 600.

Pag. 22. §. 9. I HOLD AND BELEEVE
ALL THAT THE CATHOLIKE AND
APOSTOLIKE CHVRCH] If any one
come to you and bring not this doctrine,
receiue him not into the house , nor say to
him, God saue you. 2. *Ioan.* 1.

Ambrose. He denyeth Christ that confesseth not all, things that are Christs.

Hi-

*Hilarius.*It becommeth the ministers of truth to professe true things.

Aug. lib. de fide ad Petrum, cap. 39. Most firmely hold, and no way doubt, that every Heretike, or Schismatike, baptized in the name of the Father, and of the Sonne, and of the holy Ghost, if he be not aggregated to the Catholike Church, how many almesdeeds soever he doe, although he shed his bloud for the name of Christ, can by no meanes be saved: For to every man, that holdeth not the vnitie of the Catholike Church, neither Baptisme, nor Almes, how copious soever it be, nor death for the name of Christ vndergone, can be of any value to salvation, as long as he persevereth in that hereticall, or schismaticall pravitie, which leadeth vnto death.

Cap. 40. Most firmely hold and no way doubt, that not all which are baptized within the Catholike Church shall receiue life everlasting, but they which having received baptisme do liue a right, that is, who haue abstained them from the vices and concupiscences of the flesh. For the kingdome of Heaven, as Infidels, Heretikes, and Schismatikes shall not haue it, so wicked Catholikes can never possesse it.

*Vincentius Lyrenensis.*He is a true and naturall Catholike, that loveth the truth of
God,

God, the Church, the bodie of Chrift, who before the divine religion, before the Catholike faith, preferreth nothing, not the authoritie of any man, not loue, nor wit, nor eloquence, nor Philofophie; but defpifing all thefe, and there remaining fixed and fteedfaft, whatfoever vniverfally, from all antiquitie, he knoweth the Catholike Church to haue holden, that only he decreeth with himfelfe to hold and beleeue; and whatfoever afterward he perceiveth new and vnheard of to haue beene introduced by any one, otherwife then all, or contrarie to all the Saints, that he vnderftandeth to appertaine, not to Religion, but rather to temptation.

Lin. 4. GODLY CEREMONIALL RIGHTS] He that will condemne the ceremonies of Gods Church, let him firft trie if he can himfelfe leade a humane life amongft civill men without all ceremonie; let him feparate all fubftance from his accidents and fee whether it be worth the looking vpon. As in accidents there is difference, and fome make the fubftance to be better accepted then others, for examples fake, in colour, in favour, &c. So ceremonies doe, according as they are better or worfe, fet out the fubftance of the thing wherabout they be vfed. What is any artificers

I 3

cers

cers worke, although according to the sub-
stantiall part it be wholly finished, vnlesse it
be also polite. As God gaue to his people in
the old law precepts *Morall* , *Iudiciall*, and
Ceremoniall , so in the new testament there
are *Doctrine, Sacraments,* with their ceremonies, and *Discipline. Deut.6.* Keepe the precepts of thy Lord God, & the testimonies,
and ceremonies , which he hath commanded thee .

    Lin.13. CONTINVALL PRAYER]
Luc. 18. Wee must alwaies pray and never
faile: *Vtinā dirigantur viæ meæ, ad custodiendas
iustificationes tuas. Dirige Domine Deus meus in
cōspectu tuo viam meam.* Be instant in prayer,
watching therin, with thanks-giving. *Coloss.*
4.2. Pray without intermissiō.1. *Thess.*5.17.
*Psalm.*24. *Dirige me in veritate tua & doce me
. . . . . . dirige me in semitam rectam.* 89. *Opus
manuum nostrarum dirige.*

    Pag.23. §.10. FROM A RESOLVTE
HEART] No temptation doth so soone
seaze, or overthrow, him that is well resolved, and constantly settled in his minde; as
it doth him that is doubtfull and wavering.
2.*Cor.*8.12. If the will be prompt : according to what it hath, it is accepted.

    The works of our will that spring imme-
diately from it, cannot suffer violence from
any power, but in those workes or acts that
                      are

Psalm.
118.
Psal. 5.

are of other powers, commanded by the will, shee may suffer violence.

S. Thomas. 1.2.*Q.6. A.4.* Violence, Feare, Concupiscence, Ignorance, &c. May assaile the will, but, cannot overcome it, to cause it doe a thing: for that no agent in his action can be compelled. Violence, and feare, may diminish, and make an act lesse voluntarie; Concupiscence ofter encreasseth, and maketh it more voluntarie, Ignorance maketh it, not to be voluntarie; but not involuntarie, or against ones will.

He that doth but foresee the dangers, is lesse strooken by the dint of them. The best thing, saith the Apostle, is to establish the heart with grace. And *Ecclesiastic.*2. 1. Comming to the service of God stand in iustice, and feare, and prepare thy soule for temptation. Our wavering mind addeth forces to the temptation. ^{Heb. 13. 9.}

Prosper. 3. de vita contemplativa. Every man, vntill by certaine definition he confirme himselfe in that he hath chosen; being as it were in a forked way of vncertaine deliberation, is torne in peeces by the very diversitie of wills. Vertue exhorteth, and provoketh a man, that, all ambiguitie of definition deposed, he vndertake his spirituall purpose, tha h confide, not in his owne possibilitie, but in the

I 4   mi-

miferation of our Lord, to perfever in the labour of his conflict vndertaken, 1. *Theff.* 5. 24. He is faithfull that hath called you, who alfo will doe it. They that hope in our Lord shall change their ftrength, they shall affume wings like Eagles , they sh ll runne and not labour, they shall walke and not faint .

Efai.40. *31.*

Pag.24.lin.6. AFFECTION OF WIFE OR CHILDREN] *Luc.* 14. 26. If any one come to me and hate not his father, and mother, and wife, and children, and brothers , and fifters , and moreover his owne foule , he can not be my difciple. *Idem, Matth.*10. 37.

Pag. 25. §. 11. BY COVNTRIE FARRE DIVIDED] Shee being of *Acton*, by *Long Melforde* , in the countie of *Southfolke.*

TRVE GENEROSITIE] *Seneca lib. de moribus.* The nobilitie of the mind is the generofitie of the fenfe: The nobilitie of bodie,a generous minde.

NOT IGNOBLE] Evill nobilitie it is , that by pride maketh a man ignoble before God. *Aug. ferm.* 127. *de tempore. Summa ingenuitas ifta eft , in qua fervitus Chrifti comprobatur. Off. Agath.* 5. *Feb.*

Pag. 25. §. 12. lin. 6. EDWARD THE FIRST] This was the fonne of *Henry* the
third

third, King of England, and beganne his raigne the 16. of November, 1272. the fame day that his father dyed.

Pag. 26. §. 13. lin. 8. & lin. 11. HENRIE THE 8.] By the death of his father King *Henrie* the 7. began to raigne the 22. of Aprill 1509. Of one *Arthur Plantagenet*; there is mention in *Stovv*, at the fourth yeare of this King, anno 1513.

Pag. 27. §. 14. FORCED TO GIVE OVER] In fuites of Law it is not enough to haue a iuft caufe, or good title; but a man muft haue a good head, vnderftanding and infight in the lawes, abilitie and ftrength of body to follow the fuite by ones felfe; and aboue all other things a good purfe that will never be drawne drie.

Quam præftat, pro Deo, renuntiaffe mundo: Matt. 5.
   Auferenti tunicam, dimififfe pallium!   40.

Pag. 28. §. 15. GOD FORGIVE THEM] *Pater dimitte illis*. He prayeth for his enemies, according to that; *Matth.* 5. 44. Loue your enemies, wish well to thofe that curfe you, doe good to thofe that hate yee, and pray for thofe that perfecute and reproach yee. *Idem Lu. 6. 28. & ad Rom.* 12. 14.

Bleffed are they that fuffer perfecution for iuftice, becaufe theirs is the Kingdome of heaven. You are bleffed when they shall curfe you, and shall perfecute yee, and
     I 5   fpeake

speake all evill againſt yee, for me , lying againſt the truth. *Matth.5.* 10. *Idem. Luc.6.* 22.

If ſinning, and beaten yee ſuffer : what glorie is that? but if doing well yee ſuſtaine patiently,this is grace with God. 1. *Pet.* 2. 20. *&* 3. 14. *&* 4. 14.

Pag. 29. lin. 20. I LEAVE IN MO- DESTIE TO SPEAKE OF] If I pre- ſume to ſpeake a little , I hope I ſhall not ſin

2. Cor. againſt modeſtie : *Veritatem enim dicam.*
12.6.

First,for his Eloquence he was eſteemed, where he was knowne, for an other *Cicero;* and ſo much grace was in his ſpeeche , as therewith he was able preſently to appeaſe whatſoever tumult or commotion riſen among the people . In his yonger yeares when Queene *Elizabeth* came in progreſſe to Worceſter , he made there an oration before her, at the requeſt of the citie , for which they gaue him 20. pounds : The Queene commanded alſo to giue him a re- ward , but Sir *Robert Dudley* making an- ſwere, Madame, he is a Papiſt,he Loſt that reward .

Alwaies going in circuit with the Iud- ges of Worceſtershiere he employed the ſpare time he had , in viſiting the priſons, ſpeaking with every of the priſoners in particular,exhorting them,and giving them
coun-

counsell how to answere in their owne
causes, the best way for their good, and giving them encouragement. Those that by
their cause he saw would receiue sentence
of death, he would both before, and after,
dispose to die in the most Christian máner,
and if he saw any good to be done , and
that a Priest were to be had without immi-
nent danger they should not want him :
according to his abilitie he would also releeue them with his worldly goods.

For many yeares after his death , if any
thing were done in the commonwealth a-
gainst iustice in commutation, or distribu-
tion: no other voice was heard among the
people then this alone : things were not
thus when M.r *Bel* was living, nor would
not be if now he lived.

Briefly, I may iustly returne vpon him all
those commendations which he giveth
Sir Iohn Throkmarton in the §. 16. Pag. 29.
For he had in himselfe whatsoever he required in his children , or commended in
his friends.

Pag. 31.§.17.lin.5. To wards God so
Religious] Rightly doth he call her
Religious, that did not cótent herselfe with
exercise of ordinarie perfection, but aspired
to the proper exercises of religious professió;
de-

delighting in the abnegation of her felfe, and corporall aufterities , and in the fame inftructing her children : being fo much given to prayer, as befides the office of our B. Lady, of the Dead, the Graduall, and Penitentiall Pfalmes, Hymnes, Litanies, Office of the holy Ghoft , and H. Croffe, prayers of the Manuall , which were her daily exercife: in the time of lent she would never fleepe before shee had read over the whole Paffion of our Saviour, according to one of the 4. Evangelifts, in Latin ; which she vnderftood well. Living many yeares a widow with all the care of a great familie. Shee meditated notwitftanding continually the Law of God, reading alfo, with licence of her ghoftly father , the new Teftament, with the Rhemes notes, *Sir Thomas Mores* workes, and other bookes of Controverfies verie much, by which shee often defended the Catholike faith againft the hereticall Minifters that would come to diffuade her from it ; but found her ever immoveable, as a Rock. *Ecclefiaftic.* 26. Everlafting foundations vpon a folid rocke the Commands of God in the heart of a holy woman : Whofe prayfe in holy Scripture is manifold. *Prouerb.* 11. 16. A gracious woman shall get glorie. 12. 4. A woman of vertue is a crowne to her housband. 14. 1. A wife wo-

man

man buildeth vp her houfe;and 31.30.The
woman that feareth God shall be prayfed.
18. 22. He that hath found a good wife,
hath found a great good,and shall get good
will of our Lord. *Ecclefiaftic*.25.11. Bleffed
is he that dwelleth with a prudent woman.
26.1.Bleffed is the man of a good woman,
and double is the number of his dayes.The
gift of God is a woman filent and prudent,
and no change is to be given for a well inftructed foule. 16. Grace aboue Grace,is a
modeft & faithfull woman, and no weight
is worth her continent foule. The Sunne
rifing in the higheft of Our Lord, and the
beautie of a good woman in the ornament
of her houfe. 7.26. The woman that honoreth her owne man shal appeare wife before
all. Depart not from a wife & good womã,
for her grace is aboue gold. 25.1. Beautifull before God,and before men: The con-
cord of brothers : Friendship of neighbours: Man and wife that agree well together, &c.

Line 7. VOWED CHASTITIE]
That is, conjugall chaftitie,or as they vow
that are of the third order of *S. Francis* in
the world,and amiddeft the cares therof.

I REQVIRE AND CHARGE YOV]
That is here charged, is like the charge of
old *Tobias*, laid vpon his fonne. *Tob*. 4. 3.

Sonne

Sonne if I dye, burie me, and defpife not
thy mother : Honour her all the dayes of
thy life , and doe vvhat is pleafing to her,
and doe not make her fad,&c.

Pag.33.§.18. CONTINVALL PRAYER]
Againe, the author vrgeth this point, as a
thing for this life moft neceffarie. Aske and
it shall be given. *Mat.*7.7. & 21.22.

PROVINCIALL DARKENESSE]
This terme he vfeth becaufe in refpect of
the vvhole Catholike Church, from vvhich
it received the light of faith , this Kingdome, as alfo any other, is but a Province;
and, as it is a province in the refpect of the
light , fo alfo in refpect of the darkeneffe,
which it hath falne into by shutting it felfe
from the vvhole.

So in regard of *S. Francis* whole Order,
fpread through all the vvorld , this Kingdome is called the Province of England.

Pag. 35. §. 19. FERVENCIE OF
ZEALE] The firft condition he requireth
in Prayer, is FAITH] wherof *Iacob* 1. 6.
Let him pray in faith, not wavering : for he
that ftraggereth is like a vvaue of the fea,
moved and toffed vvith the vvind. Let not
that man thinke he shall receiue any thing
from God. *Marc.*11.24. *Luc.*11.9. *Ioan.*14.
13. & 16. 23.

Prayer

Prayer is an afcent of the minde to God. *Damafcen. lib. 3. de Fide, cap.* 24.

Auguftin. Prayer is a pious affect of the minde directed to God. *Vigilate & orate vt non intretis in tentationem. Cyrillus.* Chrift prayeth with 3. companions, fo muft we; vvith *Peeter,* that is, faith; vvith *Iames,* that is, fequeftration from the vvorld, vvhich to vs is fupplated; *Iohn,* that is, fervour of grace and Charitie. Frequent prayer our Saviour taught praying the fame thing 3. times. Iterate not a vvord in thy prayer. *Ecclefiafticus* 7. That is, make it fo full as thou needeft not to fupplie that vvas by negligence omitted, & 53. The prayer of him that humbleth himfelfe penetrateth the cloudes, &c. C H A R I T I E] He that turneth away his eares from hearing the law, his prayer fhall become execrable. F E R V E N C I E] The end of prayer, well made, is more fervent then the beginning, for the motion encreafeth the heate *Ecclef.* 7. Better is the end of prayer then the beginning. Of Prayer *Clem. Alex. l. 4. & 7. ftrom.* In the laft acclamations of our prayer we ftretch forth head and hands, we ftirre our feet to heaven, by promptitude and alacritie of fpirit flying towards the effence, of which none layes hold but by intellectuall touch: we ftriue together with our fpeech to

raife

raife our bodies aboue the ground : we
ftraine our erected and eleuated foules by
defire of better and better things to goe
forward into the holy of holies, through
greatneffe of courage, fcorning to be kept
downe by the clogge of the bodie.

Pag. 35. §. 20. Of the Effects
of Prayer] Let. *Moyfes* or *Elias* fpeake.
To winne in fight; to ftop the plague ; to
binde the cloudes, and let them loofe. Aske
Helifæas, or king *Ezechias*, what it is. *S. Peeter*,
S. Gregorie, *S. Anthonie of Padua*, fome one,
or all the multitude of Thaumaturgs, fince
Chrift , or preaching of the Gofpell fhall
declare . And of the moft fweet comforts
therof, beleeue the Author here, or feeke by
experience in thy felfe, which better is, to
finde it out: enquier among the hardly nu-
merable number of Extatike Saints within
the feraphicall Order even from *S. Francis*
and *S. Giles*, vntill thefe times, wherin the
B. Mother *Louyfa* liues and many moe, of
little leffer note . בנשי Rapt, extafie, which
is an abftraction and alienation , and illu-
ftration , proceeding from God, by which
God draweth backe the foule, from aboue,
falne to inferiour things, againe from inferiour to fuperiour, and fo fhee is left halfe
dead bereaft of the fenfes . *Pythagoras* . If
thou, leauing the bodie, doeft paffe freely
in

Exod.
17.
3. Reg.
17.
4 Reg.6
17. &
20.

in to the skie, thou shalt be an immortall
God, dead to this world. *Cicero*. When the
soule is come to that state which is the highest degree of contemplatiue perfection,
then is shee ravished from all created like-
nesses, and vnderstandeth, not by acquisite
species, but by looking into the Ideas, and
by the light of them, knoweth all things:
of which light *Plato* saith, very few men in
this life are made partakers.

כונה. Attention or intention, is of so
much force in worke, as the more secret Di-
vines doe say, that by words and prayers,
nothing can be done without intention.
Hence is the commun Proverbe; Imagina-
tion maketh chance, as *Avicenna*, and others
write. Hence the Apostle, I will pray in spirit, I will pray in mind, I will sing in spirit, I
will sing also in mind: insinuating that vnlesse the mind attend, the prayer is none,
and altogether voide. Although working
in holy things, the defect of this attention
doe withstand vs, because the reasonable
number and harmonie most efficacious in
worke, is wanting: yet a greater obstacle it
is to vs, when our domestike works are
contrarie to the sacred works. *Isaias* 1.15.
When yee shall multiplie prayers I will not
heare, because your hands be full of bloud.
In things of Religion, no worke of any

K   mer-

mervailous efficacie can be done , vnlesse
some of the supernall powers be present,
spectatour, and accomplisher of the worke.
Humane nature can neither vndertake
speech, nor prayer of God , without God,
nor yet doe any divine worke without him:
for it is so weake and dull, as it hath no remedie of its nullitie, but only some portion
of divine light cōming from aboue , without which no divine thing is done by vs.
Iamblicus de Ægyptiorum mysterijs.

Those that can draw any thing more of
the spectacle of God, or of good, doe oftentimes , as it were, oversleeping themselves at the most beautifull vision , dye.
.... Then shalt thou behold it, when
thou mayest haue nothing to say of it : for
the knowledge and contemplation therof,
is silence, and rest of all the senses ; for he
that hath vnderstood it can vnderstand
nothing else, nor can he speculate any thing
else, that hath seene it, nor heare of anything
else, nor moue his bodie at all : for all the
correption of the corporall senses and motions resteth . But searching over all the
minde and all the soule, it enlighteneth and
withdraweth from the bodie, and changeth
the whole into the essence of God . For
possible it is, O my sonne ! that the soule be
deified in the bodie of a man, when it hath
                                          seene

seene the beautie of good , which is, to be
deified .... oftentimes the mind
flyeth out of the soule, and at that time the
soule neither seeth nor heareth, but is like a
brute beast . *Hermes Trismegist. clavis , fol.*
129. *a,* 6. *&* 132. *a.* 6.

Plato in Tymæo. The soule that often,and
with greatest intention contemplateth divine things, with such nourishment waxeth
so strong , and able to get out , as it over-groweth the bodie, and overgoeth it more
then the nature of the bodie is able to
beare , and with the most vehement tossings therof, doth sometimes,as it were,fly
out of it, or as it were, seeme to dissolve it.
Marsilius Ficinus de studioforum sanitate tuenda, lib,1.cap.4.

S.Bernard. *serm.* 52. *de modo bene viuendi.*
When in the sight of God thou singest
Psalmes, and Hymnes, handle that in thy
minde which thou singest with thy voice.
Let thy mind agree with thy voice,let it accord with thy tongue ; doe not thinke one
thing and sing another . If thou sing one
thing in thy mind,and another in thy voice,
thou loosest the fruit of thy labour. If thy
bodie stand in the Church; and thy minde
wander abroade, thou loosest thy reward.
Whence it is said : This people honoureth
me with their lippes , and their heart , is

K 2   farre

farre from me. But as the Apostle saith I wil
sing in spirit, I will sing also in mind, I will
sing with mouth and heart. Good therfore
it is, alwaies to pray God with mind. It is
also good with sound of voice, and Hymnes, and Psalmes, and spirituall Cantikles
to gloriefie God. *Idem in meditationib. c.8.*

Ineffable is the dignation of the Diuine
bountie, that daily seeth vs wretches, a-
verting our eares, hardening our hearts,
and nevertelesse calleth vnto vs,saying: Returne 'prevaricatours to the heart, take
heed, looke to it, for I am God. In the
Psalme God speaketh to me, and I to him:
and yet when I say a Psalme, I attend not
whose Psalme it is. Therfore I doe great
iniurie to God, when I pray him to heare
my prayer, which I that make it doe not
heare: I pray him to attend to me, and I doe
neither attend to my selfe, nor him: but
which worse is, tossing vnprofitable and
vncleane things in my heart, I cast a horrible stinke before his face.

Isaias 46.
Psal 45.

Francischus Georgius Harmonia, Cant.3. mo-
dul.20. When we come once to the first &
highest, we must rest, & goe no farther, because farther then the highest, nothing can
be give: hereof *Ieremias*: Shee shall sit solita-
rie, & hold her peace, because shee hath e-
levated her selfe aboue her selfe. And *Da-*
vid,

Psal. 4.

vid: In peace,in the thing it selfe.wil I sleepe and rest: and againe *Psalm.*65.*vulgat.*64.

לך דמיה תהלה. Silence is thy prayse God in Syon . Which said shee must be silent, because shee is now come to the place where silence is , because there every one becommeth inward and most inward with the highest ; so that forgetting all exteriour things,and separate from them all,shee hath none to vvhom shee may speake, cōversing only vvith him before vvhom there is no speech required , because he beholdeth all things; and withall,because shee beholdeth and is delighted with those things, which if she would,she cannot expresse : hence therfore she must be silent, vnlesse by the command of her Prince shee manifest something to inferiours, according to the capacitie of them that are to receiue it, for their profit . As *S. Dionys.* saith of the Angels ; That they be declarers of the divine siléce, as cleere lights,interpreting that which is in secret, &c.

Pag. 36. lin. 7. Inprisonment in an innocent cavse] *Non pœna sed causa.* As death in an innocent cause, maketh a Martyr, so imprisonment and other sufferings in like cause,maketh a Confessour : in whose number I am verie confident, in the goodnesse of God, I may

place

150

place the Author of this Testament, who,
not onely in death, but all his life, and in e-
verie occasion, hath confessed Christ and
his Church with constancie and perseve-
rance. And the caution of the Divine
word; Praise not a man in his life, is, as it
were, a command to Praise him after life:
Praise him after his consummation.

S. Max.
hom. 59
2. de S.
Eusebio

Pag.37.§.21.lin.9. YOVR SEVERALL
CALLINGS] He speaketh of states, by
which men are setled in the world to become apt members in the bodie of the
common wealth; as Governours, or Magistrates, Doctors in Theologie, Law, Medi-
cine, or Practitioners in any of the sciences,
or liberall artes. Religious in any of the
Regular Orders, that serue the commonwealth in Preaching, administring Sacraments, Sacrifices, Prayers, Comforting the
afflicted, disposing to life everlasting the
dying, and all works of mercie: in any of
the severall states of the Plebeians, or the
Mechanike arts, whatsoever, and not alone
of those that the Prince - Apostles speake
of, vocation to the faith, 2. Pet.1.10. Doe
your endeavour brothers more and more,
by good works to make sure your calling
and election. Et Ephes. 4. I beseech you
walke worthily in the vocation wherin you
are called, &c. Yet of the former callings

lings *S. Paul* seemeth to haue admonished. I. *Cor.* 7. 20. Every one in what vocation he is called , in the same let him remaine : Thou art called, to be a servant , let it not trouble thee; but if thou canneft become a free-man doe in Gods name. He that in our Lord is called a servant, is our Lords free-man: And he that is called to be a free man is the servant of Chrift.

Pag. 37. §. 22. lin. 6. T I M E, A N E N E-M I E TO T H E T H R I F T O F A D I S-T R E S S E D C O N S C I E N C E] Riches, that are feldome gotten together with a good confcience, are with more danger of detriment to the confcience , gotten toge-ther in short time. *Matth.* 19. A rich man shall hardly enter into the kingdome of heaven. *id. Marc.* 10. *And Lu.* 6. Woe be to you rich men. Whence the Apoft. I. *Tim.* 6. 17. 18. Command the rich men of this world to giue eafily.

Every rich man is either vniuft , or the heire of some vniuft man. *Hieronym. lib. 2. in Ierem. cap.* 5. *paulo ante finem, & epift. ad Hedibiam. q.* I. *in medio.* All riches defcend from iniquitie , and vnleffe one man loofe, another cannot finde , whence that com-mon faying feemeth to me moft true ; That every rich man is either vniuft, or the heire of one vniuft.

B. *Lau-*

B. Laurent. Iustinian. said that riche men could not be saved but by Almesdeeds. We burne in Avarice, and disputing against money, lay open our lappes to gold, and nothing is enough for vs . What is said of the Megarens may well be applyed to the miserable churles : They build as if they were to liue euer, they liue as if they should die the next day. *Hieron. ad Geront. de monogamia. Tom.1.*

Not he that little hath, but he that much coveteth is poore. *Seneca, lib. de paupertate.*

No man liveth so poore as he was borne : *Seneca, lib. de providentia divina.*

Children of Adam ! a covetous, and ambitious kind, hearken ; What haue you to doe with earthly riches , and temporall glorie , which neither are indeed, nor are yours ? gold and siluer is it not earth , red and white, which only mans error maketh, or rather reputeth pretious ? If they be yours take them away with you. But when a man perisheth he shall take nothing with him , neither shall his glorie descend with him . True riches therfore is not vvealth, but vertues, vvhich the conscience carrieth vvith it , to make it rich for ever . *Bernard. serm. 4. de Aduentu Domini.*

Whom God enricheth no man shall make poore. *Cyprian. Tom. 1. epist. 2.*

Those

Thofe only are good riches which we haue in hope and expectation. *Greg. Naz. orat. de Machab.*

Neither is any thing a greater terrour to vs , then left we fhould feare any thing more then God. *id. ibid.*

He is abundantly rich, that with Chrift is poore. *Hieron. ep. ad Heliodor. de vita folitaria. Eft quæftus magnus, pietas cum fufficiētia.* 1. Tim. 6.6.

The beautie of riches, is not in the facks of riche men, but in the poores fuftenance. *Amb. lib.7. epift.* 44.

The Bifhops glorie is to provide for the poores wealth, the ignominie of all Priefts is to looke only to their owne riches: *Hiero. ad Nepotian. Tomo* 1.

To the faithfull the whole world is riches. *Amb. lib.1. de Iacob. & vita beata c. vlti. Tom.* 4.

Povertie and riches, are two names of vvant and fatietie, neither is he rich that vvanteth fomething, nor he poore that vvanteth not. *Amb. Tom.3. l.7. epift.* 44. Victuals and cloathing are Chriftians riches. *Hieronym. ad Paulinum. Tom.3.*

To me all plentie vvhich is not my God is vvant. *Aug. Conf. l. 13, c.* 8.

Pag.38. §.23. lin. 6. INSTRVCTED IN LEARNING] And the reafon is, becaufe knowledge is a great helpe to ferue

K 5   God

God with; for as nothing is in the vnderstanding which was not first in the senses,
so nothing is in the will which was not first
in the vnderstanding. Discipline and sciéce
are two wings that with swift flight carrie a
man to heaven.

*Ambros.in offic.expos.Psal.*118.Life is to be
sought before Doctrine ....Good life,
even without doctrine hath grace, Doctrine without life hath no integritie ....
Againe, speaking of morall, and mysticall
things, he saith : In those is life, in these
knowledge : so that,if thou require perfection , let neither life be without knowledge, nor knowledge without life, let one
helpe another. The end of all knowledge
is to giue a man the true knowledge of his
creatour that accordingly and in truth he
may serue and worship him.

There is no secure ioy in knowing many
or hard things in the divine Writ , but in
keeping of the things that we know. *Greg.*
22. *Moral. c.4. in fine.*

As long as thou art ignorant so long must
thou learne ; and , if we beleeue the proverbe, as long as thou liuest. *Senec. lib.* 10.
epist. 77.

So great is the profunditie of Christian
letters , as I should daily profit in them, if
from my very infancie vntill decreped old
age,

age, at greatest leisure, with greatest diligence, and the best wit, I should endeavour to learne and apply my selfe to them alone. *Aug. ep. 3. Tom. 2.*

The studies of science without facts, I know not whether they doe not more involve vs. *Amb. lib. 1. offi. c. 26. in fine. Tom. 1. & lib. 2. c. 3. in medio.* Innocence, and science make a man blessed.

Pag. 33. §. 24. lin. 3. TRAYNED IN SCHOOLE TO LEARNING] Not only these two children, but of 12. 8. that lived; were, both sonnes and daughters, brought vp at schoole, all together till they vnderstood the latin tongue.

Pag. 39. §. 24. lin. 7. A GRATEFVLL ENTERTAINEMENT] Musike is not alonly so, but moreover, a thing celestiall and divine, aboue all the obiects of humane sense, and none doth so much raise the mind, or elevate the soule towards God, the chiefe and beginning of all order, of all mesure, and of all number, as this harmoniacall number, and therfore aboue all others, God is served with it in his Church; and how much it pleaseth God, so much it offendeth the divels and casteth them farre off. Consult *David* through all his facts and writings.

Mu-

Mufike ioyeth the heart, forbid it not. *Eccli.* 40. 20. & 32. 4.

Pag. 39. §. 26. lin. 1. I T E M I F F R A N-C I S] This was his firft fonne, aud dyed in childhood. I gather hence that the Author was devoted to *S. Francis,* considering that none of all his anceſtors was called by that name. This §. and the 27. and 28. were noted, as it were left vnperfeᵴ, or other wife ordained.

Pag. 41. §. 29. lin. 4. I A C T A S V P E R D O M I N V M, &c.] This was the Authors Motto, or Devize. The §. 30. and 31. were noted as before.

Pag. 44. §. 32. lin. 17. Mᵉ F R A N C I S D A N I E L L.] Here, in gratitude, and for confcience fake, I muſt acknowledge my felfe to haue perpetuall obligation to this my vncle, not only for 6. yeares of my education, but alfo for his aſſiſtance and furtherance to put me into the courfe and ſtate of life in which I am, and by the grace of God shall and will die.

The §. 33. Goeth noted as before, and where a word is left out in it, lin 21. I ſuppo-fe the Anthor would haue faid, *Vniuſtly,* but durſt not, considering the dangers of that time.

Pag. 46. §. 34. I N M O S T A M P L E M E R I T E] This §. the Author had him-felfe selfe noted with a hand monftrant, in the margent, which gaue me the firft motion of dedicating this worke to whom it is, and ought to be dedicated, as is mentioned in the epiftle dedicatorie. Here I cannot but commend and extoll the gratitude of the Author to every man of whom he had at any time receiued a benefit, according to the Apoftolicall precept. *Coloff.* 3. 15. *Grati eftote.* Vpon which precept reade *S.Bernards* fermon, entituled by him: *Againft the moft vile vice of ingratitude. Bern. ferm. de diverfis, pag.* 403. 404. *&c.* This §. was alfo noted as the others, 4. lines before the end.

Pag. 47. §. 35. lin. 7. TO VSE TRVTH] 3. *Efdras* 3. Truth furpaffeth, and over-cometh all things *&* 4. And all faid; great is the truth. *David* 116. The truth of our Lord remaineth for ever, and 117. Lord, all thy commands, all thy wayes, the beginning of thy words, are all truth. *Prou.*26. The de-ceiptful tongue loveth not truth. *Zach.*8.16. Everie one fpeake truth. *Matth.* 22. 16. *& Luc.*20.21. Thou teacheft the way of God in Truth. *& Ioan.* 14. 6. I am the way, truth, and life. *Ephef.*4.25. Laying away lyes, fpeake truth every one with his neighbour. 2. *Cor.*13. 8. We cannot any thing againft Truth. What more? all the new and old Teftament is full of the commendations of truth:

truth : and as much in the reprooving of
lying, diffimulation, and falshood. *Coloff.3.8.*
Lay away all Anger, Indignation. Malice,
Blafphemie, Foule fpeech, ly not one to another. *Idem, Ephef.4.13. & 1. Pet.2. 1.* Laying
away all malice, and all deceit, and diffimulation, and envie and detraction. *Et Heb.12.*
What defireth the foule more ftrongly then
truth. *Aug.tract. 26.in Ioã.* No man can long
beare a fained perfon : for feigned things
fall foone to their owne nature. Things that
are borne vp by truth arife from folid
ground and by time proceed to better and
better. *Seneca de clementia, lib.1.*

§.35.lin. 15. PLEASE GOOD MEN]
Paul.ad Gal. 10. If yet I should pleafe men, I
should not be the fervant of Chrift. Know
this moft certainly, that no man can pleafe
God and wicked men, your brotherhood
therfore make account that fo much more
it hath pleafed Almightie God, as it knoweth it felfe to haue difpleafed perverfe men.
*Greg.l.8. Regift. Indict. 3.c.36. Principibus pla-
cuiffe viris non infima laus eft.*

Pag.47.§.36.lin.1. DELIGHT NOT
IN RIBAWDRIE] *Apoft. ad Ephef.* 5.3.
Fornication and all maner of vncleanneffe,
or avarice , let it not be fo much as named
amongft you:or filthineffe, or foolish talke,
or fcurrilitie, which doe not appertaine to
the

the purpoſe:but rather thanksgiving.Speak
no baudie thing,for by little and little shame
with words is shaken off. *Senec l.de moribus.*
Matth. 12. 34. From the abundance of the
heart the mouth ſpeaketh. *Idem,Luc.*6.45.

Pag.48. §.37. MAKE CHOICE OF
HVMILITIE] *Prou.*15.33. Before glorie goeth humilitie. And 29.23. The pride
of a man shall humble him: and the humble of ſpirit shall attaine glorie , *&* 13.10.
Among the proude are alwaies contentiõs.
And 15.25. The houſe of the Proude our
Lord will overthrow. *Deut.* 17. 12. The
proude that will not obey the Prieſt or
Iudge,let him die.Before a fall goeth pride *Prou.*
and before a ruine,loftineſſe of ſpirit.Pride 16.18.
is not greatneſſe, but a ſwelling,& that that
ſwelleth ſeemeth great , but is not ſound.
Aug.ſerm.26.de temp. So great is the vtilitie
of human humilitie,as by his owne example
the divine ſublimitie would cõmend it(and
that moſt of all appeared in the washing of
Iudas the traitours feet.) For Proude man
had for ever beene loſt , vnleſſe humble
God had ſought him out. *Aug.tract.55.in*
Ioann. Behould O man ! what God is become for thee . Acknowledge at laſt the
doctrine of humilitie , even before thy
Doctour ſpeake. Thou wert once in Pa-
radice ſo eloquent, as to every living ſoule
thou

thou couldeſt giue a name. And for thee
thy creator,loe,lyeth an infant in a manger
and calleth not ſo much as his owne mother by her name. Thou, in the moſt ſpa-
cious orchard of fruitfull wood diddeſt
looſe thy ſelfe, neglecting obedience. He
obeying came mortall into the wide world;
that dying he might ſeeke the dead. Thou
being man wouldeſt become God , that
thou mighteſt periſh : he being God would
become mã to find out what had periſhed.
Humane pride did ſo much depreſſe thee,
as nothing but the diuine gràce could ſub-
levate thee. *Aug.Tom.10.ſerm.25.de temp.in
medio*.

Thoſe that of our Lord IESVS CHRIST
haue learned to be milde and humble of
heart, doe profit more in conſidering and
praying,then in reading and hearing. *Aug.
Epiſt.* 112. He that without humilitie doth
good works,carrieth duſt in the wind.*Aug.
ſerm.70.ad fratres in eremo.*

There is no other way that leadeth vnto
life then humilitie, which is by him defended, that, as God,ſeeth our footſteps,and
the ſame is the firſt humilitie, the ſecond
humilitie, the third humilitie, and as often
as thou ſhouldeſt aske me I would ſay the
ſame thing ; not becauſe there be not other
precepts to be ſaid : but becauſe vnleſſe
hu-

humilitie doe goe before , and waite vpon,
and follow all things that we doe, both the
things propoſed vs to looke into, and things
appoſed vs to ſticke vnto , and things impoſed vs to repreſſe vs : when we now reioyce of any good thing done: Pride wreſts
it all out of our hands. *Aug.epiſt.* 57.

A very mervailous thing it is, when humilitie of manners raigneth in the hearts of
the ſublime . Whence yee may thinke that
all the potent, when they ſauour of humilitie, they attaine the top of vertue, eſtraged,
and ſet, as it were, a farre off, and rightly by
this vertue they eftſoones pleaſe our Lord:
becauſe they humbly offer him that ſacrifice which mightie and potent men can
hardly get. It is a moſt ſubtile art of living
to hould height, and depreſſe glorie; to be
in power, and not know that we be power-
full; by beſtowing of good things, to know
ones ſelfe to be potent , and in repaying of
hurt , to be ignorant of all the value of
power . Rightly therfore of ſuch is ſaid,
Iob 36. 5. God caſteth not away the potent,
being himſelfe alſo potent : For he deſireth
to imitate God who adminiſtreth the
height of power more buſily in other mens
profits then elevated in his owne prayſes :
who being put over others, deſireth to profit them, and not to be aboue them . The

L   ſwel-

swelling of loftinesse is a crime, the order
of power none. Power God giveth, but
the elation of power, the malice of our
mind hath invented. Let vs take away that
which of our owne we brought, and the
things are good which of Gods gift we
posesse. *Creg.lib.26.Moral.c.*24.

Pag. 48. §. 38. ENTERTAINE
ALL MEN] *Leviticus* 19.31. Before the
hoarie headed arise, and honour the presence of the old man. *Prou.*22.2. The rich
and poore God made them both.

Pag. 48. §.39. lin.3. AMONG WISE
MEN] *Prou.*1. The wise man hearing will
become wiser. 3.*Reg.*10.8. Blessed are thy
servants that stand before thy face, alwaies
hearing thy wisedome. *Prou.*10. 13. In the
wise mans lippes is wisedome found, & 11.
2. Wher humilitie is, there is wisedome.

Lin.6. SVCH SHALL THEY BE
IVDGED TO BE) *Psalm.* 17. With the
holy thou shalt be holy: and with the man
that is innocent thou shalt be innocent.
With the Elect thou shalt be elected; and
with the perverse perverted.

Pag. 49. §. 40. BE NOT RASH]
Define no doubts, but hould thy sentence
in suspence: Affirme nothing without experience; for everie thing that hath appa-
rence of truth is not forthwith true; as also
what

what at firſt did ſeeme incredible is not ſtill falſe. Truth ſometimes retaineth the face of a lye, and a lye is hid vnder colour of truth. *Seneca, de 4. virtutibus.* And againe: Let nothing be ſuddaine to thee but looke into all things before hand ; for he that is prudent, ſaith not, I neuer thought that this would haue beene, becauſe he doubteth not, but expecteth; nor doth he ſuſpect, but taketh heed. Enquire the cauſe of every deed, and when thou haſt found the beginning, thou ſhalt thinke vpon the end.

Betweene an angry, and a mad man, there is but one dayes difference; the one is ever mad, the other every day angrie. *Seneca, lib.de moribus.*

Pag.49. §.41. Vſɛ ꜰᴇw woʀᴅꜱ] *Proverb.* 10.19. In much ſgeech ſinne will not be wanting : and he that keepeth his lippes, ſhall be vnderſtanding. As choʒen ſilver, is the iuſt mans tongue.

Let thy opinions be iudgements, vagabond cogitations and like to dreames receiue not ; in which if thy mind take delight, when thou haſt done and diſpoſed of all, thou remaineſt ſad : but let thy cogitation be ſtable and certaine, whether it deliberate, ſearch out, or contemplate, let it not depart from truth. Let not thy ſpeech

be

be vaine, but let it either persuade, or moué, or comfort, or command. Praise sparingly, dispraise more sparingly, for overmuch praise is as reprehensible as immoderate dispraise; that, is suspected of flatterie; this, of evill nature, or malignitie. *Seneca, lib. de 4. virtutibus.*

Loue silence, where much speech is, there is oftentimes lying; where lying, there is sinne. The speech sheweth what the man is. In the mouth of the Priest or Religious let never any word be, wherin the name of Christ soundeth not. *Tom. 4. epist. Euseb. ad Damas. de morte Hieronymi, in medio.*

WITH DISCRETION] *Coloss. 4. 6.* Your speech alwaies gracious, with a graine of salt: that you may know how to answere every man.

Yong man, speake when there is need of thee; if thou be twice asked, let thine answer haue a head. *Ecclesiastic. 32. 9.* According to the septuagint: Bring thy answer to a briefe sūme or answere cōpendiously.

Vse thy eares ofter then thy tongue, and whatsoever thou art to say, say to thy selfe before thou say it to others. *Seneca, lib. de moribus.*

§. 42. BE NOT CVRIOVS] Nothing is sweeter to men, then to speake of other mens things, and to haue care of
other

other mens matters, chiefly if it chance that they be prevented with loue or hatred towards some : from whom alwaies the truth is hidden, or, at least obscured . *Greg. Naz. in Apolog.*

Only obserue thy selfe , and keepe thy soule very vvarily . He that thinketh him-selfe to stand, let him looke he doe not fall. What seest thou a mote in thy brothers eye, and doest not see the beame in thine owne eye? *Deut. 4. 9. 1. Cor. 10. 11. Matt. 7. 3.*

O man that iudgest, thou art inexcusable, for in iudging another thou condemnest thy selfe , doing the same things that thou spendest thy iudgement vpon. *Rom. 2.*

§. 43. BE SECRET AND SILENT] *Prou.* 25. 9. Reveale not the secret of an-other. *Id.* 31. לי ייר. לי ייר. *Isaias* 24. 16. My secret to my selfe, my secret to my selfe. *Ecclesiasticus,* 32. 5. Where others hearken , povvre not out speech , and vvith importunitie haue not a vvill to seeme vvise.

Pag. 50. §. 44. lin. 3. LOOKE TO YOVR CALLING] *Ecclesiastic.* 3. 22. Seeke not things aboue thee. *Rom.* 11. 20. Be not over-vvise, but feare.

Lin. 4. LIVE IN OBEDIENCE] *Ephes.* 6. *Col.* 3, Children obey your Parents; Servants obey your Lors , and maisters. *Heb.* 13. Obey those that are put over yee.

L 3   *Tit.*

Tit. 3. 1, Admonish them to be subiect to their Princes and superiour powers, to obey their word, &c.

4.Reg.9
1. Par.
11. &
28.
Prou.21
Tob.12.
6.
1.Pet.2.
13.& 17 LEAVE KINGS AND THEIR CAVSES TO GOD] They be supreme governours vnder God. The Annoynted of God. The elected of God. Their hearts are in the hand of God, and he directeth their counsell. To hide the mysterie of the King is good: and to be subiect to him and honour him is commanded.

Prou.16
14. Lin. 8. HATH DESTROYED] The Kings anger is the messenger of death, and a wise man will appease it. In the light of the Kings face is life: and his good will is like a cloude of the evening raine.

Page 50. §. 45. VSE TEMPERANCE] *S. Aug. Tom.* 1, *l.* 1. *de lib. Arbit.* c. 13. Temperance is an affection brideling and keeping in the appetite from those things that are coveted with foule desire. *Et de morib. ecclesiæ Cath. lib.* 1. *c.* 15. Temperance is loue, yeelding it selfe entire to that is loued. Fortitude is loue, easily tolerating all things for that is loued. Iustice is loue, serving the beloved onely, and therfore rightly bearing rule. Prudence is loue, wisely selecting the things by which it is holpen, from those by which it is hindered. But this is not the loue of whosoever, but of God, that is, of the

the chiefeſt good, of the chiefeſt wiſedome, of the chiefeſt cōcord: therfore you may define it ſo, & ſay: temperance is loue keeping it ſelfe entire and vncorrupt to God, &c. And *Tom.4. l.1.83. Q.31.* Temperance is a firme and moderate rule of reaſon, over luſt and other, not right motions of the minde. The parts therof are continence, clemécie, and modeſtie. Continence, by which concupiſcence, by the governemét of counſel, is ruled. Clemencie, by which minds raſhly provoked and ſtirred vp to hatred of any one, are by gentleneſſe retained. Modeſtie, by which honeſt ſhame getteth cleere and ſtable authority. And *Q 61.* Prudence is knowledge of things to be deſired and to be ſhunned. Temperance, the refraining of concupiſcence from thoſe things that doe temporally delight, Fortitude is a firmitie of the mind againſt thoſe things that temporally moleſt vs . Iuſtice, which is diffuſed through them all , is the loue of God and our neighbour .

BEWARE OF DRVNKENNESSE] Prou.20 & 31. As a thing tumultuous, and that can keepe no ſecret forbidden by the Apoſtle. *Rom.13. & Gal. 5.* With drunkenneſſe is alwaies ioyned luxurie. *Hieron.l.3.in Ep.ad Gal.c.5.* I will never beleeue that the Drunkard is chaſt. *Hieron.in c.1. Ep.ad Titum, pag.246.*

§.46.

§. 46. lin. 2. THE RASH MAN] Is

Ecclef.
9.25.
Eccle.5.
odious in his vvord. Speake nothing rashly,
nor be hasty to bring forth thy word before
God, for God is in heaven and thou vpon
earth; therfore let thy vvords be few: for as
sleepe comes in multitude of businesse, so
the voice of the foole in multitude of
vvords.

Pag. 51. §. 47. BE CONSTANT]
Act. 23.11. Sap.5.1. The iust shall stand with
great constancie. A good man, vvhat he
thinketh he may honestly doe: although it
be laborious, he vvill doe it: although it be
losse to him, he vvill doe it: although it be
perillous, he vvill doe it: And againe, that
vvhich is dishonest, he vvill not doe it, although it bring in money, although it bring
pleasure, although it bring power. From
the honest he vvill by nothing be deterred:
to the dishonest he vvill by no hopes be in-
vited. *Seneca, lib. 10. epist. 77. in medio. Ho-
race. Iustum & tenacem propositi virum, &c.
Impauidum ferient ruinæ.*

Iacob. 1. 8. The man of two minds is vn-
constant in all his waies.

Sap. 4.12. The inconstancie of concupiscence, perverteth even the mind that is
without malice.

Eccl. 6.
& 9. &
12,
FAST IN FRIENDSHIP] There
is a friend only at table, a table fellow, but
doe

doe not thou forfake an old friend. A new
friend is like new wine . A friend cannot
be knowne in good, but in malice you shall
know him, &c.

Pag. 51. §. 48. VSE PATIENCE.] Pfal. 9.
The Poores patience will not be loft in the Prou. 19
end. A mans doctrine is knowne by hi, pa- Iacob 1
tience. In your patience you shall poffeffe
your foules. It hath a perfect worke: The
armes of the iuft are by giving vvay to o-
vercome. *Amb. lib. 1. off. cap. 5. Tom. 1.*

If any adverfitie befall thee, and it feeme
grievous and bitter to thee , beare it fo as
thou thinke nothing to haue befallen thee
but according to nature when thou readeft
naked was I borne, naked shall I go hence,
what our Lord gaue our Lord hath taken
away: and he had loft both goods and children, and thou shalt in all keepe the perfon
of a wife and iuft man, as he kept that faid:
As it pleafed our Lord fo is it done , be the
name of our Lord bleffed, &c. *Amb. lib. 1. off.
cap. 38.*

No man can be bleffed, no man becometh
a citizen of heaven , no man is conftituted
the friend of God , that among evils is
not found patient. *Aug. ferm. 32. ad fratres.*

Humane impatience will not haue the
patience of God . We wretches that will
haue God to be patient, and are out felves
L 5   im-

impatient with our enemies. If at any time we sinne, we desire God should be patient, if another sinne against vs , we will not that God haue patience with him. *Hieron. in Pfalm.* 93. *ad, vfquequo Domine peccatores gloriabuntur. Tom.*8.

FORBEARE REVENGE] That it is peculiar to God, see *Deut.*32.& 2.*Reg.* 22. *Pfal.*17.& 139.& 149.& *Rom.*12.Leaue the revenge to me and I will repay them . *Et Ezech* 9. *Eccl.*35. *Efaias* 1.&c.

If thou be Magnanimous , thou wilt never thinke thou haft iniurie done thee: thou wilt fay of thine enemie, he hath not hurt me , but had a mind to hurt me : and when thou feeft him in thy power , thou shalt efteeme it fufficient revenge , to haue beene able to revenge . Know that it is honeft and a great kind of revenge to forgiue. *Seneca, de* 4. *virtutib.l.*1.& *de Clementia lib.* 2. Clemencie is a temperance of ones mind in the power of Revenge, or, lenitie of the fuperiour to the inferiour in conftituting punishment, and crueltie is fierceneffe of mind in exacting of Punishment. He is better that contemneth an iniurie then that grieveth at it: for he that contemneth it, defpifeth it, as if he felt it not : but he that grieveth at it , is vexed with it, as if he he felt it. *Amb. lib. 1. off. c. 6. Tom. 1. Magnarum virium est negligere lædentem.*

§. 49. BE NOT TOO LIBERALL] Liberalitie is the meane betweene avarice & prodigalitie, and consequently a vertue: which alwaies holdeth the meane, flying the extreames of too much, ever a vice. Seneca, lib. de moribus

To haue, and giue to others, is an argument of a Welthie man. *Basil. hom. 29. de pœnitentia.*

Avarice in old age, is like a monster; for what greater follie is there, then as the way groweth shorter, to encrease the viaticum. *Seneca, lib. de moribus.*

These things withdraw from right: Honours, Riches, Power, and the like, which in the opinion of men are deare ; in price vile. *Seneca, lib. de Paupertate. Vide Chrysost. Tom. 5. hom. 15. ad Antioch.*

All vices wax old with a man, only avarice waxeth yong. *Aug. serm. 48. ad frat. in eremo.*

§. 50. lin. 3. BE THANKE-FVLL FOR EVERY COVRTE-SIE] Not to render thankes for benefits is foule, and so holden with all men; therfore of the vngratefull even the vngratefull doe complaine ; when notwithstanding, this same that displeaseth all, sticketh to all,

all , and so farre men goe on the contrarie side as some are to vs most odious not only after benefits, but even for benefits . He is vngratefull that denyeth the benefit he hath received: he is vngratefull that dissembleth it , he is vngratefull that repayeth it not, he is most vngratefull that forgetteth it. *Seneca lib. 3. de beneficijs.*

Some, when a gift is sent them, doe vntimely restore another, and say they owe nothing . They are to be reiected : it is a pledge to send presently another gift to him that sent to thee , and extinguish gift with gift . Sometimes being able, I will not restore a benefit , when I shall detract more from my selfe then helpe another: when he shall receiue no encrease by the receit of that, which restored me would stand me in good steed. He that maketh haste to repay, hath not the minde of a gratefull man, but of a debter. And, to speake briefely, he that desireth to repay too soone, oweth against his will , he that vnwillingly oweth, is vngratefull. *Seneca lib. 4. de beneficijs.*

Lin. 4. LET TIME BREED THE FRIENDS] Thou knowest not how great the price of friendship is, if thou doe not vnderstand that thou giuest him much to whom thou giuest a friend. A thing not in houses alone, but in ages rare, which is

no

no where more wanting , then where it is moſt of all beleeved to abound. *Seneca l.6. de benef.*

He can not be friend to man, that is vnfaithfull to God. *Ambroſ.l.3.off.c.16.& l.6. epiſt.40.* True loue is proved by conſtancie.

Slender friendſhip is that which followeth the friends felicities and riches : ſuch men ſeeme to me not to loue their friends but themſelues. *Hieron.in c.7.Micheæ.Tom.6. pag.161.& ad Ruffin. Tom.2.pag.195.*

True friendſhip muſt not diſſemble what it feeleth. Proſperitie getteth friends : Adverſitie is the ſureſt proofe of them. *Seneca, lib.de morib.ante medium.*

Pag.52. §.51. lin.3. WITH DVE REVERENCE] Let every living ſoule be ſubiect to higher powers. Rom.13

When thou ſitteſt to eate with a Prince, conſidering conſider what is before thy face , and if thou be thyne owne man, ſet thy knife to thy throate. In the middeſt of great men preſume not to ſpeake. Where Ancients are ſpeake not much. Preventing one another with honour , giue honour to whom honour is due. In the middeſt of the bretheren their Ruler ſhall be had in honour. Fooles haue decreed to yeeld to no man, nor to regard diſtinction of perſons, or degrees: on ſuch as doe regard the ſame, they

Prou. 23.

Eccl.32 13.

Rom.12. 10.
Rom.13 7.

Eccl.10 24.

they caſt the crime of flatterie , or accep-
tion of perſons:|And being great friends of
confuſion , to beware of pride in their betters,they take no heede of it in themſelves:
in ſtead of order, they ſhew irreverence.
S.Bon.ſpec.diſcip.c.6.

Pag.52.§.52. RELEEVE ALL THAT
ARE DISTRESSED] *Iacob.*1.27.Pure
and immaculate Religion before God and
the Father is this': to viſit pupils, orphans,
& widdowes in their tribulation , & keepe
ones ſelfe vnſpotted from this world .
Pſal. 40. Bleſſed is he that hath conſideration of the poore and needie , our Lord
will deliver him in the evill day. *Matth.*5.7.
Bleſſed are the mercifull, for they ſhall obtaine mercie.*Iacob.*13. Iudgement without
mercie to him that hath not done mercie.

A FRIEND] Forſake not thy friend,
and the friend of thy father. *Prou.*27.10.

Pag.52. §.53. HAVE CHARITIE
WITH ALL MEN] He ſheweth vs,with
the Apoſtle. 1.*Cor.*12.31. Yet a more excellent way : For to ſpeake with tongues of
men or Angels ; to haue the faith that re-
moveth mountaines; to feed the poore; to
yeeld the bodie to Martyrdome , is of no
value without charitie.

The latitude of the commands is charitie ; becauſe where charitie is , ſtraites are
not.

not . Wilt thou not be driuen into ſtraites
on earth? dwell in latitude . Whatſoever a
man doth to thee he cannot vex thee , becauſe thou loueſt that which hurteth not.
Charitie therfore is not brought into any
ſtraites. *Auguſtin. tract.*10. *in Epiſt. Ioan. &*
Epiſt. 62. I doe ever owe charitie , which
alone being payed holdeth me ſtill debtor.
The beſtowing of it payeth it, & although
it be beſtowed, yet is it ſtill owed, becauſe
there is no time in which it ought not to be
beſtowed: and when it is beſtowed,it is not
loſt, but rather in the beſtowing is multiplied, for it is beſtowed by having and not
by wanting it . As it cannot be beſtowed
vnleſſe it be had , neither can it be had vnleſſe it be beſtowed: And when a man be-
ſtoweth it , in the ſame man it encreaſeth,
and is ſo much more gotten as it is ofter beſtowed .... Charitie therfore is not
ſo beſtowed as money ; for beſides that in
beſtowing, this is diminiſhed,that encreaſ-
ſed,there is betweene them this difference,
that to whom wee giue money we are ſo
much the more benevolent as we ſeeke to
receiue nothing againe,but of charitie; he
cannot be a true beſtower that is not againe
a benigne exactour:for money when it is received cometh to him to whom it is given
and

and departeth from him that giveth it; but Charitie, encreaseth, not only in him that exacteth it from whom he loveth, although he doe not receiue it of him; but also he from whom he doth receiue it, then beginneth to haue it when he yeeldeth it. Wherfore I doe gladly render mutuall Charitie, and willingly receiue it: that which I receiue I doe yet require againe, that which I render I still owe.

Charitie being one and the same thing, if it fully possesse the mind, doth manifoldly enkindle it to innumerable works. *Greg. l. 10. Mor. c. 7.*

He that followeth charitie, is humble towards all. And the keeper of peace, provoketh none to brawling. *Amb. in illud 2. Tim. 2. Iuvenilia desideria fuge, Tom. 5. pag. 415.* What thou wilt haue secret, tell it no man, if thou hast not commanded thy selfe silence, how shalt thou hope for it in another. *Seneca, lib. 2. de moribus.*

Pag. 53. §. 54. EMBRACE CHASTITIE] Commended in *Iudith* 15. & 16. Exhorted, 2. *Cor.* 6. 1. *Tim.* 2. 3. 4. & 5. Chastitie without Charitie is a lampe without oyle, take away the oyle and the lampe giveth no light: take away Charitie, and Chastitie pleaseth not. *Bernard. Epist. 42.* Chastitie without her compagnions, Fast, and

and Temperance, foone decayeth, but ftrengthened with thefe helps, will eafily be crowned. *Chryfoft. hom.* 1. *in Pfalm.* 50. *Tom.* 1. *& de præparat. advent. Domini.* Chaftitie of bodie alone fufficeth not to the integritie of the heart.

The flesh cannot be corrupted, vnleffe the mind be firft corrupted. *Amb. ad virg. lapfam, c.* 4. *Tom.* 1.

Doeft thou command continence? Lord, giue that thou commandeft, and command what thou wilt. *Aug. l.* 10. *Conf. c.* 29.

To liue in flesh, not according to the flesh is not an earthly, but a heavenly life. Whence, in flesh to attaine the Angelicall life, is of more merite then to haue it: for to be an Angell is felicitie; to be a virgin, virtue: Whileft the virgin by her owne forces with grace, endeavoreth to obtaine that which the Angell hath by nature. *Hieron. ad Paul. & Euftoch. de Affump. B.* MARIÆ, *Tom.* 4.

BEWARE OF THE ALLVREMENTS OF THE HARLOT] Her lips are a dropping honniecombe. *Prou.* 5. The fornicator finneth againft his owne body. 2. *Cor.* 6.

Pag. 53. §. 55. lin. 4. CANKER OF VSVRIE] Prohibited. *Exod.* 22. 25. *Levit.* 25. 37. *Deut.* 23. 19. *Nehem.* 5. *Ezech.* 18. 8.

M *Fœnus*

Fœnus pecuniæ, funus est anima. Vſe of money is the ſoules funerall, and he that by others loſſe coveteth to be enriched, is worthy to be punished with everlaſting want. *S.Leo, ſerm.6.de ieiunio decimi menſis.*

Pag. 53. §. 56. APPLY YOVR SELVES IN COMPANIE] *Rom.* 12, 15. Reioyce with thoſe that are glad, weepe with thoſe that are ſad. *Seneca, l. de 4. virtutibus.* Let not thy povertie be vndecent, nor parſimonie vitious, nor ſimplicitie neglect, nor lenitie languishing, and if thy goods be ſlender, yet let them not be pinching ..... feare no man more then thy ſelfe ... Haue not ſcurrility, but gratefull vrbanity : let thy ieſts be without tooth , thy diſports without harme, thy laughter without noyſe, thy voice without clamour, thy gate without tumult , thy quiet not ſluggish ; and when others play, doe thou alſo ſome good and honeſt exerciſe ... Fly flatterie, and be as loth to be prayſed of the dishoneſt, as to be prayſed for dishoneſtie : be glad when thou diſpleaſeſt the evill, and thinke their evill opinions of thee , thy trueſt prayſe. Feare not bitter , but faire words ... fly vices thy ſelfe, and of others vices be neither curious ſearcher, nor bitter reprehender, but without reproaching, a correctour; ſo as with cheerefulneſſe thou prevent thy

ad-

admonition, and giue lightly way to pardon errour : Extoll not , nor deiect thou any ... Be to all benigne, but fond of none : familiar with few, equall towards all ... Be a concealour of thy vertues, as others are of their vices : a contemner of vaine glorie , and no bitter exactor of the good wherwith thou art indued ... Be docible , and covetous of wisedome, men when they teach, doe learne ; what thou knoweft, vvithout arrogancie, impart vvith thofe that require it, vvhat thou knoweft not , vvithout hiding of thy ignorance, pray others to impart it to thee.

Pag, 54. §. 57. lin. 14, BREACH OF THE DEAD MANS WILL] The lawes haue: Let them in all things obey the vvill of the Teftatour. If any one vvill doe contrarie to the will of the teftatour ; Let him goe without the inheritance . *Aug. orat. de 5. hærefib. c. 6. Tom. 6. Careat æterna hæreditate hæreticus contraveniens voluntati teftamenti* I ESV.

Pag. 55. lin. 8. TO ARTHVR MY SONNE] This was my name in baptifme, not once mentioned in all the teftament before : whence it is manifeft that thefe fragments were not written at the fame time with the Teftament, but added by the author

author after 1590. the yeare that first bere-
ved me of a yeares life.

Prima quæ vitam dedit hora carpfit.
Nullius vltima rapuit plus quam prima.

F I N I S.

E R R A T A.

Pag.	Lin.	Err.	Correct.
26.	23.	Arthour.	Arthur Plantagenet.
28.	2.	Orford.	Oxford.
29.	10.	heath.	health.
29.	13.	afforced.	afforded.
43.	14.	that doe.	that I doe.
69.	29.	falyng.	failing.
74.	14.	of the the.	of the yeares.
107.	25.	vvo.	vve.
110.	3.	Pag. 28,	Pag. 18.
156.	26.	Anthor.	Author.
165.	29.	Lors.	Lords.